Global Voices

NCTE Editorial Board: Keith Gilyard, Ronald Jobe, Joyce Kinkead, Louise Phelps, Gladys Veidemanis, Charles Suhor, chair, *ex officio*, Michael Spooner, *ex officio*.

Global Voices

Culture and Identity in the Teaching of English

Edited by

Joseph O. Milner
Wake Forest University

Carol A. Pope
North Carolina State University

National Council of Teachers of English
1111 W. Kenyon Road, Urbana, Illinois 61801-1096

ABOUT THE COVER: Our cover art was acquired from the Manu Kopere Society, Inc., of Wellington, Aotearoa, New Zealand, which specializes in contemporary and traditional Maori artwork and design. The two figures in the design represent carved *poupou*—male and female—which are featured in traditional stance with legs apart and arms raised, conveying the act of communication. The intricate background pattern is based on the art of *tukutuku*, which involves the weaving of fiber strands onto slats in a crisscross fashion and is largely done by women. The tukutuku panel and the carved poupou are traditionally found side by side, lining the walls of meeting houses.

Staff Editor: David A. Hamburg

Staff Designer: Jim Proefrock

Cover Artwork and Design: Manu Kopere © 1993

Interior Design: Doug Burnett

NCTE Stock Number: 18550-3050

© 1994 by the National Council of Teachers of English. All rights reserved. Printed in the United States of America.

It is the policy of NCTE in its journals and other publications to provide a forum for the open discussion of ideas concerning the content and the teaching of English and the language arts. Publicity accorded to any particular point of view does not imply endorsement by the Executive Committee, the Board of Directors, or the membership at large, except in the announcements of policy, where such endorsement is clearly specified.

Library of Congress Cataloging-in-Publication Data

Global voices : culture and identity in the teaching of English / edited by Joseph O. Milner, Carol A. Pope.
    p.   cm.
   "NCTE stock number 18550–3050"—T.p. verso.
   Papers originally presented at the 1990 IFTE Conference held in Auckland, N.Z.
   Includes bibliographical references.
   ISBN 0-8141-1855-0
   1. English language—Study and teaching—Foreign countries —Congresses. 2. English language—Study and teaching—Foreign speakers—Congresses. 3. Identity (Psychology)—Congresses. 4. Language and culture—Congresses. I. Milner, Joseph O'Beirne, 1937– . II. Pope, Carol Ann. III. IFTE Conference (1990 : Auckland, N.Z.)
   PE1128.A2G56   1994
   428'.007—dc20   93-41342
                                                                         CIP

Contents

Kia Ora (Greetings): Preface   ix

I. Powhiri (A Call): Initial Impressions

1. Finding Strength in Diversity
   Carol A. Pope and N. Andrew Overstreet   3

2. Tracing a Teacher's Voice
   Edward W. Milner   9

3. Different Voices, Different Dances
   Rita S. Brause   16

4. Moving beyond Babel: Toward a Global Songline
   Natalie White   19

II. Hui (General Meeting): Centerpieces

5. Divergence and Convergence in English:
   A Creative Tension?
   Katharine Perera   25

6. Keeping English Alive and Well:
   A Response to Katharine Perera
   Denny Wolfe   42

7. From the Dominant Voice to Different Voices:
   Issues of Language, Culture, and Power
   Gerald Grace   47

8. A Response to Gerald Grace
   R. Baird Shuman   63

9. Insight from the Inside: A New Perspective
   on Family Influences over Children's Television
   Viewing and Its Implications for Teachers
   of English
   Patricia Gillard   68

10. A Response to Patricia Gillard
    Bruce C. Appleby   84

11. Effecting Change in Schools
    Mary K. Healy ... 88

12. Teachers as Agents of Change:
    A Response to Mary K. Healy
    Ruie Jane Pritchard ... 101

III. Waita (Song): Classroom Practices

13. Cultural Interpretations of Language Acquisition/The
    Culture of Power: ESL Traditions, Mayan Resistance
    Response by Wendy Strachan ... 111
    Reply by Janet Giltrow ... 115

14. Sources of the Whole Language Movement
    Response by Patsy M. Ginns ... 118
    Reply by Robert E. Shafer ... 120

15. The National Curriculum for English in the United
    Kingdom: The Case Against
    Response by Joan (Mittelstaedt) Steiner ... 124
    Reply by Winifred Crombie ... 125

16. Scented Gardens for the Bland: Curriculum, Culture,
    and Controversy in the Proposed New Syllabus for
    Senior English in New Zealand Secondary Schools
    Response by Nancy S. Thompson ... 127
    Reply by Jenny Buist ... 133

17. The Errors of Our Expectations: An Ethnographic
    Study of Basic and Honors College Writers
    Response by Ann Buhman Renninger ... 136
    Reply by Deborah James and P. B. Parris ... 139

18. Organizing a Whole Language Program through the
    Use of a Loose-Leaf Notebook
    Response by Merle Yvonne Williams-Price ... 143
    Reply by Stella D. Holmes ... 145

19. Teaching Resistance
    Response by Nancy B. Lester ... 148
    Reply by Catherine Beavis ... 149

20. New Zealand Book-Based Resources: Positive Female
    Role Models, Maori Perspective
        Response by P. B. Parris   153
        Reply by Noeline Wright   156

21. Cultural Bonding through Literature
        Response by Helga M. Lewis   159
        Reply by Claire Lacattiva   160

22. Responding to Writing: Findings of a Recent Research
    Project
        Response by Dennise M. Bartelo   162
        Response by Bertadean Baker   164
        Reply by David Philips   168

23. Humane Literacy: Literary Competence and the Ways
    of Knowing
        Response by Carole Bencich   174
        Reply by Sheridan Blau   178

24. Building on Students' Strengths: Voices in the Writing
    Class
        Response by Marian Bryan   183
        Reply by William Boswell   187

IV. Poroporoaki (Farewell): Global Futures

25. Voices and Visions
        Natalie White   193

26. Different Voices, Aotearoa 1990:
    The Memories and the Messages
        Elody Rathgen   204

27. From Auckland to New York:
    A Look Ahead to 1995
        John S. Mayher   208

Editors   219

Contributors   221

Kia Ora (Greetings)

Preface

Ko te kai o te rangitira he korero.
The food of a chief is conversation.

As part of her opening welcome, Elody Rathgen, president of the International Federation for the Teaching of English and a teacher educator in New Zealand, invited those at the 1990 International Conference in Auckland, New Zealand, to dine and feast on conversation in the coming days. And feast we did! Taking as its theme "Different Voices: Language, Culture, Identity," the conference offered numerous opportunities for participants from around the world to speak, to listen, to learn, and to envision a world in which voices are not silenced but honored.

The surrendering of ourselves to the process of listening, talking, thinking, and exploring resulted in a rich professional experience which mirrored the value of learning by listening, talking, exploring with our students. Consumed by the global voices of teachers, students, teacher educators, and international leaders, we spoke often of how valuable an experience attending such a conference would be for English language arts teachers everywhere. Thus we decided to reconstruct the conference in a text which would reflect the dialogue, the spirit of conversation that was established in Auckland. We wish through this volume to give you a sense of the stimulating exchanges that occurred at the conference and have continued across and within continents since that time.

In an attempt to universalize the themes and messages of the 1990 IFTE Conference while simultaneously not forsaking the particularity of the event, we include here an interspersing of participants' descriptions of their experiences at the conference as well as the implications which they drew from the sessions they attended. Throughout the text there are also allusions to New Zealand and its indigenous Maori culture. This melding first occurs in the table of contents and the arrangement of the text. Because we endeavored to honor the Maori culture as part of the conference, we chose to use the Maori language for the major divisions in the text. Therefore, the preface becomes the *Kia Ora* (greetings); the introductory essays, the *Powhiri* (the call, the invitation); the keynote speeches of the conference, the *Hui* (general meetings); the classroom practices discussions, the *Waiata* (song); and the essays about the history and future of IFTE conferences, the *Poroporoaki* (farewell). These are terms often used at the IFTE Conference and seem appropriate to what we attempt here. We trust that we are not taking too many liberties with the translations.

Even though this text by necessity represents the spirit and the content of the 1990 IFTE Conference through writing and reading, it also enables us to reinforce the value of speaking, listening, and viewing that was emphasized at the conference. Besides honoring the value of talking, acknowledging the importance of listening to students' voices, and emphasizing the significance of viewing, we also had ample opportunity at the conference to experience films that focused on New Zealand writers and their writing and to read poetry, hear writers read and/or recite their own or others' work, and exchange and explore ideas in numerous informal settings.

We would also be remiss if we did not mention the pervasive influence of Rose Pere—a Maori educator, leader, visionary—who guided the initial *Powhiri*, where everyone was called together, invited to join the culture of the conference, and asked to share the feast of conversation. Her message, which goes beyond the limitations of this text, was grounded in the power of language, the importance of talk as she shared the ancient Maori teachings. Urged to honor our own and others' uniqueness ("Each of us is perfect"), we were reminded that we are all related, that the most important component of the universe is People, and that we must share responsibility for other people and for Nature. From Tili Afamasaga (Western Samoa), Keri Kaa (New Zealand), and Rex Horoi (Solomon Islands), we heard similar messages about the value and importance of strong oral traditions and were warned that we invalidate a language by ignoring it. Keri Kaa's admonition, "Poets ought to be responsible for language change," provoked much thought and consideration. Even though these persons and their emphases on oral tradition are not explicitly represented here, their collective message and the spirit of their significant voices undergird this entire volume. Every section which follows reinforces the value of individual learners and teachers, each of whom brings a unique persona and language to his or her interactions.

This book contains offerings for numerous audiences—classroom teachers, supervising teachers, field evaluators, historians, university methods faculty, leaders in every area of English language arts instruction. Therefore, it lends itself to various reading approaches. You may scan the text to glean ideas for instruction, to discover the history of IFTE conferences, to learn about writers' impressions of New Zealand and the conference, to eavesdrop on the dialogue between presenters and responders to sessions, or to hear the tone-setting voices of the keynote speakers. Or you may choose to read this text straight through, imaging or reliving the 1990 IFTE Conference. No matter your choice, you will hear voices that will stimulate thinking and encourage collaboration through diversity: convergence via divergence.

I Powhiri (A Call)

Initial Impressions

A variety of voices blended in New Zealand for the 1990 International Federation of Teaching English (IFTE) Conference—classroom teachers, school administrators, teacher educators, historians, writers, artists, parents, students, theorists, researchers, practitioners. In this first section of *Global Voices* we introduce a few of those voices who were willing to share their impressions of New Zealand, of their journeys, and of their IFTE experience.

Andrew Overstreet, who brought the unusual perspective of a U.S. school superintendent, discusses with Carol Pope in "Finding Strength in Diversity" the understanding he reached about English language arts instruction around the world while at the conference. They explore the effect of being observers of New Zealand's educational attempts to honor its indigenous peoples as well as their culture and the challenges Andy has faced since his return from New Zealand as a school-system leader who values human diversity and believes in its power for all students.

Edward Milner, a poet and high school teacher, provides us with a glimpse into the journal he kept while on his trip to New Zealand and the IFTE Conference. In it you will find some intriguing stories about his visits to New Zealand classrooms, a chronology of conference events, and some conclusions he drew as a result of the issues explored at the conference. His farewell poem to new found colleagues serves as an invitation to continue the conversations begun in New Zealand.

In "Different Voices, Different Dances" Rita Brause considers the implications of the two different Maori dance presentations that were performed on the opening night of the conference. Using dance as a reflection of cultural voice, Rita considers the implications of traditional and contemporary dance interpretations and draws some provocative conclusions about the importance of nurturing the present as well as the past.

A scholar and historian of international English conferences since Dartmouth in 1966, Natalie White tells the poignant story, in "Moving beyond Babel: Toward a Global Songline," of her journey to New Zealand. In a startling occurrence aboard the airplane en route to the conference, Natalie witnesses "the thin red line," which can represent the lives of students we touch in the classroom as well as the different voices that coalesced at the conference.

Each of the essays in this Initial Impressions section touches on the themes of *Global Voices*—the virtues and values of diversity, the importance of dialogue, the challenge implicit in not silencing any voices, and the call for honoring various cultures. The 1990 IFTE Conference drew many individuals, countries, and cultures together in order to explore ways of extending these themes to instructional settings and daily life around the world.

1 Finding Strength in Diversity

Carol A. Pope and N. Andrew Overstreet

So what is a superintendent of schools doing at an international conference on teaching English? When we first discussed the possibility of Andy's attending this conference with me, we decided that it would be a valuable experience. Both of us knew, however, that Andy had some reservations. Would he feel out of place among English educators? Would he be bored by esoteric discussions of literature and writing style? And what could he learn that would be helpful in his role as superintendent? We figured that visiting the "home" of Reading Recovery and developmentally appropriate Instruction could not be all bad, and Andy had recently been supporting writing-across-the-curriculum and literature-based reading programs in his school system. At the very least, we assumed he would discover how cultures around the world approach English language arts instruction—an area we believe to be crucial because it supports learning in all content areas. Much to our surprise, we found awaiting us in New Zealand an eye-opening experience about the global as well as national significance of culturally diverse voices in schools—not just in English language arts classes but in all classes.

Since our return from New Zealand, we frequently talk about that trip's effects on our lives, my instruction, and Andy's perspective as a school-system leader. The following strands represent the themes of these discussions.

English Language Arts Instruction

Although Andy had been to numerous content-focused conferences and had even been to NCTE's Annual Convention on occasion, I found that he spoke often in New Zealand of the universal themes regarding the teaching of English that he observed at the large sessions, the small-group discussions, and the workshops. He was surprised to find that the issues regarding teaching English are similar worldwide and that many of the "best" ways of confronting these issues have been discovered in these various settings simultaneously. "All these people are grappling with the same issues," he pronounced one day. Andy had heard discussions about providing meaningful classroom experiences for students: making schoolwork valuable to students; engaging students with content and process; selecting appropriate materials to engage students and draw them into the content; building on student language and experiences; providing opportunities which challenge students to accept responsibility for their own learning; encouraging students to think independently—and he was amazed at the continuity.

In a recent conversation about that continuity Andy remarked that he was startled by the philosophical congruence he witnessed from around the world regarding the teaching of English. As he explains, "It appears to me that we *do* know how to teach English and how to foster learning in the English language arts classroom. However, it distresses me to say that what I heard in New Zealand regarding instruction does not represent what I grew up thinking English was all about in school. Nor does this perspective represent what I have seen happening in many English teachers' classes that I have observed in the past twenty years. In fact, I suspect that many of the traditional English teachers I have known as a student and as an administrator would have been mightily disturbed by the emphasis on collaborative talk and learning, the importance of using language to think aloud or in writing, the focus on accepting students' personal responses to literature, the value of television as a learning tool, and the call for respecting the language which students bring with them in to school. The IFTE Conference was not a *convention,* nor was it about *convention;* it was about honoring diversity and the many voices that represent that diversity."

As I watch and listen to Andy in his work, I see that IFTE's emphasis on diversity has galvanized his own attempts as a superintendent to speak for *all* children, to honor the culture and language of each child, and to encourage the establishment of classroom environments which build on the individual contributions of every student. It has also supported his commitment to removing barriers that have marginalized many students because of their cultural background, their experiences, or their language. He often speaks of the necessity of abandoning our "factory model" of schooling, in which students function only as homogeneous products to be assembled, in favor of developing a more learner-centered approach in which both the teacher and the student are unique learners in the classroom; the teacher is a leader rather than a line worker; and the student is a growing, changing human being rather than a sellable product.

Cultural Diversity

Each of the school systems where we have worked has been located in a racially, ethnically, and culturally diverse setting, so our realities have been heterogeneous. However, our attendance at "Different Voices" heightened our awareness of what a strong feature that heterogeneity can be in our American culture. Of course, we give lip service to equality in the United States, but our behavior in schools actually fosters sameness rather than difference. We expect students to conform, to follow the rules, to blend in rather than remain unique. Exploring this concept at a world level enabled both of us to see the subtle prejudice in our locally diverse culture, one which is becoming more diverse daily, and gave us a renewed insight.

When I asked Andy about his view on this issue of cultural diversity from the perspective of a school superintendent, he acknowledged that cultural pluralism is a characteristic of our "united" states, just as it is in our school systems. However, he was struck during the IFTE Conference that we do not yet understand what to do with that diversity in school systems, in schools, in classrooms. "Throughout the conference," he said, "I kept thinking of the power we are overlooking in our schools and considering possible ways to bridge that gap."

In recent months I have heard Andy address various groups—school board members, parents, church groups, teachers—and he always speaks of how we must abandon "Granpa's" curriculum in favor of content and approaches that build on current student needs, not on adult needs. He reinforces over and over that if we think of our students first, we must acknowledge and honor the diversity that they bring throughout schools' doors and into the classrooms.

Unique Setting

Given the importance of the "Different Voices" theme which we explored at the IFTE Conference, no better setting could have been selected than New Zealand. Oh, yes, we could have gotten a "different voices" perspective in Ottawa, in London, or in New York; but for us the full impact of the message was strengthened by being far away from our own home, from the center of our world, and from our own hemisphere.

In New Zealand the educational leaders have been developing a curriculum which honors the cultural diversity of their historic homeland. By studying the indigenous peoples of this land (the Maoris), by attempting to preserve and respect the Maori culture (its literature, its language, its customs, its habits, its contributions to this rich land), New Zealanders have chosen not only to honor their heritage but to keep it alive.

This effort is not without its critics; in fact, during and since our visit to New Zealand, there have been some setbacks regarding the teaching of the Maori culture in schools. However, being outsiders who could observe this discussion gave us clarity we could not have gained by being in our own country or in one so like our own. We could see, as outsiders, the class system that will be so difficult to dismantle in New Zealand; and seeing that division made us admire the work of the country even more. As we talked and listened to a sales clerk in Rotorua (the seat of the Maori culture) tell us that a large number of Maoris are on government subsistence "because they don't want to work," we were reminded of similar U.S. voices. How many times have we heard such remarks made about our American Indians and our African Americans? Yet, within two hours of those prejudicial remarks, we also heard a Maori father speak with pride and gratitude (and shame) that his children now come home from school and teach *him* the Maori language that he never learned, in fact was forbidden to learn, when he was growing up. The pride at knowing that his heritage would not die but would live through his children was evident in his words, his damp eyes, and his wide smile.

This "outsider" perspective in New Zealand prompted us to wonder how the United States would be different today if we had not been so intent on squeezing out, on extracting diversity in order to create a "standard" American English and experience. How would we as a people be different if we had valued the American Indians, not disenfranchised them? Would we be a richer, stronger, healthier people today had we not all but annihilated an indigenous culture, quieted the native voices of our country?

Sociopolitical Issues

It is worth noting here that the 1990 IFTE Conference took place at a time when world-shaking events were taking place: the Berlin Wall had fallen in November 1989; the fall of communism and the breakup of the Soviet Union were not far behind. The theme, the message of the conference—valuing different voices—certainly represented the energy that propelled these vast changes. The empowerment of the individual, of individual peoples, is a message whose time has come in many parts of the world.

At the IFTE Conference we constantly returned to the issue of equity across cultures, within countries, and within educational settings. In particular, within the context of English language arts instruction, we have found that we cannot ignore political, ideological issues that reflect the larger sociopolitical issues of our time. Nor can we ignore the potential upheaval which may come, as it has come around the world, when we empower those who have heretofore been silenced.

In fact, Andy's genuine question made me think about empowerment even more: "Are we truly ready to listen, hear, and respond to the diverse voices which might emerge in our classrooms? Are we, as educators and citizens, ready for the overthrow of the status quo as we give choice to marginalized voices? Are we ready to confront those citizens who would prefer to keep some groups quiet and 'in their place'?" These are questions which both of us try to address as we explore different instructional and governance venues with students, teachers, parents, and school board members.

Future Challenges

The 1990 IFTE Conference was a microcosm of a larger world—one which merged culturally, linguistically diverse voices in New Zealand. Ever aware of the demographics which indicate that the world, our society, our schools will continue to grow more dissimilar in ethnicity, race, culture, and age, will we still try to accommodate this diversity through forced homogeneity? Or will we learn the lesson of history that repressed peoples (particularly those who have been oppressed into sameness) will rise up, regain power, and often return to isolated tribalism in order to rediscover their heritage?

Surely, with past and more immediate examples in process, we will learn the lesson of different voices, strain to hear their harmony, and move forward in a unified way based on the strength of heterogeneity rather than the weakness of forced homogeneity. We, as human beings and as educators, must build identities in positive ways so as not to separate and destroy our own potential as a people, as a world.

To confront the challenges of the future and an ever-shrinking world, we must acknowledge and interweave the common thread—our human diversity.

When I asked Andy what one message from the IFTE Conference he would share with the leaders of any school system (teachers, principals, central office administrators, school board members), he responded, "It would be this: each of us can apply the 'Different Voices' theme in our own settings—whether they be classrooms or world communities. We must acknowledge and honor our cultural diversity, and we must use that diversity to build strength. We can accomplish this challenging task in schools by empowering teachers who themselves can empower students; but we must model at every level—national, state, local/central office, principal's office, classroom—the value of cultural pluralism in our world so that the children of today will be tolerant, accepting, and appreciative of those who are different from themselves."

If all of us in education would practice and model this acceptance, perhaps the world and school would be a place that welcomes the voices of many, rather than of only a few.

2 Tracing a Teacher's Voice

Edward W. Milner

The conference was a major attraction to North Carolina Writing Project participants because of our interest in improving writing in our own classrooms, in continuing our international visits to writing projects (two years ago in England and Wales and this time in New Zealand), and in preparing for a continuation of our role as ambassadors of the Writing Project to other countries.

New Zealand

We left Hawaii, after a two-day stop, on the night of Sunday, August 19, and as we traveled 3,925 miles to New Zealand, we gained only two hours, but we lost a whole day. Monday was gone, and it was now Tuesday, the 21st of August. We emerged from a night's sleep on the plane to see the clouds and sunshine of Auckland, New Zealand. Auckland is an isthmus between two large bays, one on the Pacific side, and the other on the side of the Tasman Sea. New Zealand is about twice as large as North Carolina, with half the population. Its native population is about one percent of the total, but whereas the "Pakehas" (anyone not a Maori) are celebrating their 150th anniversary, the Maori are celebrating their one thousandth year of settlement in New Zealand. Auckland is almost exactly on the same parallel as Charlotte, North Carolina, but its weather is slightly more tropical owing to the trade winds and the insular nature of the country. The two New Zealand islands stretch for more than a thousand miles so that the southern (remember, they are south of the equator) tip of the South Island has mountains and glaciers and fjords, whereas the northern tip has tropical fruits, trees, and birds.

Like the colonists in North America, the colonial whites here first fell on their knees, and then on the aborigines. The Maoris were given treaties that were perhaps neither as bad nor as dishonorable as ours in the United States, but were still a source of discontent. And if we expected to go to an international conference on English and avoid that issue, we were mistaken. So we came to an island paradise that was waking to the realities of civil disobedience. Our planners and our leaders were Maori or pro-Maori in their actions and attitudes. This perspective made for an exciting conference.

New Zealand Schools

On our first day in New Zealand, the Level III Writing Group visited various schools in Auckland. My group visited the Papatoetoe and the Mangere schools in the southern part of Auckland. They resembled schools we had visited in England and Wales in that they were built on an open school basis (both structurally and pedagogically). We were mostly concerned about writing, but did occasionally visit a social studies or math class. In math and social studies it might be they should take off their hat to us, while in writing and language arts, it should be the other way about, for the students' work in these classes was truly accomplished.

On the second day, we visited an entirely different kind of community, Thames, which was at the intersection of the mainland and the Coromandel Peninsula. This community had started off a hundred years ago as a gold-rush town, so it was imply a long strip of stores and offices, hospitals and schools, businesses and a few light industries. The schools, however, were much like the ones we had seen the day before. In both schools, there were systematic efforts to teach Maori, the language of the natives. What was absolutely delightful was the greeting (dancing, singing, and spear brandishing) of these K–6 students. We were given a package of gifts, and in exchange, I sang one of my songs and had the "warriors and maidens" accompany me in so doing. As in Wales, two years before, the first question the children raised was whether or not I had been to Graceland and to Disneyworld. "Oh, well, at least he plays a guitar." While I do use the guitar to facilitate observation as well as education, at the same time, I get to talk openly with the children and see them at their work. Their labors at organization and fluency are about like those of our students, but their publications, their storybooks, are wonderful and unlike any I have ever seen.

I should also note here that in New Zealand, as in the United Kingdom, the principal is the head teacher. At the same time, the principal is slightly more authoritative and controlling than principals in the United States. In my own area of expertise, there is nothing abroad like the bulletin boards and shareware in the states. Computers are used rationally, whether it is at Papatoetoe in Auckland, or in

Wales. They are used to take roll, allow the teachers and students a word processor, and provide databases for students in math and science. But there is not the rampant individualism, with all of its virtues and vices, that exists in the USA.

IFTE Conference

Friday, Aug. 24: After two days of school visits, we were ready for the conference. We registered for our workshops and papers (this took up half of the conference time; the other half was taken up by speakers, panels, readings, teas, and meals). We attended a *powhiri* (a calling up by the women of the conference; speeches from selected elders; *waiatas,* or songs, that we sang throughout the conference; greetings; kissing or rubbing noses), then had dinner, followed by Kahurangi dancers, informal eating and drinking.

Saturday, Aug. 25: Following the "Defining and Facing the Issues" theme, we had a speaker (Rose Pere), tea, and a *hui*. (A *hui* is a meeting in a hall where cushions are provided. The members remove their shoes at the door and enter quietly. A *waiata* or two is sung, and the speaker may speak but also dance and chant, if so inclined.) Speakers at this meeting also included representatives from the United States, Canada, United Kingdom, Australia, Samoa, and the Solomon Islands. Following lunch we had another speaker (an aborigine from Australia, who was much in alliance with the Maori) and then a group session, followed by afternoon discussions, reception, and dinner. After dinner there was a magnificent film on the New Zealand artist Janet Frame.

Sunday, Aug. 26: The theme of this day, "Exploring the Issues," featured a British speaker, Katharine Perera, followed by workshop and paper sessions for the rest of the day, interspersed with films, meals, tea, and writers reading their own work. The sessions I attended included one by an American in Hong Kong who married a Chinese and has reared bilingual children. Of the two workshops I attended, one was a panel of three that offered many tips on publishing children's literature. The other workshop I attended was a film on village life in New Zealand.

Monday, Aug. 27: Reinforcing the theme, "Relating the Issues to Teaching and Learning," was speaker Patricia Gillard, a member of the Australian Broadcasting Tribunal. Our panel, after tea, included speakers from television, dance, and drama. The paper for the day was on how to use the microcomputer in teaching, written by three Americans. One workshop I attended discussed how to use television in teaching, and another dealt with how to use popular music.

Tuesday, Aug. 28: The speaker, Mary K. Healy, who focused the day's theme, "Effecting Change," was from the Puente Project in Los Angeles. In my first workshop there as a continuation of this presentation, a bilingual effort at a community college focusing on English and writing. I also attended a workshop which focused on children's storybooks. What was impressive about this was the first speaker, a librarian in New Zealand, who showed literally hundreds of children's books that were especially illustrative of modern art. The second speaker was from Papatoetoe, which we had visited. The children's artwork in their storybooks was as impressive as the modern art on the covers and served well as illustrations for these children's stories. And the children's created stories were also engaging.

During this session I also discovered how it makes sense in an open classroom to facilitate language with audio-visual prompts. A little music may prompt an otherwise reticent speaker-thinker. A little color and line may give concrete encouragement to those with learning problems. The storybook is this "hint," twofold. First, the storybook presents the finished product, the marketable, sellable product. Second, it also purveys a highly finished art form, an art form that has improved rapidly over the last thirty years. Finally, the storybook gives something for students to shoot for as they criticize their work, print in their illustrations, and bind their pages for final publication.

An intriguing evening session included a panel, mostly of Maori women, which addressed the issues of change and lamented that the women's liberation movement among the Pakeha women completely failed to understand the role of the Maori woman in Maori culture. We left the question undecided as we went to our various groups at the conference dinner.

Wednesday, Aug. 29: The speaker for the closing day—which took as its theme "Facing the Future"—was Gerald Grace, an education professor from the United Kingdom. Following the morning tea was the *Poroporoaki,* or ceremonial farewell, to which all were urged to speak. My contribution to this ceremony is included at the end of this text. We then had lunch and departed.

Bound for Home

Our journey home began with a daylong trip back to Hawaii. By recrossing the equator and the International Date Line, we regained the day we lost, but still lost several hours. (In case you are wondering, it is true that the water empties from your sink in a counterclockwise fashion above the equator and clockwise below it.) From Honolulu we traveled through the night to Dallas, Texas, losing six more hours.

In Dallas, while awaiting the last leg of our journey, our group round-robin told of our experiences, what we had learned, and what we had found. I offered that the conference, with its Pakeha-Maori dichotomy, provided me with insight into the whole of the English language.

Conclusions

As a result of my attendance at the 1990 IFTE Conference, I reached some tentative conclusions about "different voices" that I have arranged here by the daily themes of the conference.

"Defining and Facing the Issues": Colonialism has foisted its language and values on the colonialized. Sadly, many languages have been destroyed or lost. The least we can do is become bilingual. In the USA this is most difficult. Do we start with Ashati or Swahili, Cherokee or Zuni? At the same time, we must make every effort to retain English as the common or predominant language. We must not settle for writing; we must also publish and disseminate.

"Exploring the Issues": English will be unintelligible from country to country as Latin was in the Middle Ages or Portuguese is today, unless we look at the issues. We cannot legislate a common language. We try to standardize or make it uniform at peril. Though we do not speak English the same way Shakespeare did, we can still understand his language. Some countries update and upgrade, but they put the historical language out of reach. Some countries try to make it uniform today, but this alienates us from the past spoken and read language. We have many things going for us, and English is a universal language, but it is a tender fabric that can be destroyed.

"Relating the Issues to Teaching and Learning": Teaching writing is one of the ways to retain English. Lots of writing, less of legislation. Use of the computer may mechanize it, or it may help to increase fluency. If computer writing is evaluated quantitatively, its purposes will not be well served; but if it is evaluated qualitatively, we may see a recovery and a flowering of language.

"Effecting Change": Change will take place only from room to room and from teacher to teacher. "Teacher-bashing" is the last way of effecting change. Having teachers involved in the creation and evaluation of the curriculum and instruction is a positive way to effect change. Much change, especially on machines, may be mindless. Care must be taken to have rational approaches to networks and systems. Networking by telecommunications, or distance education, is emerging slowly but steadily. It is well to network individually and then from group to group. Issues involving all minorities and equity all must be open to the insights of other issues such as television and the computer.

"Facing the Future": Homemade television will serve to educate makers of tapes that reality and truth are constructed. Slowly people will begin to demythologize the propaganda spawned by mass media. We will become better informed voters and better thinkers. Similarly, homemade programming will demythologize computer programs and writing that are mindless and mechanical.

As I relate my IFTE experiences to my own teaching, I see a discrepancy between the interdisciplinary approach of language and the monodisciplinary approach of computer programming. The workshops that I attended, the classrooms that I visited, and the conference that I enjoyed were, all of them, open and rich in texture. A machine class, by its very nature, symbolizes a closed system, a removal of ambiguity. Yet, if writing is to include the whole person, the whole curriculum, then it must begin with the recognition that the teacher is a whole person and the student is a whole person. Learning takes place between and among them. The days of the posturing, arrogant, "know-it-all" teacher are over. We must learn to learn from each other. As Freire reminds us, the bank account image will not work in education.

The whole thrust of "Different Voices" was staked on this issue. We see it here in the USA in the battles between formal English and variations of English used by various ethnic groups. The message for me at the conference was that English has many pitfalls. If we make its use a state-regulated affair, it will be cut off from its practitioners in other countries that are English speaking. On the other hand, if we make it strictly a modern handbag, accommodating all of its various current usages, it can be cut off from its history as is the case with the Dutch language.

Our best future lies in lots of writing, lots of publication, little standardization or laws, continuous communication with other countries, and, above all, a multidisciplinary approach involving art, story, writing, criticism, and publication. My motto is that while I do not teach English, I do attempt to humanize the machine. I teach writing.

I have used music; and since this conference, I have used storybooks and artwork as prompts for writing sessions in computer programming. Computers can be used to facilitate surgically precise bombing, or they can be used to facilitate international understanding.

My Poroporoaki

I do not teach English;
My job is to humanize the machine.
I do teach writing.
Here, I have written songs and poems and drawn pictures.
As a stranger, I have been embraced as friend.
I have been ecstatic with your beauty,
Laughed at meals,
Moved by the motion of the dance
Cried at the films,
We all seek and are sought by the holy.
Our holy grasps us and shakes us,
Is terrifying and mysterious.
I thank you kind and peaceful people
For your offerings of beauty.
Sometimes terrifying, sometimes mysterious,
But always holy.
When you come to my land and my
State and my city and my school and my
Home, I will embrace you, I will
Dance with you. I will
Cry with you, and I will ask
You to say your
Poetry and sing your
Songs to me.

3 Different Voices, Different Dances

Rita S. Brause

"I didn't know dance was an area of your expertise," Carol remarked as we were talking about plans for this volume. "It's not," I quickly responded. "But it is an area of interest, particularly as it reflects a community's voices and values."

Participants at the IFTE Conference in New Zealand were invited to "taste New Zealand culture"—particularly the Maori culture. We were introduced to many customs. Our daily ritual included leaving our shoes at the door of the meeting room, sitting on the floor to listen to the plenary session speakers, and singing brief songs at the opening and closing ceremonies. In addition to the conventional "academic" sessions and workshops, the program included two entertainment sessions: one of traditional Maori dances and a second which displayed contemporary New Zealand dancing, heavily influenced by Maori traditions. It is the contrast between these two sessions on which I will focus.

Immediately following our communal dinner in the cafeteria, a group of secondary students performed traditional Maori dances. These adolescents had carefully learned a set of dances, which had been passed down from previous generations. They twirled the same colored balls, they wore the same skirts, and they copied the face marking of their forebears. The conference attendees had viewed these same steps and the same costumes at selected tourist attractions on the North Island. There were few differences—causing some to consider any changes as errors.

The students danced the same steps their grandparents performed some fifty years previous. Their dances represented how the Maori warded off danger by making loud noises and distorting their faces as they prepared for warring and hand-to-hand combat, activities remote from the contemporary experiences of these adolescents. Despite their alien nature, these student-dancers conveyed an assurance that they had learned the dances well. And those teachers who were concerned with their learning these dances focused on their duplication of precise gestures and sounds. The dancing, which previously had a strong utilitarian purpose, now existed to document the past—and to entertain others.

The dancers were conveying the voices of the ancestors, who lived in worlds dramatically different from the experiences with which these adolescents were struggling on a daily basis. In the interest of tradition, they were denied their own voices. These dances were not their dances; rather, they were dances of their ancestors. And we never got to hear the voices of these adolescents. The enthusiasm which they displayed was attributable to their "performing" for their teachers and their teachers' peers, not their ability to get their message across to others. Their voices were absent from this event.

A little later that same evening, in a different setting, we viewed a second group of dancers—professionals. They not only performed the "traditional" dances, but they infused their dances with contemporary rhythms and movements. (The traditional dances contrasted with "their" dances.) Their dances reflected an awareness of the outdatedness of hand-to-hand combat. They represented more contemporary human concerns: love and romance as well as disputation and anger. And there was a more international flavor to these dances. They reflected an influence of dances and music from other cultures as well. These dances reflected the fact that no longer were the New Zealanders—or the Maoris, for that matter—isolated on the Island of the Long White Cloud. They were members of a worldly community. Their society was interdependent with other cultures—twentieth century people living exciting, unpredictable lives. These changed perspectives on life were reflected in their dances. These dancers were enthusiastic about their dancing. They seemed to come alive as they danced, and the audience did as well. In contrast to the traditional dancing, which involved neither the dancers nor the audience, there was a real sense during the contemporary dance session that the voices of all the people in the room were reflected somehow in some aspect of the dance.

Following the contemporary dance, there was much hushed discussion among the audience. (It was hushed since people did not want to offend others, and there was no real forum for formal discussion.) There were those who loved the contemporary and those who dismissed it—preferring the traditional. (I did not hear anyone advocate the coexistence of both.) I think this discussion really marked the essence of the conference—and its focus on *different voices*.

It seems to me that those who venerated the traditional and dismissed the new were denying New Zealanders (and particularly Maoris) participation in the contemporary world—to have a voice which would include their heritage as well as modern, universal advances. By analogy, any group which would be restricted to its past would be similarly handicapped by this action. I think this desire of wanting to sustain others' traditions, particularly to the exclusion of any contemporary influences, serves to deny those individuals an opportunity to grow—to have their own voice—to join the larger world. The import of that observation became clear from participating in the conference.

I know how difficult it has been for me to find my own voice. I take it as my professional responsibility never to silence others and, more important, to encourage others to let us hear their different voices. Let us not reify traditions but use them to learn and grow. Auckland's theme will resonate for a long time as we explore how we may nurture the different voices and dances which need to be heard and seen.

4 Moving beyond Babel: Toward a Global Songline

Natalie White

The "Different Voices" of the 1990 International were to sound issues of gender, race, and class within the conference theme of "Language, Culture, Identity." This, the Fifth International Conference on the Teaching of English in *Aotearoa*, the Maori word for New Zealand, went far beyond Babel, all the way to Eden—to Mt. Eden, the community in Auckland where the conference was held. Resonances of past international English conferences dating back to 1966 Dartmouth (the seminar which started the international movement in English education) were embedded in my own journey to New Zealand in August 1990.

Strangers we all were, collected in an airplane, leaving the City of the Angels from the decidedly pedestrian Los Angeles International. Erratic representatives of the human family, we were not bonded in community; having the sanctity of anonymity, we confessed in casual dialogue the horrors of "the job," the pressures of living, the continuing saga of S & L scandals, a declining economy, political debauchery, the increasing horrors over Kuwait. Passengers in thin air, we were "out of time," looking, as from Olympus, at the mindless squabbles playing out in the world below us. We were, ironically, out over the serene Pacific, bound for Honolulu: comfortable, safe, reserved—yet pilgrims all. From many stations and walks of life, from different cultures, of many languages, we endured our time out of time in ho-hum boredom and mindless chatter—as dusk fell and intermittent shivers of turbulence resonated against the thin metal shell surrounding us. Dark storm clouds formed; as the storm descended, the timbre deepened to low growls.

Nearby a passenger coughed—a strange cough, choking, gagging, escalating into a sound like none I've heard. Muffled noises brought sudden movement while we went our egocentric ways. For me, it was marking the text of my paper to be delivered in Auckland;

textual precision was my mental set. Abruptly, all of us on this ship in thin air were to be plummeted into the deepest measures of our human context. At that moment pure professional, I was coolly reserved, ignorant of my fellows, "together" in the vernacular—isolated in my own skin. Stirred by a sudden breeze, I recognized a flight attendant running through the cabin. Strange. Back to the purification rite I was performing on text. Footfalls again as she ran past, this time carrying oxygen. Out of context came sudden knowledge: a passenger near me, a companion on this journey, another pilgrim soul had become suddenly, violently, perhaps critically ill. Work ceased, my thought became something like prayer; caught in unknown, I knew the darkness, the disarray, began to see the descending storm in this life, as in all our lives.

Trying not to see the drama unfolding too near me, I looked for escape toward the window. Storm clouds visibly and all-too-quickly descended from above; heavy curtains of black were closing out the light. Too like the Middle East, this angry storm shook the many links of the great chain of being. The night-dark face of the Pacific was an impenetrable ink blot below us. What remained was the little left of the sunset becoming a thin, blood-red line, etching the black-curtained sky, the deep, dark sea—etching the darkness with scarlet, gules, with the blood-red memory of the descending light of the sun. Symbolist, imagist, English teacher that I am, meaning struck me. "Hold, hold" became my prayer for the passenger; "hold to that thin, red line." The ocean below, the depths, the impenetrable depths, the storm, the heavy black clouds—too near, the dogs of war, the horsemen of the Apocalypse, riding fast. The passenger, herself fighting to hold to that thin, red line, for her a lifeline, was merely fifteen years old. She was to teach me something of that thin line, something of the pilgrim journey in the classroom that I had never seen.

Even now, in recollection, the time is strangely finite, collapsing upon itself, yet seeming an eternity. We turned back toward the mainland; urgent attention was needed or the child might die. The physician on board, the captain, the crew, even the corporation which flew us could do but little. Several times as we flew toward San Francisco, her breathing stopped. By the time of our arrival, several cylinders of oxygen were empty. Little more than a twenty minutes' lease on life remained in the tank when we landed. Teams of paramedics, police rushed on board. We would remain on the ground while she was stabilized; then the waiting ambulance would take her to a hospital, and we would turn back toward our delayed South Pacific idylls.

Of these pilgrims in the plane, some continued reading, talking with quiet acceptance, even respect. They worked with her, finally brought her to the point where she could weakly squeeze the fingers of an attendant. Others wanted to gawk and stare, hoping for a sideshow, a circus, the parade of another's anguish. Like the hordes who will gather at a traffic accident or watch a fire, some, flushed with excitement, stood on their knees, not praying but, facing the rear of the airplane, straining to glimpse the unfolding drama. They were members of no community but, loosened by anonymity perhaps, or desiring the small comfort of story against unrecognized angst, were fighting the gods, fate, mortality: taking small power from powerlessness. A small line formed at the ground-telephone; people waited to give a play-by-play to awaiting relatives.

I had become blank, somehow hollowed by long hours of distance and dismay. Blindly, in chaotic context, I, too, was trying to form a story, a teacher's story about a stricken child and the importance of what we do and what we give through text, toward the human context of life and living, a story I had learned best in my study of the first International, the Dartmouth Seminar. Now I could see all too clearly the tensions in the multiple relationships each English teacher melds into ongoing classroom discourse, toward personal, social, and cognitive growth. All of us have suffered the death of children we still love: by accident, by disease, drug or substance abuse, by suicide, in gang warfare—but never had the angel hovered so near, never had the line felt so thin, nor had I wondered what we could offer to the shudder of a child's final moment, what we offer our students, our society through that thin, red line. Suddenly, irreversibly, I was to come to know it, to understand its essence, to touch its fragile truth. That line, has, like our children, many faces. It holds back the tension of raging storms above, stands against the abyss of the deep, dark fathoms of seas below. Teaching, we mediate that thin, red line:

> As *bloodline*, it carries the signature of our DNA in familial traits, ethnicity; in the oxygen which darkens it resides the inspiration of our living breath, the vehicle of dialogue through speech; there couple nutrients to sustain both body and mind.
>
> As *time line*, it connects the wisdom, the insights, the inspirations of all ages.
>
> As *song line*, it marks, stories, celebrates the events of our days on this earth.

As a *line of communication,* it becomes a chorus, and sometimes a celebration, an entertainment within our global community, putting us in touch with the sisters, the brothers of our common humanity.

As tensions gather like storm clouds around us, the thin, red line becomes a lifeline for us all. In Auckland, as we met to consider the issues of race, of gender, of class, in sounding our different voices, we were to communicate, to connect to form and to hold to that thin, red line: bloodline, yes, time line, song line—lifeline for us all, for that nature which sustains us.

II Hui (General Meeting)

Centerpieces

Now that we have given you a sense of the context out of which the respondents in this book write, we present four plenary papers that articulate and underscore the central ideas of the IFTE Conference and this text. Since the conference out of which the essays arise set out to undercut privileged language and valorized cultures, the qualities of participation, equality, and interaction were essential features of our meetings. Nevertheless, the words of these four speakers more than any others seemed to shape the conference and mark its movement from reflection on different voices to celebration of actions which had promoted them. For each of these centerpiece presentations, as in the section to follow, a response is offered to capture the dialogical flavor of the original setting. The responses are not only insightful but carry the original thought forward and measure out the parallels found in the respondents' own worlds.

Katharine Perera's lecture brilliantly explores the tension in language between the vitality which creates diversity and the regularity which promotes cohesion. She wants to avoid the insensitivity which once required children to leave their home language at the threshold of the school, but she also wants to prevent English as the world language from becoming many languages that are indecipherable by peoples of different lands. She seeks a middle way which takes a modest first step toward solidifying awareness of Standard English (if there is such) by shaping instruction so as to confront all students with the myriad dialects that surround them in daily life.

Gerald Grace exhorts more boldly that English teachers stop playing the role of culture cop, that we stop thinking that something powerful about "our" culture is reflected in an elegance and rightness of Standard English. He decries the haughty sense that being "cultured" means being thoroughly permeated by Western manners, knowledge, and perception. Affirming different voices means allowing others to hold the floor, allowing yourself to listen to those voices, allowing yourself to be instructed by them. With that global perspective, all language will seem lively and powerful and good.

Patricia Gillard moves from this sense of embracing diversity in language to a celebration of differences in the wider realm of mass media. Her study of how twenty-three families watch television helps us to see that just as we privilege one dialect over another we also valorize one kind of television viewing over another. She shows the connection between both *what* and *how* television is watched and the social class circumstances which inform both that content and style. She cautions teachers to honor students' home styles in this matter just as we must in language. We are enriched by the diversity, she argues, and should teach from an awareness of this reality rather than denigrate our students' viewing content or style because it is not our own.

Mary K. Healy brings these fine essays to a natural close. She presents a strong picture of her own professional development, which flows from maturing as a teacher in her own school to growing in a community of teachers as an original member of the Bay Area Writing Project. Both of those professional steps could have been taken without intersecting our central thrust, celebrating different voices. But as she moves to the leadership of the Puente Project, she transfers the process of her own personal and professional growth experiences to a process that helps others grow who have been on the margin. Those were the other voices of the Mexican Americans who had not been successful in the academic world of California's huge educational structure. She took as her mission the support of able students who had been marginalized culturally and would have had, in spite of their talent, little hope of success in advanced academic programs. She helped them believe in themselves and helped them push open doors which had long since been closed to them. So the four essays progress naturally from the initial step of openness to language diversity to the active state of promoting ways marginalized voices can be heard in the academic world and given new life chances.

5 Divergence and Convergence in English: A Creative Tension?

Katharine Perera

> *A language as it evolves is subjected always to two conflicting pressures simultaneously: the pressure towards convergence or homogeneity, which facilitates communication within a perceived speech community, and the pressure towards divergence or heterogeneity.*
>
> (Harris, 1988: 4–5)

In Charles Dickens's novel *Our Mutual Friend,* Betty Higden, who has adopted a foundling called Sloppy, says of him: "Sloppy is a beautiful reader of a newspaper. He do the Police in different voices."

T. S. Eliot used the second sentence—"He do the Police in different voices"—as the working title of his poem "The Waste Land." So the conference title, "Different Voices," has not only linguistic and cultural meanings but literary resonances, too; it captures well the range of concerns, interests, and responsibilities that teachers of English share.

It is those different voices that participants in the conference are considering and celebrating; and because it is an international conference, those taking part represent some of the great diversity in the language that we all call English—including a number of varieties of English that Dickens would never have come across 150 or so years ago. But for an English person like me, it is not necessary to travel 12,000 miles to the other side of the world to hear such diversity. Quite apart from the presence in Britain of Commonwealth expatriates with a high public profile—people like Kiri Te Kanawa, Germaine Greer, Clive James, Trevor McDonald—and of very popular television programmes like "Dallas" and "Neighbours," there is enormous variety in the pronunciation of English within the very small compass of the British Isles. The amount of diversity of pronunciation within a language in any geographical area is directly related to the length of time that it has been spoken there. So there is more diversity in English within the British Isles than there is within North America, and more there than in South Africa, Australia, and New Zealand, where English has a shorter history as a mother tongue. (I am deliberately omitting the Caribbean from this account because the situation there is so linguistically complex.)

We are usually more sensitive to the social and regional differences in the language within our own country than elsewhere. So, although I can readily distinguish the regional accents of Liverpool, Manchester, and Birmingham—cities within a hundred miles of each other—I am not at all good at distinguishing Canadian from American English. I have to hope the speaker will say *out* and *about*, so that I can listen for the distinctively Canadian pronunciation [ʌʊt n̩ ə'bʌʊt]. Similarly, I can easily mistake a South African for an Australian, unless I can get her to say *start the car*, in which case I shall recognize the difference between the South African [stɒit ðə kɒ:] and the Australian [sta:t ðə ka]. Again, to my ears many Australians and New Zealanders sound the same, unless the speaker helpfully says something like *this biscuit*, when the contrast between the characteristically New Zealand pronunciation [ðəs baskət] and the Australian [ðis biskit] will enlighten me.

These are differences of pronunciation, but there are considerable differences of vocabulary among the numerous varieties of English, too. As an example of regional variation within England, we can take some of the words for a narrow passageway between buildings. This is variously called an *alley*, a *backsie*, a *ginnel*, *jigger*, a *jinnel*, and a *snicket*. Turning to international variation, we find that British speakers refer to a *pavement*, whereas Americans talk about a *sidewalk*, and in Australia and New Zealand *footpath* seems more usual. I have illustrated variations using words of native English stock, but a particular characteristic of English outside the British Isles is the admixture of words from indigenous languages; so in North American English there are words like *moccasin* and *toboggan*, which come from Algonquin; in Caribbean English there is *duppy* (ghost) and *okra*, which come from West African languages; in Singapore English we find *kampong* and *satay* from Malay; in Australian English, words that come from Aboriginal languages include *corroboree* (a noisy gathering), *dingo*, and *billabong*; and the New Zealand hosts of our conference have all adopted into their English Maori words like *hongi*, *marae*, and *pakeha*.

There is no doubt that—at least among native-speaker varieties of English—it is in pronunciation and vocabulary that the greatest variation is to be found. But there are, in addition, some differences in grammar between the various standard forms of English. For example, in New Zealand and Australia, when making *I used to go* negative, it is possible to say *I usedn't go*, whereas in Britain *I used not to go* or *I didn't use(d) to go* would be more usual. There are considerably more grammatical differences between Standard British English and North American English. For example, Americans can *appeal a decision*, whereas Britons *appeal against* it; British English speakers say, *Last year that coat fitted me*, whereas Americans say, *Last year that coat fit me*; and so on.

These are only the briefest illustrations; we all know other examples of our own, as the differences amongst the standard forms of the different international varieties of English are now so numerous that they fill an increasing number of academic articles and books. What this means is that, in a sense, none of us can say that we are native speakers of *English*; rather we are native speakers of British English, American English, New Zealand English, and so on. The corollary of this is that we don't have native speaker intuitions about what is right in other varieties. I know, for example, that Canadians say [ʌʊt n̩ ə'bʌʊt]; I also know that they don't use the pronunciation [ʌʊ] in all the /aʊ/ words, like *loud, round, bounce*, etc.—but I have no way of knowing which words have the characteristically Canadian pronunciation and which do not. So, if I tried to talk like a Canadian, I would be bound to make mistakes. Similarly, I know that Scottish English speakers say *outwith* in some, but not all, of the contexts where I say *outside*, but I am not at all sure how to differentiate those contexts.

So far, this discussion of variety in English has been largely from the point of view of the hearer and has been based on the fact that we are generally able to identify English speakers' regional origins from the way they speak. But distinctive forms of language are very important to *speakers*, too, because of what they convey about affiliations, loyalties, and cultural identity. There is plenty of evidence for this. Amongst the earliest empirical studies was one published in 1963 by the American sociolinguist, William Labov, in which he reported his linguistic investigation on Martha's Vineyard, an island three miles off the coast of Massachusetts. At the time of Labov's study there were 6,000 native Vineyarders, many of them direct descendants of seventeenth-century English settlers. Because the island is isolated from the mainland, some traditional pronunciations have survived—notably the vowel sounds in words like *nice* and *right, house* and *found*, where the first element of the diphthong is produced more centrally in the mouth than it is in General American—so we find pronunciations like *a nice house* [ə nəis həʊs] in Martha's Vineyard, compared with [ə nais haʊs] elsewhere. From an economic point of view, the island is in decline because of the collapse of traditional industries like fishing and farming, and the islanders are increasingly dependent on tourism. Every summer the indigenous population of 6,000 is swelled by some 42,000 wealthy summer visitors from the mainland, many of whom own second homes there or rent houses for a month or more. What happened during the 1950s in the face of this influx was that the distinctive island pronunciation, which had been gradually dying out in the early part of this century, gained a new popularity and status among Vineyarders. Furthermore, Labov was able to show that speakers' broadness of accent was directly related not to social class or education or the other indices we are used to but to their feelings about the island. From tape recordings of interviews with sixty-five informants, Labov was able to quantify the degree of centralization of the two diphthongs, with a high score representing the broadest local accent. He also assessed whether the informants were noticeably positive about the island (expressing pride in being a Vineyarder), or negative (being eager to leave), or neutral. His study revealed a strong relationship between pronunciation and sense of cultural identity: those islanders with the highest degree of centralization of these two diphthongs were those who were most positive about the island, and vice versa.

Studies like this show how important it is that we take account of group loyalties and cultural identity in planning and delivering the English curriculum. Recently, I have had some involvement in devising a National Curriculum for English in England and Wales, so I should like to say a little about how we dealt with this issue.

It is the first time that there has been a National Curriculum in Britain. For each curriculum subject, the government set up a working party charged with the task of establishing

> clear objectives—[which are called] attainment targets—for the knowledge, skills and understanding which pupils of different abilities and maturities should be expected to have acquired at ... the key ages of 7, 11, 14, and 16; and, to promote them, programmes of study describing the content, skills and processes which need to be covered during each key stage of compulsory education. (D. E. S., 1989, appendix 2)

The English curriculum working party was set up in April 1988 under the chairship of Professor Brian Cox, and I was one of the nine members of that committee. Our final report—which is popularly known as the Cox Report, though its proper title is *English for Ages 5 to 16*—had to be produced by May 1989. After a brief period of consultation and some minor amendments, our recommendations became law in April 1990.[1]

The Cox Committee was appointed in a climate of political dismay about the supposed declining standards of English in British schools, and there is no doubt in my mind that the government hoped and expected that our report would call for "a return to basics," with an insistence on the exclusive use of Standard English from the moment that children walked through the school gates at the age of five. If so, they were disappointed. In an attempt to take account of the linguistic, social, cultural, and educational complexities of this issue, the report includes statements of principle like this (see also Cox, 1991: chapter 31):

> A policy is required which recognises the educational and social importance of Standard English, but also respects the language background of the pupils. (D. E. S., 1989: 4.36)

> No child should be expected to cast off the language and culture of the home as he or she crosses the school threshold. (D. E. S., 1989: 2.7, quoting The Bullock Report, D. E. S., 1975: 286)

> A child's native language (including his or her native dialect) is an intimate part of individual and social identity. (D. E. S., 1989: 4.33)

> Schools should teach Standard English in ways which do not denigrate the non-standard dialects spoken by many pupils. (D. E. S., 1989: 4.36)

But how were these principles put into practices in programmes of study and attainment targets? A major way was by making the notion of language variety explicit within the curriculum. So the programme of study for 10-year-olds includes this requirement:

> Teachers should help children to make an account of any differences in grammar or vocabulary between the local dialect of English and Standard English, recognising that local speech forms play an important part in establishing a sense of group identity. (D. E. S., 1989: 17.43; Cox, 1991: 201)

As far as attainments are concerned, what secondary school pupils are expected to be able to do between the ages of 12 and 16 includes the following:

> Pupils should be able to:
> —talk about variations in vocabulary between different regional or social groups;

—talk about some grammatical differences between spoken Standard English and a non-standard variety;
—talk about some of the factors that influence people's attitudes to the way other people speak.

(D. E. S., 1989: 15.24; Cox, 1991: 158–61)

Our hope was that in an atmosphere of enquiry rather than proscription, pupils would be able to explore something of the great diversity of English and come to recognise some of the different functions that are served by both standard and nonstandard varieties.

One way into such an exploration is to collect examples from printed sources that draw attention in one way or another to the kind of English that is being used. Below are just four examples that I collected from British newspapers during a period of just a few months. The first one relates to a demonstration in Dorchester against the planned introduction of the poll tax. Dorchester is a small country town in rural England. The poll tax is a new method of calculating local taxation; it is deeply unpopular and is widely held to be inequitable.[2] The demonstration occurred at about the same time as a number of ugly and violent poll tax riots in inner-city areas.

(1) "We haven't had a march here in living memory," said the policeman in a thick West Country accent. "My superintendent's living memory is even longer, and he don't know of one."

Here, the focus on the policeman's rural accent and the use of the traditional dialect form *don't*—which may well have been put into the policeman's mouth by the journalist—are both designed to show that anti-poll tax feeling is not confined to militant, left-wing, inner-city dwellers but is strong in old-fashioned, conservative areas, too. Sometimes when writers put dialect expressions in people's mouths they get them wrong, and that is the point at issue in the second example, a line given by a white American writer to Dr. Martin Luther King, Jr., in a new musical about King's life. It is intended to represent Black American English vernacular:

(2) "Them victuals, they smell like soul food."

The black American poet Maya Angelou, who wrote the lyrics for the musical, was so incensed at this portrayal of Dr. King that she publicly dissociated herself from the whole enterprise, saying, "He would never have said that. It's written by someone who thinks black English is bad English." There is a happier example (3), which refers to the release of the American hostage Frank Reed from captivity in Beirut:

(3) When Mr Reed got off the plane in Washington on Friday night, he referred to Mr Keenan and Mr McCarthy as "my mates," a British expression that he learned from them during captivity.

In this example, Frank Reed's adoption of the British hostages' variety of English in preference to his own (which I imagine would be "buddies") is a powerful way of expressing his continuing sense of solidarity with them in their continuing captivity. The fourth example, which I find amusing, comes from *The Observer*, an up-market Sunday newspaper, on August 5, 1990, the day after the Queen Mother's ninetieth birthday:

(4) We made a reference to the Queen Mother (Gawd Bless 'er).

The unconventional spelling is intended to convey a working-class Cockney pronunciation. By this, the paper is trying to have it both ways: that is, to express affectionate sentiments towards the Queen Mother and yet at the same time to distance itself from those sentiments by suggesting that they are the preserve of the working classes.

So far I have given some illustrations of diversity in English, showing how such diversity can be related to linguistic and cultural identity. We need now to consider whether linguistic divergence is on the increase or not. As far as regional variation in Britain is concerned, what is certainly true is that there are now public and respected figures, particularly in radio and television broadcasting, who speak with noticeably regional accents, whereas only twenty years or so ago that was very rare. So we have national weather forecasters, for example, with Hampshire, Yorkshire, and Scottish accents.

It is also the case that, internationally, there is a growing tendency for different national forms of English to gain recognition and acceptance. The two major forms of Standard English are still Southern British and General American. American English has had a clearly separate identity from British English for nearly two hundred years. This divergence was given great impetus by the antipathy felt towards Britain at the time of the Revolution: for example, in 1802 the United States Congress recorded the first use of the phrase "the American language." Shortly afterwards, Thomas Jefferson wrote,

> There are so many differences between us and England . . . that we must be left far behind the march of circumstances were we to hold ourselves rigorously to their standard [language]. . . . Judicious neology can alone give strength and copiousness to language, and enable it to be the vehicle of new ideas. (cited in McCrum, Crann & MacNeil, 1986: 237)

Then in 1828 Noah Webster published his *American Dictionary of the English Language,* which not only codified distinctively American spellings but also had a far-reaching effect on vocabulary and pronunciation. It is reasonable to say, therefore, that since that date, there have been two codified, standardized varieties of English. It probably was not until this century that there were more. It seems that it was only during the 1940s, for example, that it became acceptable for public broadcasters in Australia to use distinctively Australian forms of the language, and the publication of Sydney Baker's book *The Australian Language* in 1945 was an important step on the road to the establishment of an Australian standard. The first dictionary of New Zealand English was published in 1979. There are now many books with titles like *New Englishes, Modern Englishes,* and so on, referring to the varieties of English used as official languages and as a medium of education in the Caribbean, Singapore, and India.

The obvious question that arises from this is: How far can divergence go before these different varieties become different, mutually unintelligible languages? It is a question that has been asked before, of course, and various scholars have attempted to give an answer. The following quotation, for example, comes from Randolph Quirk, formerly professor of English language at London University:

> In some places . . . quite extreme permissiveness has been actually encouraged. Where this trend has coincided with political movements towards community identity . . . counter-standard policies have become especially radical without anyone . . . having much clear perception of the long-term implications. (Quirk, 1981: 151–52).

Quirk, who on the whole seems to me fairly optimistic about the survival of English worldwide, nevertheless believes that the long-term implication of the encouragement of nonstandard varieties at the expense of standard varieties is the breakup of the language. Robert Burchfield, former chief editor of the Oxford English dictionaries and an expatriate New Zealander, is more pessimistic because he believes that even the standard varieties are diverging to a serious extent:

> Even as English spreads around the globe, it is beginning to break up. Within two or three centuries, Britons, Americans and Australians will be unable to understand each other. "Australia and New Zealand are moving quite swiftly," says Dr Robert Burchfield. "They will take about the same time as Americans to move right out of sight." (*The Sunday Times,* 21.1, 1990)

The analogy can be made with Latin, which was widely spoken throughout the Roman Empire and which broke up into the different Romance languages which we know today as French, Spanish, Portuguese, and so on. Below, I have given the conference title, "Different Voices," in the six main Romance languages; it is striking that even this simple phrase is different in each of the languages:

(5) voix differentes French
    voces diferentes Spanish
    vozes diferentes Portuguese
    veus diferents Catalan
    voci differenti Italian
    voci diferite Romanian

A more modern example can be found in Portuguese. I was recently at an international conference in Hungary, where I spent some time talking to a Brazilian whose mother tongue was Portuguese. He told me that he found it easier to understand lectures that were delivered in English than those in the Portuguese spoken by participants from Portugal. In other words, in the last three hundred years, the forms of Portuguese spoken in Portugal and Brazil have diverged so considerably that they are no longer always mutually intelligible.

Unlike the examples of Latin and Portuguese, however, there are some factors in the situation of English today which tend towards convergence. For example, the use of English as the international language of airline pilots, pop songs, television, and films; the existence of great international publishing houses with offices in London, New York, and Sydney and a commercial interest in publishing books in a form of English that is intelligible worldwide. I am currently very aware of the standardising power of publishing houses because I am acting as the subject editor for a section in a new encyclopedia on language and linguistics to be published by the British publisher Pergamon; it insists that all contributors must follow American rather than British spelling conventions.

I believe that there is a crucial need for these two opposing forces of divergence and convergence to be balanced in a creative tension, with each holding the other in check. If divergence becomes the stronger force, then English will fragment into different languages; if convergence is dominant, many speakers will lose their individual cultural identity. In formulating my view in this way, I have made it clear that I believe it would be regrettable if English were to break up—if a similar conference in, say, two hundred years' time necessitated headphones for all participants and a small army of interpreters. If that view is shared, it raises the question of what we can do about it, since merely to express anxiety about what might happen to the language in the next two hundred years would not be very productive.

First of all, to start negatively, I do not believe there is any place for some kind of linguistic academy or international committee to legislate on English usage worldwide. There is no evidence that such a body would have any beneficial effect at all.

Nor do I believe that it is feasible to construct a special, simplified variety of English that would be nobody's mother tongue, specifically for the purpose of international communication. Professor Quirk (1981: 155) has made such a suggestion and has given some indication of what the characteristics of "Nuclear English" would be. He says it would have to be both communicatively adequate and decidedly easier to learn than any variety of natural English. In describing how English might be adapted and made simpler, he suggests, for example, that the whole range of our notoriously difficult tag questions would be replaced by one form such as *Isn't that right?* So, instead of: *It was raining, wasn't it? I can leave, can't I?* and *You must hurry, mustn't you?* there would be just *It was raining, isn't that right? I can leave, isn't that right?* and *You must hurry, isn't that right?* (In fact, some varieties of English already have the even simpler one-word lexical tag *right*, e.g., *You must hurry, right?*) Although such suggestions are constructive and thought provoking, I do not believe that they would work, because Nuclear English would be cut off from its living roots. A language that is nobody's mother tongue is on the way to becoming a dead language, just as Latin became a dead language, even though it had been used as the pan-European language of religion and legal affairs for many centuries.

To turn now to some positive suggestions, there are five things that we might bear in mind as we think of the English curriculum in our own countries. First, although it sounds trivial, I am sure that having the same name for our different varieties of English helps. That is because the sense of what constitutes two varieties of one language and what constitutes two different languages does not lie just in linguistic features such as vocabulary and grammar, but also in the perceptions and attitudes of the speech community. These perceptions are powerfully influenced by names. Generally speaking, people assume that a different name means a different language. So they will talk of speaking both Hindi and Urdu, or Dutch and Flemish, when in fact each of the members of those pairs is so similar to each other that it is like my saying that I speak two languages, English and American, on the grounds that I know that in the States and Canada I would have to put trash in a garbage can and baggage in the trunk of a car whereas in England I put rubbish in a dustbin and luggage in the boot. Therefore, if we are to avoid language fragmentation, I think an important starting point is to maintain the rather cumbersome labels "Jamaican English," "Australian English," "New Zealand English," "American English," and so on, rather than to promote the simpler and emotionally more appealing names "Jamaican," "Australian," and "American," etc.

Next, I am convinced that the strongest protection against the breakup of the language is our shared writing system. Although we all sound very different when we talk to each other, when we write to each other many of those differences disappear. The inherently conservative nature of written language puts a brake on the natural processes of language change and ensures that the different patterns of change in our various countries is still related to the same core. We are all used to the complaint that English orthography is absurdly complex and that it is no longer related in any straightforward way to the sounds of speech. If English spelling were to be reformed so that pronunciation was more directly represented, the obvious question is whose pronunciation would be chosen? We can see the effect of relating spelling more directly to pronunciation by looking at literary examples, as there are a number of writers who have used nonconventional spellings to reflect the speech around them: we can think of Emily Brontë and D. H. Lawrence in Britain, and of Louise Bennett and Mikey Smith in the Caribbean. At (6) I have given an extract from a 13-year-old's reworking of the story of the Pied Piper that has spellings that attempt to capture the Geordie (Tyneside) accent, where *town*, for example, is [tun] and *called* is [ka:ld]:

> (6) Thor wes yence a toon caaled Newcastle on Tyne an' this toon wes full o' moggies. Thor wes moggies aal ower, moggies gobblin spuggies an' gliffin bairns, nickin tetties an' yowling aal neet. Soon the toon's folk wes really sick. They went to the Pollis an' yammered, "Yees are aal fyuls. Thor ir moggies runnin aal ower. Howway, man, dee sommic."[3] (Lesley, age 13)

I am convinced that there is great value in trying to convey the distinctive characteristics of our different voices in this way in literature; I am equally convinced that it would be disastrous if variant spellings for each of the different national standard forms of English were institutionalized and used in all types of writing. We would have a number of mutually unintelligible languages in a much shorter time than two hundred years. Therefore, I think it would be helpful if, instead of bemoaning the absence of regular sound-symbol correspondences in our orthography, we took the opportunity to point out to pupils that our writing system is neutral as far as pronunciation is concerned and does not reflect any one accent of English better than any other. In passing, it is also worth noticing that the conservatism of the writing system allows us still to read and understand works written four hundred years ago, despite the fact that there have been such substantial sound changes in that time that we would have great difficulty in comprehending the *spoken* language of that period. To make that point, here is just half a line from *Hamlet,* using a made-up spelling that reflects for us how Shakespeare would have pronounced it:

(7) 'Own fair dafter and no more' (Shakespeare, *Hamlet* II.ii. 435)

Unless you remember the play very well, you may have difficulty in recognising that as *One fair daughter and no more.* Shakespeare would have pronounced *one* to rhyme with *bone,* logically enough, and *daughter* to rhyme with *after*—as *laughter* still does. If English spelling had been changed over the years to keep it in line with sound changes, the works of Shakespeare would all be as hard to relate to our modern language as that half line is. So, our much-criticized spelling has the inestimable advantage that it is not tied to pronunciation and, therefore, is widely intelligible across space and time.

It may seem that spelling reform is so unlikely as to be not worth thinking about, but it is worth noticing that the spelling of Dutch was reformed in 1863, 1945, and again in 1953; so there have been four different spelling systems in the past 150 years, with the effect that it is harder for the Dutch than for us to read literature from earlier periods. Furthermore, they are currently working on another set of reforms. In Britain a bill drawn up by the Simplified Spelling Society was put before Parliament in 1949, and although it was defeated, it was by only three votes. Another bill in 1953 actually passed its first reading but was withdrawn because of opposition by the Ministry of Education.

It would be possible, though, to think of spelling reform *without* planning to tie the spelling to a particular pronunciation of English. If in any of the countries where English is spoken as either a mother tongue or as an official language, there were to be serious consideration given to proposals for spelling reform, it would be essential for all the other English-speaking countries to be involved as well. If the spelling were to be changed to any noticeable extent, then it would have to be done in concert; and this would entail the setting-up of some kind of international committee. I have already referred dismissively to such a body, but only in connection with the regulation of language *structure*. It is much more feasible to regulate *spelling* by decree, and indeed there are successful precedents for such concerted action. For example, the current reform of the Dutch spelling system is being undertaken by a joint committee from the Netherlands and Belgium because the two countries, which both accepted the earlier spelling reforms, are determined that their writing systems should not diverge. Another example can be found in Malay, the official national language of both Malaysia and Indonesia. Malay used to be spelt differently in the two countries (reflecting the orthographies of the British and Dutch colonisers, respectively). In the early 1970s a joint committee was set up and a new Union spelling was accepted. In some cases the Malaysian spelling was adopted by both countries, as in *jalan* at (8); in other cases, a completely new spelling was agreed upon, as in *cakap*:

(8) **Indonesian spelling**	**Malay spelling**	**Union spelling**
djalan	jalan	jalan
tjakap	chakap	cakap

So, at least in the written form, the two slightly different varieties have converged.

My third suggestion, which applies only to native speakers of English, is paradoxical. That is, in order to sustain the unity of English we need to bring as much linguistic variety as possible into the classroom. The reason for this is people's attitudes toward language. We have already seen that the boundaries between languages cannot be drawn solely on the basis of linguistic features but depend partly on people's perceptions. Whether we understand a speaker of another variety depends partly on the variety itself—on how different it is from our own; partly on the speaker—on his or her clarity, speed, etc.; but also partly on us—on whether we listen with the *will* to understand. if we have a narrow conception of what English is, then there is a greater likelihood that when we meet a markedly different variety we shall react negatively, saying, in effect, "That's not English—I don't understand a word of it." If, on the other hand, we have been frequently exposed to forms of English other than our own, we are less likely to take a monolithic view of what English is and more likely to make an attempt to understand an unfamiliar variety. In this way, we still perceive the different Englishes as one language instead of several.

Fourthly, one way in which we can bring this variety into the classroom is by making available literature from cultures other than our own. For those of us who have been brought up on an almost exclusive diet of literature written in Britain, there is not only American and Canadian literature but also an increasing wealth of English works written in India, Africa, the Caribbean, Australia, and New Zealand. It is partly through reading works such as these that we gain our passive competence in other forms of English. After all, there is no need for us to be able to *speak* in "different voices"; what matters is that we *understand* them when we hear them. I was delighted that the Cox Committee made the reading of literature from other cultures a requirement for older secondary pupils:

> Pupils should be able to:
> Read a range of poetry, fiction, literary non-fiction, and drama, including some works written before the 20th century and *works from different cultures*. (D. E. S., 1989: 16.21)

What is less pleasing is that one of the last-minute alterations the government made before these statements of attainment became law in 1990 was to remove the phrase *works from different cultures*. The requirement remains in the programmes of study, so I am guardedly optimistic that they will still find their way into our classrooms, but the alteration is a striking illustration of official reluctance to give any prominence to the notion of cultural and linguistic diversity.

The fifth thing we can do if we do not want English to fragment is to ensure that all pupils have the opportunity to acquire a standard form of the language, because these will always have more in common with each other than nonstandard varieties will. Pupils, of course, have the right to choose never to use the standard form if they feel it undermines their own social and cultural identity, but if they are not taught it, then they do not have that choice. I hope it is clear from what I have said already that I am not suggesting that there should be just two accepted Standard Englishes. On the contrary, I think it is right that each English-speaking country should have its own standard form which reflects its own national identity, its own distinctive "voice." What matters is that these worldwide Standard Englishes should be mutually intelligible.

For those countries where English is an official language and a medium of education but *not* generally a mother tongue—for example, India and Singapore—it is necessary to consider how national distinctiveness can be combined with external intelligibility. (It seems to me essential that external intelligibility should be an educational goal; otherwise, one of the most important reasons for adopting an alien language is vitiated.) With regard to the three aspects of language—pronunciation, vocabulary, and grammar—it is pronunciation that is usually the most immediately distinctive aspect. Considerable variation of individual sounds is possible without losing external intelligibility. For example, the vowel sound /ei/ in *face* is pronounced in widely different ways in England—[iə] in Newcastle, [æi] in London—without comprehension breaking down. But what does cause problems of intelligibility is when stress and rhythm are markedly different from native speaker varieties. So the pronunciation *atMOSphere*, for example, can render the word unintelligible to native speakers.

Vocabulary can afford to be distinctive. If we take the case of Indian English, then there are loan words like *gurdwara* (temple), new compounds like *mixy-grinder* (food blender), and hybrid Indian-English compounds like *newspaper wallah* (newspaper seller). The presence of these words shows that the language has put down roots, has become part of the country's cultural identity.

Grammar, on the other hand, needs particular care, if widespread comprehensibility is to be maintained. Take just one example from the tense and aspect system: If an Indian says, *I am doing it,* where a native speaker would say, *I have been doing it,* then misunderstanding may arise and, unlike the case of an unfamiliar word, it may well be misunderstanding that goes unrecognised and unrepaired.

The Cox Committee considered that a right understanding of the nature and functions of Standard English is so important that the report contains a whole chapter on it; it is featured, too, in the programmes of study and statements of attainment. Here are two brief examples:

> Teachers should explain how Standard English has come to have a wide social and geographical currency and to be the form of English most frequently used on formal, public occasions and in writing. (D. E. S., 1989: 17.43; Cox, 1991: 201)

> Pupils should be able to:
> write in Standard English (except where non-standard forms are needed for literary purposes, e.g., in dialogue in a story or playscript.) (D. E. S., 1989: 17.34; Cox, 1991: 172)

Some English teachers have felt that this emphasis on Standard English is at odds with the committee's statements of respect for pupil's own language varieties. I am sure that this is not the case, and that a regional and a standard variety of English can both be part of a native speaker's language competence. I believe that teaching a standard form is important, partly because in any culture it is those who have access to the standard language who have access to power, but also because it is important for the future of the language, since, internationally, it is the Standard Englishes that will hold the language together and prevent our enriching diversity from becoming an impoverishing fragmentation. It has been suggested that, in countries outside Britain and the United States, there will always be only a small number of people who will want or need the international connections that are facilitated by a common language, and that to impose a standard form on the many for the sake of the few is to give insufficient weight to questions of linguistic and cultural identity. But this is to misunderstand what happens when languages diverge. The advantages of speaking a widely understood variety of English are not confined to international businesspeople or jet-setting tourists. Today, literate people throughout the English-speaking world are able to read all the vast wealth of books, newspapers, and so on that are printed in English. It is obvious that it would not be commercially viable for publishers to produce the full range of this material in all the languages that would result if the current varieties of English were to diverge to the point where mutual intelligibility was lost. Therefore, divergent varieties with relatively small numbers of speakers would have few publications, whether literary, political, academic, or social; consequently, all members of such speech communities would be the poorer. It is for this reason, above all, that while acclaiming the fact that we can celebrate our different voices, I also rejoice that we still share a common tongue.

Notes

1. The Report of the English Working Group, which appeared in 1989 and was popularly known as the Cox Report, is no longer available (and was never available outside Great Britain), but much of it has been incorporated into a book by Brian Cox (1991). Therefore, when I quote from the report, I have given both the original source and, where possible, the more accessible reference.

2. The poll tax was, in fact, largely abandoned by the Conservative Government after Margaret Thatcher's forced resignation in November 1990.

3. I am indebted to Professor Ron Carter, National Director of the LINC Project, for this example.

References

Cox, B. (1991). *Cox on Cox*. London: Hodder & Stoughton.

Department of Education and Science (1989). *English for ages 5 to 16* (The Cox Report). London: H. M. S. O.

Harris, M. (1988). The Romance languages. In M. Harris & N. Vincent (Eds.), *The Romance languages*. London: Routledge.

Labov, W. (1963). The social motivation of a sound change. *Word, 19*, 273–309.

McCrum, R., Cran, W. & MacNeil, R. (1986). *The story of English*. London: Faber & Faber.

Quirk, R. (1981). International communication and the concept of Nuclear English. In L. E. Smith (Ed.), *English for cross-cultural communication*. London: Macmillan.

6 Keeping English Alive and Well: A Response to Katharine Perera

Denny Wolfe

Some sat on a bare floor, some in chairs, and some lay comfortably on mats. As all of us surveyed this gathering of hundreds of teachers from nearly everywhere in the English-speaking world, we contemplated our differences and our similarities—our separate and mutual interests, issues, and identities. We eagerly awaited whatever might come.

The setting for this scene was Auckland, New Zealand, Aug. 26, 1990. The occasion was the Fifth Congress of the International Federation of Teachers of English (IFTE). Many had traveled thousands of miles to assemble in this place for days and nights of cross-cultural exchange about English teaching. Expectations were high, as most came with an openness to having patterns of thinking challenged and habits of mind tested by colleagues from schools serving many cultures.

The keynote speaker on this day was Katharine Perera, a linguist from the University of Manchester in the United Kingdom. Her topic was "Divergence and Convergence in English: A Creative Tension?" What a fitting subject for this audience, an audience feeling the very tension she was about to describe. Perera began by reminding us eloquently of how varieties of spoken English in many parts of the world reflect our similarities and differences—English in the British Isles, in North America, in South Africa, in Australia, in New Zealand. In pronunciation and vocabulary, great variation exists, reflecting both speakers' and listeners' cultural identities and affiliations.

As I listened to the first part of her talk, I thought of the many cultural variations of pronunciation, vocabulary, and grammar that exist in classrooms throughout the United States. I remembered anew how important it is for us as teachers to acknowledge, accept, and respect these variations of student talk. Only by doing so can we hope to create classroom learning environments where students feel safe enough to take the risks necessary for growth, for full participation in the educational enterprise. The 1991 Cox Report in the United Kingdom, *English for Ages 5 to 16*, acknowledges this point, as Perera noted: "A policy is required which recognizes the educational and social importance of Standard English, but also respects the language background of the pupils." We must not attempt to take away from students the language they know, I thought. To do so is to rob them of their instruments for learning. By teaching them to value their language—and by showing that we also value it—we can then help them see the importance of learning Standard English. But not before.

This attitude toward teaching is illustrated by the story of the monster and the watermelon. It seems that an anthropologist walked into a primitive village one day and saw the villagers huddling and quaking and pointing to an object in the field, which they said was a monster. Upon inspecting the object, the anthropologist found it was merely a watermelon. He told the villagers, "This is no monster. It is a watermelon, a gourd, with juicy red pulp, good to eat," whereupon the villagers killed him. Days later another anthropologist entered the village, witnessed the same scene, and inspected the "monster" in the field. But this anthropologist drew his machete, sliced up the watermelon, and threw the pieces into the woods. He trampled on the rinds, pounded his chest, and returned to the villagers. And they made him king. Over time, he taught them the difference between a monster and a watermelon. Good teaching works this way. Good teachers know they must honor and respect students' values, customs, and worldviews. Since language is central to these things, good teachers value and respect that, too. Then, and perhaps only then, can teachers teach new things—like Standard English, for example.

Divergence in language use is a fact of linguistic life, literally. Without such divergence, language dies. It is divergence that keeps language vital and dynamic, qualities essential to health of any kind. And it is this very divergence that keeps Standard English alive and well. It, too, must change in order to flourish. Split infinitives, sentences that end with prepositions, distinctions between *who* and *whom*, nominative case pronouns always following linking verbs—these are but a few examples of Standard English features that were entrenched in the American language not so long ago. But only the most persevering purist, or indomitable elitist, would always insist on those usages today in spoken American English.

Halfway through her talk, Perera asked the cogent question, "How far can divergence go before these different varieties become different, mutually unintelligible languages?" She cited several scholars, including Randolph Quirk and Robert Burchfield, who worry about the alleged breakup of the English language. Their concern is that English seems to be diverging to such an extent that one day a conference like IFTE could indeed require translators, although everyone would claim to be speaking English. Perera pointed to Latin, which ultimately diverged into French, Spanish, Portuguese, and the rest of the Romance languages. Clearly, the case of Latin offers a historical and dramatic precedent for the potential occurrence of such a linguistic phenomenon.

Sensibly, Perera observed that it would be futile to attempt to "legislate" a Standard English. It would be equally naive and lame to invent an artificial ("nuclear") English for international use, although some have seriously proposed both of these strategies to combat extreme divergence. Perera makes five suggestions for preserving English: (1) keeping the same name—English—for the varieties that exist; (2) maintaining a shared writing system that has far more similarities than differences; (3) maintaining an attitude of acceptance of linguistic variety, coupled with a will to understand the varieties; (4) expanding the canon to include literature of other cultures; and (5) working to ensure that students acquire some appropriate form of Standard English in each corner of the English-speaking world. Her arguments for and discussions of these five suggestions are lucid, rational, and practical.

On her first point, we have a concrete choice. We can decide to keep the name *English* for all the varieties that exist. Such a decision is plausible both to make and to enforce—if need be, through government agencies. Her second point—to maintain a shared writing system—is both possible and probable. The politics, economics, and culture of the publishing industry will ensure the perpetuation of a shared writing system. Her last three suggestions, however, are much trickier. And they all have to do with what English teachers do in schools. Because they are tricky and because they rely upon teachers, they are also difficult to implement in a universal, consistent way. To make them feasible requires diligence by those who prepare teachers, by teachers themselves, by curriculum planners, and by school policymakers.

Her third point, calling for the acceptance of varieties of English and a will to understand them, demands a teaching force that values linguistic diversity and relates to students in such a way as to *inspire the will* to comprehend dialectal differentiation. This is an enlightened and a noble goal of English teaching. In almost any classroom in America, for example, many dialects exist. Some attention in the curriculum must be given to recognizing, accepting, studying, and understanding these dialects. Until such attention is seriously included in the curriculum of more schools, we run the risk of not only losing English but perhaps our society, as well. We need a spirit of togetherness in spite of our separateness, if we are to maintain standards of anything. The current movement toward cooperative learning is a hopeful direction in schools. To increase cooperation and diminish competitiveness simply *must* become a major agenda item for schools as they approach the twenty-first century.

Perera's fourth suggestion—to include more literature from other cultures—is, of course, controversial. Debates about the "canon" rage on. But the argument to expand the literature curriculum for the purpose of illustrating linguistic variety is a refreshing and compelling one. Generally, those who argue for preserving the canon as it exists (i.e., the "dead white guys," as they are referred to by many American students) talk of the need to maintain and perpetuate a common core of shared experiences and values. Those who argue for expansion lament the exclusion of many superbly gifted female and multicultural writers from the literature curriculum. To include the need to illustrate *linguistic variety* in a literature curriculum strengthens the expansionists' case.

Perera's last suggestion—to ensure that students acquire Standard English—on the surface, seems naive. How can we as teachers "ensure" that students learn anything—historical concepts, mathematical formulas, the scientific method, and so on? The realistic answer is that we cannot. The processes of teaching and learning, the complexities of schools and society, the contemporary pressures of parenting—all of these and more are powerful forces against "ensuring" acquisition of a standard form of English by all students. Yet, in spite of all these forces, professional teachers try, and many succeed. What seems clear is that teachers have little chance of helping students acquire a standard form of English if schools do not admit and respect the dialects students bring with them into classrooms. Again, only if they feel valued, accepted, and respected will students care to learn anything—and this includes Standard English.

Divergence and convergence appear to be independent concepts; yet, without things diverging, there is nothing to converge. As

English teachers, we must revel in the rich, colorful, and expressive varieties that exist in the English language; at the same time, we must help students value and master what Perera calls "a common tongue." Through "different voices," it is both possible and desirable to maintain one.

7 From the Dominant Voice to Different Voices: Issues of Language, Culture, and Power

Gerald Grace

Tena koutou, tena koutou katoa.
Tena koe Karen, tena koe Paul, tena koe Keri.
Greetings to you all.
Greetings to Karen, to Paul, and to Keri.

I am very pleased to be back in Aotearoa, New Zealand, and honoured to have been asked to speak at this conference. What I'm going to do is to attempt to review, in four parts, some of the main emphases of this conference: theory, history, policy, and practice and strategy. These have been the four main emphases within the discourse of this conference and of its papers and of its workshops.

My argument, in brief, will be as follows:

First, that a major theme of the conference could be summed up in the expression, "from the dominant voice to different voices." I will then look at the different ways in which we have theorized the concept of the dominant voice.

Secondly, that English teachers need to appreciate the historical, political, and ideological context in which English and its teachers are constituted (i.e., the transformation to different voices is not going to be easy). It's going to be a long struggle, and Rose Pere, right at the beginning of this conference, reminded us that you have to know your history, because knowing your history gives you strength and lets you know what you're up against. And I'm going to try and indicate that for English and its teachers.

Thirdly, that the conference has, in all its discussions and busyness, been setting an agenda for policy and has provided a richness of practical ideas for empowering different voices. It's been very impressive, a great experience.

But, fourthly, that in itself, the agenda to empower different voices will not be enough. The transformations of English which have been proposed in this conference have a politics as well as a culture. And the politics of transformation will require teachers to have a strategy and to make allies. Teachers of English, probably more so than teachers in other subject areas, cannot afford to be political innocents.

I will begin, then, by addressing what I take to have been a major theme of this conference—the move from the dominant voice to different voices—and to look at how we have theorized, in our various settings, this notion of dominant voice.

From the Dominant Voice to Different Voices

When educational language policy and practice are examined historically and comparatively across a wide range of societies, the existence of what I want to call "historically dominant voices" is soon apparent to the student and to the adult. By "dominant voices," I mean a language/power relationship. Those who are in power in various contexts seek to empower their language in any interaction with other languages. Language thus becomes, among other things, a mediated power relationship.

The dominant voice seeks to define the world in terms of the categories and ideologies of the powerful. It is the voice which speaks for most of the time with confidence and with apparent authority. We in the United Kingdom know a particular voice that speaks, most of the time, with confidence and with apparent authority. It is the voice which defines correctness and appropriateness, sense and non-sense, faith, morals, and the needs of society and the individual.

Where there is no opposing concept or practice of democracy, of partnership, of consultation and participation, of dialogue and mutual respect, and of power sharing, then the dominant voice is the voice of imposition. It is the voice of hierarchy and of cultural, political, economic, and personal imperialism.

In its various manifestations in history and in contemporary societies, the dominant voice or, more precisely, the agencies of the dominant voice, have in general a uniform intention. This intention is the reproduction of the dominant voice within the person and within various subject populations. The intention is to get the person or the community to speak "correctly," i.e., to speak in the approved form, both linguistically and ideologically.

The process of the reproduction of the dominant voice, of speaking "correctly," is not simply a linguistic matter, although it is certainly that; it is a matter also of personal, cultural, and political identity. For what is being attempted in the reproduction of the dominant voice is the cultural and ideological transformation of the person and the community.

In practice, however, the reproduction of the dominant voice is a complex and contested process with at least three consequences: (1) Some who are subject to it internalize it and gradually cease to speak in a different voice; (2) some retreat from it into what Paulo Freire has called a "culture of silence," in which the linguistics and cultural confidence of the person and the community has been undermined and the capacity to speak in a different voice is weakened; and (3) where circumstances permit, some resist the dominant voice by continuing to speak "in a different voice" and encouraging others to do likewise.

I referred earlier to historically dominant voices, and it is important for us all, as students of education and language policy, to have a historical understanding, as well as a contemporary understanding, of the range of phenomena which can be referred to as "dominant voices."

Dominant voices have been and are those of state power and bureaucracy; of church and religious agencies; of political and ideological apparatuses of various types. In certain societies the voice of the party has, until recently, been the dominant voice, while different voices have been under constraint. In other societies the dominant voice is becoming that of free-market economics and New Right political and moral ideology. Here, different voices may be heard, but often in the mode which has been characterized as "repressive tolerance." That is to say, the voices are heard, but they are not engaged with.

The dominant voice has also been associated with the power relations of class, race, imperialism, and gender. Throughout history, dominant classes and regions have sought to impose their language and culture upon other classes and other regions. This imposition has frequently been attempted through the agency of formal education systems, through the aptly named schooling process. It has been justified in the name of civilisation. In Britain the Victorian middle classes referred to the refining and uplifting of the lower classes. This, in their view, was the mission of education: to refine the lower orders and to uplift them, but not too far. It has been justified in the name of social and economic progress, called "modernization," and it has been justified in the name of equality of educational opportunity.

Dominant groups, through the process of colonial conquest and imperialism, have not only invaded the economic and political space of other peoples, but also their linguistic and cultural space. As part of the imperial process, these groups have imposed the dominant voice, the voice of a colonizing power and its agents. The English language, in the context of imperialism, has been a classic example of the imposed dominant voice, and teachers of English, we must remember, have historically been agents of that process.

Finally, within the wider social context, the power relations of gender have structured and shaped both language content and language use. The maleness of language has dominated for centuries, and during those centuries, men have spoken for much of the time while women have been forced either into the culture of silence or into marginalized forms of language. But not at this conference, they haven't! That's for certain.

When I got my invitation to speak, I said, in the usual modest way that white, middle-class professors have of responding to such letters, "Yes, I'd be pleased to come. Perhaps it would be a good idea if I started." The committee considered, wrote back, and said, "We're putting you last, Gerald." I thought, "Right. We know where we are." Then I reflected and thought, "But of course, the conference is Different Voices; they don't want a white male from England talking first. They're going to have women; and, you'll notice, I'm the only male keynote speaker, and I'm put in at the end, by kind permission!"

It made me think of David Lodge's wonderful comment, "English, white, male, middle-class, middle-aged . . . all sources for contemporary discredit." So I'm very glad you allowed me to come. But the dominant voice has not only existed at the larger social structural level of state bureaucracy and party; of the church and religion; of capitalism and the market; of the community and interest groups; and of class, race, and gender relations. It has also existed within educational systems, frequently as the dominant voice of the teacher.

There is now enough evidence to show that in school classrooms, especially secondary school classrooms, teachers speak for most of the time. There is, in short, a *pedagogical dominant voice*. One of its functions, historically, has been to constrain, rather than to facilitate, the existence of different voices within the classroom.

It's a voice you will hear frequently in English secondaries. If you go into many English secondary schools, you will hear, "Sit up there. Look this way. Don't just stare at me. Why aren't you writing notes? Do you think this is a holiday camp?"

At some time, we must seriously reflect on how the formal institution of school does this to people. What is it doing to those teachers that it turns them into the pedagogical dominant voice? Why can't they enter into the humane and dialogic relations that I'm sure would be the ideal of many of them? Somehow, they end up hectoring their classes. Now, that's something to do with the way we organize schooling, and we've certainly got to change that.

This international conference on the teaching of English has set for itself the theme "Different Voices: Language, Culture, Identity." As the NZATE organizing committee has expressed it, "In planning this conference in New Zealand we have committed ourselves to honouring the partnership promised a hundred and fifty years ago in the Treaty of Waitangi. The tangata whenua, people of the land of New Zealand, are the Maori, and as we move toward the end of the twentieth century with a history of over one thousand years of Maori settlement and a hundred and fifty years of pakeha occupation, New Zealanders are searching for their identity, both as individuals and as a nation. We believe that this reflects a worldwide movement by indigenous peoples that cannot and must not be ignored."

What NZATE signalled right at the beginning of this conference was its commitment to a partnership model of language use and cultural exchange in Aotearoa/New Zealand between the Maori and the pakeha communities. This was a radical start to the conference. These historical agents of the dominant voice in New Zealand, the English language, were declaring their commitment to, respect for, and sensitivity towards a partnership status with a different voice, the Maori language. They were calling for an end to a dominance/subordination relationship between the two major languages of Aotearoa/New Zealand.

Other speakers, presenters of papers, and conveners of workshops have taken up the themes of partnership, of different voices, and of overcoming dominance/subordination relationships and have widened the application of these themes to include the different voices of other indigenous peoples, of working-class youth, of women and girls, of social and political critics, and of pupils and students as participants rather than simply as recipients of the educational process.

Now, it must be said that these sorts of emphases and commitments represent a radical break with historical traditions in the teaching of the English language. These traditions have been largely about dominance rather than difference: the dominance of class-related forms of the language; the dominance of gender-related forms of the language; the dominance of certain structural and literary forms of the language; and the dominance of teachers of English in the role of oracles and transmitters of the subject called English.

Before we can begin to look at future directions for the teaching of English and before we can begin to celebrate and to implement English in a different voice, we must recognize that there will be no simple transformation. Historical traditions have power and are remarkably enduring. New forms of dominance in language and in culture constantly threaten. In other words, English as a subject, and as an activity, is a site of struggle—culturally, socially, politically, and ideologically. Teachers of English need to be fully aware of the historical and contemporary struggles over the nature of English. The radical project of this conference, empowering different voices, must take into account the nature and the power of the forces working against such a project.

Different voices cannot simply be empowered by international conferences per se; nor can they be empowered simply by the professional commitments of teachers. A strategy of transformation is required if teachers of English are to empower different voices. In forming that strategy, at least three things are necessary: (1) an awareness of the historical and contemporary expectations for English; (2) a developed, professional agenda for transforming the subject; and (3) a responsible, democratic, or, if you prefer, consultative plan of action to win support for that agenda within the school, the community, and the wider society.

The Historical, Political, and Ideological Context of English Teaching

I start then with the importance of knowing your history. That was a point emphasized by Margaret Gill, who said that English teachers need to know more about the history of their own group. Teachers in general and teachers in English in particular need to know more about the history, the sociology, and the politics of their own professional occupation and how teachers and the activity of teaching have been constituted by powerful ideologies and external agencies at various times. After many years of relative neglect, there is now available a body of literature and research studies on this subject.

For teachers in general there are texts such as *Teachers Work* by Bob Connell (1985) and Michael Apple's *Teachers and Texts,* which came out in 1986. Two texts which I have been associated with are *Teachers, Ideology, and Control: A Study in Urban Education,* which was my study of inner-city teachers in London (1978), and *Teachers: The Culture and Politics of Work,* which I edited with Martin Lawn in 1987.

For teachers of English in particular, there is Margaret Mathieson's classic, *The Preachers of Culture: A Study of English and Its Teachers* (1975), and a recent collection by Ivor Goodson and Peter Medway, *Bringing English to Order: The History and Politics of a School Subject.* (1990).

If you examine the literature on teachers, it is possible to view the struggle over what English is and what should be the role of the English teacher in three historical and political phases.

In the first phase, which we could call the "historical mission" of English and its teachers, both the subject and its agents constituted dominant voices. Teachers of English were expected to be, in that superb phrase of Matthew Arnold in his "Culture and Anarchy," "preachers of culture."

The culture of English to be preached was that of the dominant social order—both in class and gender terms—and in the wider empire, that of the imperial race. The correlates of English in this mission were a notion of class culture called "civilisation," a notion of race culture called "civilisation," and a notion of gender culture called "scholarship."

English was expected to contribute to the enhancement of morality and internal social order through the refining effects of great literature; the hegemony of the English people, through the spread of its language to every quarter of the globe; and a general notion of disciplined schooling and scholarship through an emphasis on correctness of speech, grammar, and syntactical detail and appropriateness of expression and style—what was called, in short, "standards."

The concept of standards and how they were to be enforced was a concept of discipline and order. It had correlates with moral, social, and political discipline. We can see that in the current reaction of certain groups that want to bring back grammar, the desire to bring back social, moral, and political discipline.

Let me just give you two examples from this historical phase—those from Matthew Arnold's "Culture and Anarchy." I always thought he should have called it "Culture *or* Anarchy," because that's one of the central messages of the book. This is his vision of culture: "Culture seeks to do away with classes, to make the best that has been thought and known in the world current everywhere. To make all men live in an atmosphere of sweetness and light" (Grace, 1978, p. 20).

Just do a critical content analysis of that. "Culture seeks to do away with classes." Well that's very helpful. That means we don't have to redistribute power and money, we just have to get people to share culture and we've solved the problem. You've got internal social control through culture. No need to change anything else. That's message one: "To make the best that has been known and thought in the world current everywhere." Well, who is to decide what is the best that has been thought and known in the world? It leaves that unsaid. And the last is a classic: "To make all men live in an atmosphere of sweetness and light"—so we know what the women can do!

The second quotation is from Robert Morgan's article, "The Englishness of English Teaching." He is quoting, as he rightly describes it, a remarkable 1867 tract by James George, an Ontario minister of religion, which asserted that the very first of the lessons which God had commissioned England to do, was to teach the planet, "a noble language, embodying the richest scientific and literary treasures found anywhere" (Goodson & Medway, pp. 197–241).

The Rev. James George believed that each language accorded with the mentality of the people. I quote: "Hence a highly civilized race will ever have a highly accomplished language. The English language strikingly illustrates this. It is very generally held that a certain mixture of blood, drawn from the noblest branches of the human family, produces the finest race of men. The English tongue is in all senses a very noble one, . . . Great Britain is, on a grand scale, engaged in teaching this noble tongue to the world" (Morgan, pp. 209–210). Now that was a mission, that was a vision and His Reverence had it and it had force in the world. And don't think it's gone away. It had force in the world; and it still has force in the world.

The second historical phase for English and its teachers is much shorter, and covers the period from the 1950s until the 1980s. In this phase some teachers of English and some professional associations of teachers of English began a process of radical revision of the subject and of its teaching.

Although there were different emphases at different times between the 1950s and 1980s, a common element was that the role of the teacher as a preacher of culture and as an agent of the dominant voice was rejected. An oppositional culture of English teaching was formed which wanted to celebrate students' self-expression and creativity and the linguistic and social resources of subordinated social groups. The names associated with this oppositional culture of English, James Britten, Douglas Barnes, Harold Rosen, John Dixon, Nancy Martin, are well known to you all.

In a recent article dealing with this period, Stephen Ball and others, under the title "Literacy, Politics and the Teachers of English," have commented, "Here the English teacher was no longer to be missionary, disseminating the values of civilization, but an anthropologist, mapping and collecting the values and culture of subordinate groups. Initially the working class, later girls and blacks. The notion of literature is profoundly expanded here to encompass all that can be said or written" (Ball et al., p. 58).

Later a more explicitly political form of English teaching developed which wanted to engage more directly with the language/power relation. Chris Searle's book *Classrooms of Resistance* (1975) was one of the expressions of this move.

The notion of critical literacy, as opposed to domesticated literacy, was derived from the writings of Paulo Freire and theorized by a range of writers, including Aronowitz and Giroux: "Critical literacy responds to the cultural capital of a specific group or class and looks at the way in which it can be confirmed and also at the ways in which the dominant society disconfirms students, by either ignoring or denigrating the knowledge and experiences of their everyday lives. The unit of analysis is here social and the key concern is not with individual interest but with individual and collective empowerment" (1987, p. 183). Now in New Zealand such ideas have recently been given powerful expression in the text *Literacy, Schooling and Revolution* (1987) by Colin Lankshear and Moira Lawler of Auckland University.

Alongside these oppositional developments, which frequently have had a class focus, some English teachers have signalled the alliance of their subject with the growth of multicultural, bicultural and anti-racist initiatives in education. English teachers have also been in the forefront of curricular and pedagogical reform which recognises the importance of gender bias and of sexism in educational theory and practice. English teachers have mediated the work of Dale Spender to many of their colleagues.

In short, during this second historical phase of English teaching, a positive commitment has been made by English teachers to be facilitators of different voices in class, race, and gender terms. But we have to remember that this second phase of English teaching has taken place in a social, economic and political context in which various forms of educational progressivism have been able to flourish. The external conditions have been relatively good economically, ideologically, politically. In terms of an important ethic of relatively autonomous educational practice, they have been related to a respect for teachers as informed professionals. But that period now is, I think, under deep threat, and I want to turn now to the voices of the contemporary struggle.

Now, we are in the third phase, the 1990s, where the external conditions, and especially the ideological and political conditions, are not so good in many societies. Related to various forms of economic crises or of constructed crises, a reassertion of conservative forms, of social, cultural, and political ideology can be discerned.

At the same time, new forms of radical conservatism, in the shape of free-market economics and of New Right social and moral doctrines, have come to power in a number of societies. There *are* different voices in the third phase of English teaching. They are not only the voices of those who support projects of cultural emancipation and liberation, they are also the voices of those who criticize and oppose such projects.

The counterattack to the progressiveness of English teaching in the sixties, seventies, and eighties began in the seventies and has gathered force since that time. While a section of English teachers has been working to empower different voices, a section of the mass media has been working to empower the voices of the critics of that enterprise.

A political, ideological, and media conjunction can be seen at work in a number of countries, criticising, resisting, and undermining attempts by English teachers to widen both the conception of their subject and the practice of their subject. There is, in other words, a vigorous contemporary struggle about the nature of English and the role of its teachers.

We have constantly said during this conference that we must listen to different voices, but I think we want to be selective. We want to hear the different voices not too different from ours, more reassuring. By that we have generally meant to hear the voices of other ethnic communities, working class, girls and women; but if we are to have a strategy in the struggle over English, we have to listen to the voices of these critics. What are the critics saying about people such as yourselves? What will this talk be reported as or the whole conference be reported as?

English teachers are often portrayed as sentimental, woolly liberals or worse, trendies, lefties, feminists, and lesbians (used as terms of abuse). Progressive English teachers are seen to be subverting the subject, lowering standards, and betraying the parents.

Just listen to some of these voices of the critics. I take most of my examples from England, but I know that you can provide them all from your own country. Here's Stuart Froome, in his one-person dissenting comment on the Bullock Report, "Language for Life," back in 1975:

> My own observation in a number of schools [note the rigour of his research design and methodology] leads me to the belief that in the zeal for creativity by teachers today, there is not the vigorous critical marking of spelling, punctuation and grammatical errors which there used to be, while the traditional systematic doing of corrections is fast disappearing. This has led in my view to the wretched solipsisms exhibited in students' written work.

Notice that term, "wretched solipsisms." Laurie Walker pointed out in his historical study of the patrolling of the language that the terms used are full of moral outrage. Historically talk was about "vicious use of language." Froome doesn't use "vicious" use of language, but he uses "wretched." It's full of moral outrage.

Here is the *Spectator*, March 18, 1988, responding to the Kingman Report on the Teaching of English:

> When scenting victory one is supposed to wipe the smirk off one's face and talk of a victory for common sense. I can contrive no such view. I read it with a song in my heart and a smile on my lips for the report rehabilitates and revives in the most uncompromising and irrefutable fashion, the rigorous study of formal, correct, standard English. It is the grammarian's resurrection. (Ball et al., p. 73)

Here is the Conservative Monday Club publication of 1985 on "Education in a Multiracial Society"(Ball et al., p. 78):

> To say that British history, English literature, the civilisation of Western Europe should have pride of place in our schools is not to argue from a sense of superiority. It is to argue for relevance.

This is actually a formulation of a new racism, the new racisms that are appearing everywhere. The old racisms said, "There is superiority of races and we will tell you what they are and we will rank them for you if you like, very exactly." That was the old racism, which was in power and is still in power in some areas. Now racists realize they can no longer maintain that position. The formulation is changed to "these are really questions of relevances or national identities and no one is saying anyone is better than anyone else; it's just that this is relevant and this is not relevant."

These arguments and voices will be heard here in Aotearoa/ New Zealand, and they are heard in Britain as the counterattack against multicultural and anti-racist education in Britain gathers strength. It is the argument of, "But is it relevant to our concerns, the concerns of a modern world?"

The voices of the critics, of what might be called *cultural reaction*, can be heard in North America, Britain, Australia, and in New Zealand. We need to make as close a study of the themes of the cultural reaction as we do of the themes of this conference.

Finding a Strategy: Making Allies

This conference has been formulating an agenda to empower different voices. The common denominator through all of these discussions has been a principle of respect and empowerment for different voices which have for too long been suppressed or silenced or marginalized. The voice of the Maori; the voice of the Koori; the voice of African Americans; the voice of Latino students; the voice of other ethnic communities; the voice of working-class youth and community; the voice of girls and women; and within educational institutions, the voice of the pupil and the student.

This is not because the teachers of English gathered here are a collection of cultural and political extremists. On the contrary, it is *not* teachers of English gathered here who are extremists; it is those who would deny the principle of respect and the principle of empowerment for different voices. Those are the extremists.

Note how the concept and the language of "extremism" has been appropriated by the media, so that it is always used in a one-sided fashion. Those who speak *for* empowering voices will be called extremists. Those who speak *against* it, what are they speaking for?— the silencing of different voices. Although their views are called responsible, middle-ground, balanced, or whatever, they are nothing of the sort. These people are extremists who are trying to silence different voices by appropriating language, and it is our business to try and fight that appropriation.

What this conference has said is empower different voices but do not throw out Standard English in order to do this. We have not said this. The conference has recognised throughout, in Eve's most powerful phrase, that people are enhanced by being "two-way strong," linguistically and culturally, rather than simply being one-way strong. Keri Kaa pointed out to us how she had to learn at an early age how to switch language codes, and she did that and she grew powerful in that and it can be seen to be a cultural strength and not a weakness.

So we are *not* saying displace Standard English with different voices, we are saying bring them into a partnership relation. We are saying we want to express the world comprehensively. We have recognized that Standard English has important social, political, and cultural functions. It cannot be denied. But at the same time we have recognised the power of other Englishes and of a whole range of other, different voices. As Katharine Perera said to us, we have learned to celebrate our different languages and rejoice in our common tongue. That is our position of principle.

That's fine principle, but can it be implemented in practice? Do these ideas have a life outside conferences such as this or are they just, in the words of the *Daily Mail,* "trendy piety"?

It is clear from this conference that they are very practical principles for action and there is already much valuable professional experience about how they can be applied. Look at the titles of the workshops and the papers, what we might call the "voices of practical application" in this conference.

They are, for instance, "One Language, Varied Voices: Celebrating Women in the Classroom"; "Through the Eyes of Another Language"; "Cross-cultural Readings of Literature"; "Establishing Connections between Communities and Curriculum"; "Using a Diversity of Voices within and across Classrooms"; "The Collaborative Use of Microcomputers"; "Cultural Bonding through Literature"; "Passport to Power: Mastering the Written Word"; "The Puente Project." And how much practical wisdom we learned yesterday from Mary K. Healy, through that account of the Puente Project. Who could say these were just theoretical, trendy ideas? This was a project that had practical engagement and was succeeding in very practical ways.

The conference proceedings, when they are published, will demonstrate quite explicitly that a coherent agenda exists for empowering different voices both at the level of principle and at the level of practical application in classrooms.

Some people will think this is surely sufficient. We have the agenda, we have the practical examples and, paraphrasing the famous Air New Zealand announcement, they will say our position should be,

"Trust your English teachers, they know what to do." But it's not enough. The project of empowering different voices will not succeed simply because a group of English teachers has got a well-worked-out agenda for it.

Another element in the strategy of transformation is required, and that is to win allies for change.

If English teachers internationally want the project of empowering different voices to succeed and to be sustained over time, so that it involves a more fundamental transformation of the educational process rather than simply of language and literature teaching, they will have to make allies: within the school, within the parental group, within the community, and within the wider society. English teachers must be prepared to enter into an educative and working relationship with those constituencies who need to understand and support this project:

- their principals and professional colleagues within the school
- the boards of education, the boards of trustees, the boards of governors
- the parents
- the community and the business interests
- the mass media and the politicians

Each of these constituencies has the potential to obstruct, subvert, and to terminate projects for the empowering of different voices. They have to be brought into a relation of alliance, rather than opposition, if at all possible. But is it possible? Can English teachers alone affect such a major task of education and integration? Obviously, there has to be a search for the allies who are already there, and there are allies: in the school, in the community, in the wider society. Then, with the assistance of those allies, the wider educational project must be attempted. And again, the Puente Project gave us great hope and gave us a model of how that can be done.

We cannot hide behind the walls of the school or the college or the international conference setting. When our colleagues misunderstand the project, we must be prepared to discuss these misunderstandings and, perhaps more fruitfully, get them to work with us. When the parents have reservations about the project or even direct hostility to it, we must engage them in dialogue and again invite them to work with us. When business interests are convinced that this is going to be bad for business, we must patiently try to show them that, on the contrary, it's going to be good for business; but that's not the reason we are doing it.

When the mass media persistently and, in some cases, maliciously misrepresent the project, we must ask to talk with the editors and the reporters. We must ask for right to reply, time and space in the media, and we must try to change their adversarial stance to what we are doing.

Of course, I am not expecting you to go out and bless the media, by no means. But I am saying, you've got to get out there and talk to them and you've got to sustain it, even when they're very unresponsive and quite offensive—because that gap has got to be bridged, or the projects that this conference wants to advance will not happen.

When the politicians think that there will be votes, as they frequently do, in vigorously attacking the project that this conference is committed to, we must try to demonstrate that, on the contrary, there is powerful community and parental support for what is being done, and we must invite them to come along on the project (for a photo opportunity of course), to be present at the project, and we must try to win them to it.

I will close with the quotation of Margaret Mathieson, in which she tries to express what are the contemporary challenges of the teachers of English:

> English today has come to be viewed less as a subject and more as a way of life. During the past one hundred years it has been held increasingly responsible for humanizing all the nation's children through literature, through creative use of their native languages and through critical discrimination between art and the products of commercial entertainment.
>
> Viewed as a network of activities, inside which children can achieve emotional, social and moral development, English has come to be seen as the school subject which, more than any other, requires teachers to have outstanding personal qualities. At every stage of the subject's growth, during which new hopes have been invested in it, as a liberating force, fresh demands have been made for inspirational teachers. (p. 211)

Now this conference has given us fresh demands, but at the same time it has given us the vision and, above all, the spirit to respond to them.

Kia ora tatou.

References

Apple, M. (1986). *Teachers and texts.* London: Routledge and Kegan Paul.

Arnold, M. (Ed.). (1935). *Culture and anarchy.* Cambridge University Press.

Aronowitz, S., & Giroux H. (1987). *Education under siege: The conservative, liberal and radical debate over schooling.* London: Routledge and Kegan Paul.

Ball, S., et al. (1990). Literacy, politics and the teaching of English. In I. Goodson & P. Medway (Eds.), *Bringing English to order: The history and politics of a school subject.* London: Falmer Press.

Connell, R. (1985). *Teacher's work.* Sidney: Allen and Unwin.

Freire, P. (1973). *Education for critical consciousness.* London: Sheed and Ward.

Freire, P. (1985). *The politics of education: Culture, power and liberation.* London: Macmillan.

Goodson, I., and Medway, P. (1990). *Bringing English to order: The history and politics of a school subject.* London: Falmer Press.

Grace, G. (1978). *Teachers, ideology and control: A study in urban education.* London: Routledge and Kegan Paul.

Lankshear, C., and Lawler, M. (1987). *Literacy, schooling and revolution.* London: Falmer Press.

Lawn, M., and Grace, G. (Eds.). (1987). *Teachers: The culture and politics of work.* London: Falmer Press.

Mathieson, M. (1975). *The preachers of culture: A study of English and its teachers.* London: Allen and Unwin.

Morgan, R. (1990). The Englishness of English teaching. In I. Goodson & P. Medway (Eds.). *Bringing English to order: The history and politics of a school subject* (chap. 7). London: Falmer Press.

Searle, C. (1975). *Classrooms of resistance.* London: Writers' and Readers' Co-operative.

Walker, L. (1990). The ideology and political of English grammar. In I. Goodson & P. Medway (Eds.). *Bringing English to order: The history and politics of a school subject* (chap. 5). London: Falmer Press.

8 A Response to Gerald Grace

R. Baird Shuman

Gerald Grace reaches the crux of his paper halfway into it when he says that there exists "a vigorous contemporary struggle about the nature of English and the role of its teachers." Earlier in the paper he asks, "Why cannot they [teachers] enter into the humane and dialogic relations that I'm sure would be the ideal of many of them?"

The "Different Voices" Conference of the International Federation of Teachers of English that met in Auckland, New Zealand, in August 1990, did not consider matters relating to English; rather, it cast its gaze upon the *Englishes* that are used throughout the world. The simple act of pluralizing the proper noun is a first, important step toward achieving the ends that Grace envisions in a paper that is concerned with the theory, history, policy, and practice of English teaching. He suggests practical strategies for implementing a new attitude and heightening a consciousness of the need to revise how people view the English language as it is commonly used in the intellectual, commercial, and governmental enterprises of far-flung English speaking societies.

Where English is used, according to Grace, a standard dialect of the language is usually favored. This favoritism is directly connected to the politics of power. In Britain and in parts of the world where British influence still holds sway, the BBC or public school dialect is preferred. Many opportunities are foreclosed to those who have not mastered this form of English. In the United States, the so-called Network Standard variety of English—or something closely approximating it—is expected of those who hold the key positions in society.

One might question whether this situation poses a real or a phantom problem. Is not English a universal language, the international language of air controllers, business executives, bankers, scientists, and intellectuals? This being the case, does it not follow that anyone who aspires to positions of power and influence should adopt the accepted form of that universal language?

The problems this sort of thinking poses are numerous: the reasoning that has led people to think in such ways are essentially reductive and are honeycombed with errors in logic based upon a misunderstanding of the correlation that exists between language and thought and on a failure to define satisfactorily such terms as "accepted form."

Grace quotes the Rev. James George as saying that "a highly civilized race will ever have a highly accomplished language. The English language strikingly illustrates this." This smug statement stems from abysmal ignorance. It represents the sort of imperialistic view that has long pervaded the thinking of dominant English speakers when they discuss the place of their language in the world order.

If it is a given for Mr. George that his society represents a pinnacle of civilization, it must follow that the language of that civilization is highly accomplished. This premise, however, is based upon a perception of civilization so parochial as to have little meaning and questionable validity.

Grace touches on this point when he says, "While a section of English teachers has been working to empower different voices, a section of the mass media has been working to empower the voices of the critics of this enterprise." The mass media are perhaps the most strident conservative voices in the dominant-language dispute, and they are pervasive, reaching millions of people who feel threatened by ethnic difference.

Lev Vygotsky postulates what language conservatives seem often to ignore: "Progress in thought and progress in speech are not parallel."[1] In his later essay, "Thought and Word," Voygotsky reminds his audience that "since generalizations and concepts are undeniably acts of thought, we may regard meaning as a phenomenon of thinking. It does not follow, however, that meaning formally belongs in two different spheres of psychic life."[2]

In his essay, "Language, Mind, and Reality,"[3] Benjamin Lee Whorf takes a similar stand in addressing the relativity of language and the parochialism of how people usually view it: "What we call 'scientific thought' is a specialization of the western Indo-European type of language, which has developed not only a set of different dialectics, but actually a set of different languages."[4] Whorf goes on to show how such advanced scientific topics as Albert Einstein's theories of relativity can not easily be articulated in Indo-European languages because these languages presuppose time-space associations that are not wholly compatible with Einstein's theories, which are best expressed in another, less verbal language, the calculus. Whorf goes on to demonstrate that because of the time/space concepts of their language, the Hopi Indians can cope better linguistically with Einstein's theories than speakers of Indo-European languages are able to.

Buckminster Fuller made a similar suggestion that demonstrates how hard it is to kill old truths that have been proved to be untruths: "[T]he words *up* and *down*, which we all use without much thinking, were invented to accommodate our multimillion-year-old misconception that we lived on a flat world extending laterally to infinity."[5] Much of our language relating to spatial relationships is moored in the long-discredited concept of a geocentric universe and a flat Earth: in common parlance, the earth still has four corners, the moon rises, and the sun sets.

Other so-called primitive languages—notably some of the Indian languages Whorf investigated—avoid such pitfalls because these languages reveal that Indian conceptions of time-space are closer to those of modern physics than to those of people limited to Indo-European languages. This theory is reinforced by what we know about the amazingly sophisticated Mayan and Aztec calendars, for example.

In his research into British teachers' language attitudes and their relation to social class, William Dubberley concludes that "the majority of teachers [in his study] has a deficit model of the working class culture within the community and that their explanation as to the failure of working class pupils *was pathological.*"[6]

The situation in the United States is no better. Teachers make false equations between language use and intelligence, thereby subtly foreclosing to many students possibilities that their inherent intellects should make available to them and often wrecking their self-esteem in the process. Few teachers, for example, recognize that if African American students from the inner city say, "I got three brother," they are speaking with greater accuracy than their middle-class compatriots who say, "I have three brothers."

In the first example, the noun *brother* is preceded by the plural marker *three*. To add *-s*, a second plural marker, is a redundancy. Network Standard English, nevertheless, observes the convention and frowns upon a departure from it, even if that departure makes perfect sense logically.

Paulo Freire's extensive studies in education made him realize that when a prestige dialect is in place, many members of a society whose own natural dialect tacitly excludes them from positions of power retreat into silence.[7] The implications of this insight are of incredible social and economic importance. Whorf shows that all higher-level thinking is dependent on language. He shows as well that the structure of the language people use influences their perception and understanding of themselves and of their environments; in other words, language is a—perhaps *the*—major force in shaping one's cosmos.[8]

Whorf believes, further, that "the higher mind or 'unconscious' of a Papuan headhunter can mathematize quite as well as that of Einstein."[9] This environmental view of human development has broad implications. Whorf is not necessarily suggesting that the Papuan headhunter, transferred to another environment, would develop into an Einstein. Rather, he suggests throughout his writing that individual perceptions of the universe are decisively shaped by language and that the perceptions of so-called primitives cannot be blandly dismissed as incorrect perceptions. Hopi perceptions of time/space, as reflected in the Hopi language, are, from a physical standpoint, infinitely more sophisticated than Indo-European perceptions of this phenomenon.

Some of the most significant thinkers about matters of language would subscribe to Gerald Grace's observation that "we [those connected with the IFTE Conference] are *not* saying displace Standard English with different voices; we are saying bring them into a partnership relation" [Grace's italics]. Grace calls for educators to become activists who help the public, through the media and other means, to understand the implications of trying to impose single, approved varieties of English upon societies. Only when English teachers are more fully exposed to linguistic theory than they currently are in most teacher training programs will such activism be likely to develop and flourish.

Notes

1. L. S. Vygotsky. "The Genetic Roots of Thought and Speech," in *Thought and Language,* edited and translated by Eugenia Hanfmann and Gertrude Vakar. Cambridge, MA: The M.I.T. Press, 1962, p. 33.

2. "Thought and Word," Ibid., p. 129.

3. *The Theosophist.* (Madras, India), 63:1 (January, 1942), pp. 281–291 and 63:2 (April, 1942), pp. 25–37. Reprinted in *Etc., A Review of General Semantics,* 9 (1952), pp. 167–188 and in *Language, Thought and Reality,* edited by John B. Carroll. Cambridge, MA: The M.I.T. Press, 1956, p. 246–270.

4. Whorf, *Language, Thought, and Reality,* p. 246.

5. In "Breaking the Shell of Permitted Ignorance," in *R. Buckminster Fuller on Education*, edited by Peter H. Wagschal and Robert D. Kahn. Amherst, MA: The University of Massachusetts Press, 1979, p. [9]. Fuller's italics.

6. William Dubberley. "Social Class and the Process of Schooling—A Case Study of a Comprehensive School in a Mining Community," in *Progress and Inequality in Comprehensive Education*, edited by Anthony G. Green and Stephen J. Ball. London: Routledge, 1988, p. 200. Italics added.

7. See Paulo Freire's *Pedagogy of the Oppressed*, translated by Myra Bergman Ramos. New York: Herder and Herder, 1970.

8. See Stuart Chase's Foreword in *Language, Thought, and Reality*, p. vi.

9. Ibid., p. 257.

References

Freire, P. (1970). *Pedagogy of the oppressed* (M. Bergman Ramos, Trans.). New York: Herder and Herder.

Fuller, R. B. (1979). *R. Buckminster Fuller on education* (P. H. Wagschal & R. D. Kahn, Eds.). Amherst: The University of Massachusetts Press.

Grace, G. (1990, August). *From the dominant voice to different voices: Issues of language, culture, and power.* Paper presented at the different voices conference of the International Federation for the Teaching of English, Auckland, New Zealand.

Green, A. G., & Ball, S. (Eds.). (1988). *Progress and inequality in comprehensive education.* London: Routledge.

Vygotsky, L. S. (1962). *Thought and language* (E. Hanfmann & G. Vakar, Eds. and Trans.). Cambridge, MA: The M.I.T. University Press.

Whorf, B. L. (1956). *Language, thought and reality* (J. B. Carroll, Ed.). Cambridge, MA: The M.I.T. Press.

9 Insight from the Inside: A New Perspective on Family Influences over Children's Television Viewing and Its Implications for Teachers of English

Patricia Gillard

Introduction

The subject of television is rarely discussed with detached disinterest by teachers. Attitudes range all the way from wanting to see the set banned from school classrooms and, if possible, the lounge rooms at home, to placing children's television experience in the centre of discussion and working out from there.

What is less recognised is the influence of teachers' own viewing experience on the assumptions they make about the television medium, especially how it is and should be used. These assumptions provide a framework within which methods and contents for teaching about television are adopted.

As a former high school English teacher turned television researcher, I would like to issue some challenges based on research in children's own homes which describes the different ways families use TV. These days, I am less comfortable in classrooms, so that I do not claim expertise in applying these "insights from the inside" (of family TV rooms) to particular teaching programs. What I do want to emphasise is the importance of considering television use at home when its treatment as part of English programs is being considered at school.

One of the great falsehoods about children's viewing, which teachers need to reexamine, is that it is "zombie-like" or completely passive (see Palmer, 1986b). Children, like adults, have definite tastes in TV shows. Ever since TV was introduced, children have been known to be the most physically active members of the audience, the ones most likely to move in and out of the TV room during advertisements (Allen, 1965), the group who are least worried about the TV set as an object and those most likely to "play" with the switches and hand sets (Gillard, 1989). As the medium diversifies into video games, videodiscs, and forms of "virtual reality" it is children who are the most adaptive. They are not "captured."

Research evidence notwithstanding, the notions of a "passive audience" viewing a "nasty medium" still stick. They are usually based on opinions of the worth of television programs rather than an understanding of how people make use of the medium as part of their leisure. It is certainly simpler to work from the assumption that TV as a whole is bad for children and the more they view, the worse it is. Unfortunately, this simple assumption is very misleading.

An Ethnography of Children's Viewing at Home

The study to be discussed here started with very different assumptions, using ethnographic methods similar to those applied in research and evaluation in schools. (See, for example, Woods, 1979; Stubbs & Delamont, 1976.)

Ethnography begins, not with a well-developed theory but with a few major concepts. Observation and other forms of investigation in the natural setting are then used to gradually piece together a description of what is going on. Central to this approach is the inclusion of the definitions of their own experience by those who are studied. The research does not set up camp, then tick boxes. Instead, detailed notes are kept as he or she is immersed in the setting, until regularities of behaviour can be discerned.

For my study, this meant a description of television viewing that took into account the perspectives of the children and families who were being studied: how they defined television viewing, how they arranged their time and their living space to accommodate this activity.

In this chapter, I want to look first at some of the detail of the research because it took place in people's lounge rooms, and there is a lot to see there. I will outline what was discovered about TV rules, as well as the impact that different kinds of family situations had on children's viewing. The significance of these findings for English teaching will be outlined in the discussion.

Methods Used in Research

In 1982 and 1983, I carried out a large-scale observation study of twenty-three children in the two age groups 8 to 9 years and 11 to 12 years. Researchers observed them watching TV at home for nine hours, writing down the details of what they said and did during this time, and the TV they watched.

With this 200 hours of observations, "maps" of their TV rooms and interviews with mother and child, I have since gone on to write an ethnography of children's viewing.

The families in which we observed came from all areas of Sydney, Australia, and included a great variety of social classes and family types.

Television Rules

For this study, television rules were defined as any statements about TV behaviour, or parents' attitudes, that were made during interviews, or imposed during observations.

Each family differed from others in the operation of TV rules. They covered such subjects as amount of viewing, time for viewing, programs, tasks to be performed, things not to do, and where and how to sit. Some families said they had "no rules."

One of the most interesting findings was the differences between the rules given by child and parent in the same family. Table 1 illustrates this. Children were very literal and concrete in their account of TV rules, speaking from their daily experience. Parents, on the other hand, gave more general statements.

By comparing the diaries of actual viewing, it was also found that most rules were broken, especially those which limited the amount of time spent viewing (see table 2). However, rules were not broken by much, and served to define what was generally acceptable.

The Influence of Family Types

During the analysis, patterns were discovered which identified certain kinds of family processes with the use of particular rules. I have grouped the families under headings which describe the kind of control exercised.

Time Control

Eight families had rules about when or how much television children could view. Some of these families also restricted programs. The families were similar in their economic status and family formation. In every case, the children lived in a large and comfortable home with both parents and at least one sibling. All of the fathers were professionals with established and well-paying jobs. All of the mothers were at home full time.

Table 1. Younger Boys—Television Rules as Stated by Mother, Child, or Both

Child	Mother Rule	Child Rule	Common
Alexander		Don't turn on TV nothing good on	Ask permission before turning on TV
Tom	No TV if fight with sister or jobs not done Homework first	Don't change channel until TV warmed up, picture visible Don't throw anything at TV Turn channel knob carefully	
Len	Turn TV off when mother gets up in morning No late movie No excessive violence/horror Not TV on days off school	Do not have TV on too loud	
John	No continuous viewing in afternoon No bad sitcoms	Not too much morning TV	Only watch TV in morning when ready for school* Prefer watch news Prefer watch SBS*
Hugh	No eating with TV* No morning TV No TV after 8:30 p.m.		
Tony	Father discourages commercial stations*		No viewing before 5 p.m.*

*Rules which were broken during the observation period

As table 3 shows, these children watched little TV over the three days they were observed, and much of that viewing was of noncommercial stations (government-funded ABC and SBS). On the other hand, they seemed to have access to a wide range of other leisure activities.

When they did watch TV, these children made the most of their short viewing time by paying close attention to the screen. They were all intent viewers, with the three youngest girls also making comments

Table 2. Girls' Television Behaviour Which Broke Family Rules

Child	Stated Rule	Viewing Event
Amy	One hour a day	Half hour extra one day
Elizabeth	No afternoon TV	Viewed at 5:30 p.m. once
Suzi	Homework first	TV before homework once
	ABC and SBS only	One commercial program
Jennifer	Don't sit too close	Sat close often
	Ask before view	Did not ask
	Prefer ABC	Commercial TV two days
Emma	No TV if no music practice	Disregarded two days
	Homework first	Disregarded once
	1 hour a day	Half hour extra, two days.
Stacey	Don't block view of others	Blocked view of father
	"Skippy & Matchmates"	Sister priority one day
	Priority over sister	Sat close
	Don't sit too close	
Stephanie	No TV before 7 p.m.	Watched at 6 p.m. third night
	No TV till 6:30 p.m.	
	No sex, violence	Watched "Dukes of Hazzard"
Peggy	Bed 8:30 p.m. if school next day	Bed 9 p.m. one night
Josephine	Mark viewing in TV guide	Did not mark programs
Toni	No morning TV	TV one morning
Leslie	No "Brady Bunch"	Watched "Brady Bunch" once

and interacting with television programs in an expressive manner, for example:

> Leslie has been watching television for half an hour when "Brady Bunch" begins. The reception is very poor so she adjusts the aerial, then gets comfortable, lying flat out on the bed on her stomach, with hands propping up her head. She helps her little sister onto the bed, who lies down in the same way. For the next ten minutes she doesn't move. The younger sister hits her on the head with a bear, but Leslie says nothing and ignores her. Her sister hits her again, but Leslie just gazes at the TV. Her sister pulls her hair and her clothes. Very quietly, without looking at her, Leslie speaks to her sister. Leslie: "Bel, please."

Table 3. "Control of Time" and Children's Viewing

Child	Structured	Hours	Station
Suzi, 8	Ballet Swimming Acting Singing	2.5	ABC, SBS, commercial
Amy, 8	Tennis Pottery	4	ABC
Emma, 8	Brownies Piano Swimming	5.5	Mostly ABC
Elizabeth, 9	Ballet Swimming	1.5	ABC
Leslie, 11	Flute Piano Orchestra	2	Mostly commercial
Stephanie, 12	Sailing Soccer	3.5	Commercial
Alexander, 8	Organ Youth club	3.5	SBS, commercial
Peter, 11	Fishing	2.5	ABC

Program Control

Children for whom there were restrictions on specific programs or program types were a very heterogeneous group in the amount and type of viewing and their access to other leisure activities (see table 4). The common element was the importance of the mother's relationship with the child and her significance in the family structure. The mothers of four of the five children were actively engaged in tertiary study or professional work and had a sole child at home. In three of these families there was no resident father and the mother was the main provider.

Mother's work or study made it very difficult to directly supervise the times children viewed or to structure routines which would restrict viewing. Instead, mothers made known their general preferences to the child with positive comments on shows they liked and criticism and explanation if they disagreed with their child's program choice. Most of the mothers spent some of their time co-viewing with children, a significant factor considering that they spent less time at home because of their work.

Len's mother, for example said she did not like him watching shows with excessive horror and violence. His favourite program, "The Incredible Hulk," had occasional violent scenes, so she usually watched it with him. During one fight sequence, Len started biting his

Table 4. "Control of Programs" and Children's Viewing

Child	Structured	Hours	Station
Jennifer, 8	Brownies Dancing	10	Mostly commercial
Toni, 12	Irish Dancing Physical Culture Organ Musicals	9	Mostly commercial
Josephine, 12	Ballet	9	Mostly commercial
Len, 8	Police Boys Club	8.5	Commercial, ABC
John, 8	None	6	Commercial, ABC

nails, then moved along the lounge to be reassured by physical contact with his mother.

All of the children, with the exception of Toni, were very active viewers in that they commented on the program and asked questions while they were watching. Few of the children watched intently for long.

Situational Constraint

This group began by being labelled as the "no rules" group because mothers usually stated that "everyone agreed" or there were "no rules." Most of the children in this group lived in small houses and flats in poorer areas of Sydney. The fathers did clerical or manual work and, if they lived with the family, were present most of the time during the observations.

As table 5 shows, all but one of the children watched many hours of TV during the three days, mostly commercial stations.

Observation of the behaviour of children showed that, far from being unrestricted in their viewing, the limitations imposed by little space and the presence of other family members meant that television viewing followed a set pattern most days and did not often reflect the choices or preferences of the individual child. Where the pressure of accommodating all the family in one room led to conflict in the use of space, children had to be mindful of where they established themselves and how they chose to view, for fear of being in the way. The TV routines therefore arose from the ways family members used the space rather than being consciously defined by parents.

Table 5. "Situational Constraint" and Children's Viewing

Child	Structured	Hours	Station
Judy, 8	Brownies	8.5	Mostly commercial
Tom, 8	Soccer Swimming Cubs	4.5	Commercial
Will, 11	Cricket	10.5	Commercial
Phillip, 12	Tennis	19	Commercial
Chris, 12	None	13.5	Commercial

Children in this group were among the most physically active when they viewed and were seen to do a variety of leisure activities in the area surrounding the TV set:

> *(Tom is sitting in his beanbag watching "Wheel of Fortune." His cousin and little sister are beside him on the floor and his mother is preparing dinner in the kitchen, watching TV at the same time. After a commercial break, his mother sits down to watch the next segment. His cousin gives the little sister a ride on her back in front of the TV set.)*
>
> *Tom:* Oh rats, she's got 1,200.
>
> *Mother:* No she didn't.
>
> *(Tom attempts to answer to a question from the program.)*
>
> *Tom:* The Northern Territory.
>
> *Mother:* No. There's one letter before . . .
>
> *Tom:* Close, though. At least I tried.
>
> *Mother:* Umm.
>
> *Tom:* I've got it right before. *(To his cousin)* Does "fantasy" end in 'm'?
>
> *(His little sister wants a ride.)*
>
> *Tom:* OK, then.
>
> *(Tom gets up to play horsey with his sister and moves into the next room, where he can still see the set. His mother goes into the kitchen when the ads come on and calls them to have dinner.)*

Survey Results

In a random survey of 486 Sydney children which followed the observations, differences between the children in their activity while viewing were found to be related to the number of hours of TV they watched and, to a lesser extent, family socioeconomic status (defined by father's occupation).

The survey found a significant positive correlation between viewer activity (a measure which used pictures of activities children were instructed to circle if they "usually" did them) and total television viewing. ($r=44$, $p=.001$, $n=446$). The more television children watched, the greater the number of activities they performed around the set. Interestingly, the children who watched more TV in wealthier families were also more active as viewers. (When the effects of SES were controlled using partial correlation, the relationship between viewer activity and the amount of television was still significant. $r=41$, $p=.001$, $n=446$).

The Importance of Family Context

There are other studies which relate family living patterns or affluence to children's viewing. The term "family culture" has even been adopted as a general description of routine family patterns.

A New Zealand Example

A recent survey of sixty-four children and fifty-nine parents by Christchurch Polytechnic, New Zealand, reveals such a pattern. The research, *Square Eyes? The Viewing Habits of Christchurch 10 Year Olds* (1990), is unusual in its inclusion of questions about *how* children watched TV and the rules which restricted their viewing. The report describes major differences between the viewing of children in the two schools studied, and these viewing styles are partly explained by the location of the schools in areas markedly different in affluence.

We think we have identified two ways children watch television through our survey. What is interesting is that it differs between schools.

Exclusive Viewing

Television is used selectively. When it is on, it is watched intensively. It is a controlled activity often allotted the same amount of time daily, regardless of programming. If a show clashes with the family routine, it is missed or videotaped for later. For the children, bedtime is bedtime, regardless of what the TV guide says. Parents turn off the TV set at the first sign of distraction—indicated by levels of simultaneous activity (since "no one can do two things at once"). Parents have the final say on the time, type, and amount of television watched, and they exercise that right.

Television as a Background

Television has a very different role in the family routine. It accompanies many activities. The set is on longer and the family members tune in and out as they please. The children have a "waiting" mode. Sometimes the set is on because of force of habit; other times it provides companionship, entertainment, and relaxation. Viewers make choices while viewing rather than plan beforehand. The family is more likely to eat in front of the television set in order to see the odd show that clashes with their routine. Simultaneous activity is not viewed as "distracting" but as part of the viewing process. There are fewer restrictions on what is watched.

It is our impression that many children at school A watch television in this way. Being selective about what is viewed has its merits but may close off the potential to try new programmes, the unfamiliar. Viewing a wide range of programmes has its merits but can get to a level where television is the prime concern when organising the day just to fit them all in. What is important is *how* the child interacts with what he or she views when viewing under these types of conditions (1990, pp. 19–20).

An American Example

The differences in Australian families identified in my research find some parallels in the work of an American researcher who described the "time culture" of three families in relation to television.

Bryce (1987) studied three families intensively for a total of one month each, broken up into different times of the year. She went so far as to live in the same house with two families and next door to the third, participating fully in the families' activities during her stay. She documented their television-related behaviour by the use of field observations, tapes of family interaction, interviews, and observation of eye-gaze direction during TV viewing. Family documents such as the children's report cards were also collected.

One of the major dimensions which Bryce has identified as an important influence on the way television is used within families is the way they organize time. She uses the concept of "Monochronic" time, which emphasizes schedules, segmentation, and promptness, and "Polychronic" time, which is characterized as several things happening at once, to distinguish between families. In the family which displayed Monochronic characteristics, children were discouraged from doing other things while viewing. They planned their viewing schedule and paid closer attention to the TV screen. By contrast, a second family, which operated according to a Polychronic, temporal arrangement, used TV as one of several activities, as well as employing its program times to decide when other activities would be done. Attention to TV in this family was more intermittent.

My study supports the general trend of Bryce's results and relates this time culture to the mother's role in structuring the leisure time and activities of the family. In Australia, the ways mothers did this seemed also to be related to social class. In wealthier families, mothers were at home full time, supervising the routines and leisure activities of the household, and this involved greater control of children's viewing.

Main Findings

The findings which seem most relevant to the question of how children view can be summarised as follows:

- The more TV is on, the more likely children are to engage in other activities as they view. This suggests that children adapt to their TV environment. *How* they view may be the most important aspect of TV viewing because it differentiates between children in the ways that they "see" and therefore, presumably, what they learn from what they see.

- A definition of TV viewing as watching particular *programs*, rather than a continuing activity taking place with other events, assumes a particular style of viewing which is typical of families who structure their time and generally have more leisure options. This pattern is probably typical of many teachers as well. The view that TV is an inferior use of leisure time and that other media, such as books, are superior, is associated with this particular program-related definition of television.

- Families where TV is a major source of leisure and where it is switched on for much of the time are less likely to perceive the need for "control." On the other hand, viewing is more likely to be a shared activity and a part of being "at home."

- Where TV is a major source of leisure, there is likely to be less difference between what adults and children view.

- In families where women work away from the household, alternative ways of dealing with TV will usually be adopted, such as discussion with children of program content and deliberate co-viewing with children.

Implications for Classroom Practice

It is important that teachers be aware of the importance of family contexts in deciding the *nature* of children's TV viewing. Because children are part of their particular family TV culture, they cannot easily change their own behaviour without altering the routines of the whole household. Whether they be in very "controlled" TV families or those which profess to have "no rules," children are not able to change their household routines. They are more likely to be defensive and resist the teacher's perspectives.

The following kinds of actions on the part of a teacher may represent an imposition of his or her values about TV viewing (partly derived, no doubt, from the teacher's own family) which cuts right across those of the child's style of viewing at home. I've chosen these because they are very common practices (I have done these things myself) which are even suggested in many teacher's guides.

Don't:

- measure the time spent viewing TV with the purpose of encouraging students to "reduce" it;
- list programs viewed by students and exhort students to watch "better" programs;
- set television viewing in opposition to other "preferred" uses of leisure time such as reading;
- prohibit students from doing homework in front of TV.

Instead of this oppositional stance to television, it is important that English teachers find out what are the major viewing contexts of their own students.

The question of *how* children view is more important than how much they view or the programs they list because their *style* of viewing will also determine the meanings they take from television. There will be many children for whom "watching TV" will be synonymous with watching particular programs. But there will be others who think of TV in terms of their few favourite programs as well as what stands out from the current crop of ads and anything else that they have noticed in passing.

It may be that television as they understand it, sitting in their TV rooms at home, is not easily identified with a series of discrete programs. Some of the most recent work in popular culture (Cranny-Francis, 1988) suggests that genre is a more useful way to analyse television content than specific programs or program types.

The messages that are taken from television by students, or the text that is constructed from television (using the language of cultural studies) may be a very disjointed one, full of misunderstandings and complex associations. Or it may be oversimplistic, ignoring the nuances which more concentrated viewing, or exposure to film or non-commercial television allows. Whatever it is that your students understand as "TV," you can assume it is not quite the same as your own understanding.

It will be important as a teacher to establish *how* your particular group of students watch TV, and then what they make of it, before you choose which content to discuss. In other words, you may want to be a bit of an ethnographer yourself and find out how they "construct" their television experience as a guide to what and how you could teach. It is very likely that within one class you could identify a number of different ways of using TV. With some sensitive handling, the differences between students could be used as a resource.

The diversification of TV technologies, such as computer games, videodiscs, etc., and the interactive capabilities they offer can be discussed in the same way. How do you use it? What do you get from it? Let's watch, talk, reconstruct.

I am speaking here of a starting point which is located in students' experience and which builds from that. Of course, a teacher will want to make demands on students' thinking, to enlarge their ability to make judgements, to get them to test the TV versions with their own experience, to see how much more the television medium can stretch itself in providing images of ourselves. However, this will not be successful if the first step involves a criticism of students' everyday TV activity. Teachers' assumptions and values about TV which are in direct opposition to family practices are likely to be ignored and resisted.

The Importance of the Broadcasting Environment for Teaching about Television

In emphasising the family context for television viewing, it is important also to acknowledge the power of broadcasting environments in different countries to define what "television" means in the experience of teachers and students. The quality and diversity of programs available on TV in your country will influence your own attitude to the medium and your use of TV. This will be true of the students you teach as well. They will bring more limited resources into the classroom in terms of their own viewing, if what is provided is repetitive or poorly produced.

Without regulatory support, children as an audience are not usually provided with quality programs of their own on a regular basis. In a deregulated system it may be more difficult to work from students' experience towards a more varied and critical understanding of television. People find it hard to imagine television programs which they have not experienced.

In Australia, teachers have access to a variety of programming, some of it quality children's programs. The broadcasting environment includes two publicly owned channels, the ABC and SBS (the latter a multicultural TV station). In addition, the three commercial networks are also required to show five hours a week minimum of quality programs for primary-aged children and two and a half hours for preschoolers. Sixteen hours a year of new Australian children's drama is also mandatory. The effect of this regulation is to create a small niche for quality children's television and to acknowledge children's needs as a special television audience.

In the absence of variety and quality, which students themselves have learnt to take for granted, it may be important to co-operate with the groups in your country who are using other means of screening quality programs, such as special children's or video libraries. Some English teachers may even see it as an extension of their professional role to influence their government and broadcasters to provide regular quality programs for children.

Whenever I've done research on television with children or adolescents, I've taped a reservoir of energy and enjoyment and a desire to share their TV experience. Perhaps they are surprised that an adult is interested. They "love" TV. They know it well and celebrate it in the playground, but keep it to themselves around disapproving adults.

It may be that you as English teachers come from a different culture than your students, when it comes to television. I urge you, all the same, to accept their perspectives as a starting point and to work *with* students in the exploration of this fantastic medium.

References

Allen, C. L. (1965). Photographing the TV audience. *Journal of Advertising Research 5*, pp. 2–8.

Bryce, J. W. (1987). Family time and television use. In T. R. Lindlof (Ed.), *Natural Audiences: Qualitative Research of Media Uses and Effects*. New Jersey: Ablex.

Cranny-Francis, A. (1988). The moving image: Film and television. In G. Kress (Ed.), *Communication and Culture*, pp. 157–180.

Gillard, P. (1989). *An ethnography of children's television viewing in the family context*. Unpublished Ph.D. dissertation, University of NSW.

Palmer, P. (1986a). *Girls and television*. Sydney: New South Wales Ministry of Education.

Palmer, P. (1986b). *The lively audience*. Sydney: Allen & Unwin.

Square eyes? The viewing habits of Christchurch 10 year olds. (1990). Research Syndicate Media Studies Centre, Christchurch Polytechnic.

Stubbs, M. & Delamont, S. (Eds.). (1976). *Explorations in classroom observation*. London: Wiley.

Woods, P. (1979). *The divided school*. London: Routledge and Kegan Paul.

10 A Response to Patricia Gillard

Bruce C. Appleby

When I first heard Patricia Gillard give this talk at the IFTE conference in Auckland in 1987, I was impressed by her insights and her research. I am pleased to be able to react to what she has said and written, as she has posed dramatic and important questions about how we react to children's viewing of television and how we deal with television in our English/language arts classrooms. Given the various reports that fill our newspapers, professional journals, and popular magazines about the horrors of children's television viewing and how much time is spent in front of the television set that should be spent studying and reading, Gillard's research is particularly refreshing. She makes us aware of how we have overreacted and of how we have not done enough similar research in the United States.

Immediately in her introduction, Gillard touches on a sore point. When she mentions the cry to ban television from school classrooms, one immediately thinks of the commercial cable Channel One now available in many classrooms and the cry that went up when such an idea was first broached. It's interesting to note, now that such fare has been around for a few years, just how little we hear about it and how the minds of our students have not been softened by its attack on their sensibilities. We live in a commercial-filled environment and we cannot escape from the constant bombardment of commercial appeals.

"[T]he influence of teachers' own viewing experience on the assumptions they make about the television medium . . . " is a subject that needs much further research and investigation. As we experience "the graying of the profession" in 1992, we are seeing the retirement of a generation of teachers who did not grow up with television in the home as a constant factor, a segment of the profession who have not had a television set always present in their lives. I was 23 years old before I "lived" with a television set. There are fewer and fewer teachers of English/language arts who have not had the same television history as their students. Why not use these similar histories as a starting block for the incorporation of the study of television in our classrooms?

Equally important is Gillard's early assertion that it is a falsehood to assume that children view television in a "zombie-like" state, completely passive vegetables (Where do you think the term "couch potato" comes from?) who have no taste or discrimination in what they watch. Indeed, I would contend that the term "couch potatoes" is far more accurately attributed to adults than it is to children.

Recently, the Nielsen Company has come under fire for its inability to accurately measure who is watching what on television in its survey homes. Since the cost of television advertising is directly tied to information on the captive audience at specific times within a broadcast, Nielsen has been working hard to get a more accurate description of the viewing habits of *all* members of a household. Videotaped studies indicate that it is the children in a household who are most likely to move in and out of the television-viewing environment, despite (in Gillard's words) "the notions of a 'passive audience' viewing a 'nasty medium' [that] still sticks."

Gillard's use of ethnographic research techniques allows her to come to conclusions and to make observations that researchers in our country need to emulate. Many of her conclusions about children watching television in Australia are equally true in the U.S. Most rules established by parents as to what and how much television can be watched are routinely broken.

It is curious to note that in the eight families that Gillard observed where there was time control (the first category in her study of the influence of family types), all the fathers were professionals and the mothers were at home full time. I doubt if this would be true of professional homes in the U.S., and particularly question whether in such a group all the mothers would be home full time. Certainly, this fact would give a partial explanation as to why there was less television viewing and why there was a wide range of leisure activities. In less affluent homes, television is going to dominate more because of the smaller space and because of the lack of funds for a wider range of leisure activities. As Gillard points out, in those families where she looked at program control (the second of her categories under family types), the main provider was a single mother. Since the mother was less likely to directly supervise all the children's television viewing, her preferences were stated. It is curious that these mothers spent time co-viewing with their children. One wonders if this may not be seen as "quality time" with the children.

These observations are borne out when the "situational constraint" group is discussed, for these families were the poorest and—not surprisingly—viewed the most television. One cannot ignore the sociological importance of the fact that this group had less space in which to view and the children had less of a voice in deciding what was watched. And one cannot be surprised when Gillard reports that there was a significant positive correlation between the amount of television viewed and the number of activities performed around the television set.

As Gillard emphasizes so strongly, teachers must be aware of the family context when discussing or dealing with the television viewing habits of their students. Children do not control family routine and family use of time. To attempt to change the television viewing habits of our students is to attempt to change the family structure and routines. Teachers must realize this most important fact and how it relates to their *own* television viewing habits before they move to impose their television values on their students. Gillard's list of "don'ts" for teachers is enlightened and excellent. An oppositional stance is doomed to failure.

By looking at the genre that students watch, particularly through relating the genre of television to the genre of literature, teachers can move on to looking at *how* students watch television. By combining a study of the television genre viewed with the context of viewing, then relating this to what we are doing when we approach reading and writing, we can integrate television into our work in language arts. By approaching television as text, as worthy of study as any other text, we can remove our value judgments and make such study enriching rather than condemning. By dealing with the diversity of television technologies—computer games, videodiscs, videotapes, interactive fiction—and by approaching such study as enriching, we can have influence not through the laying on of our values but by getting our students to think about and analyze what television is to them.

The quality and diversity of programs available cannot be ignored. Too often, when television in our culture is discussed, it is from an assumption that all people have cable available and utilize it. This isn't true, as I can testify by the fact that I still rely on "rabbit-ears" antennae, here in my house in the woods. I do envy the Australian variety of quality programming for children, with its two publicly owned channels and the requirements for quality children's programming on the commercial stations. The wider and much less expensive availability of videotapes in our country gives us a different advantage, with what can be done with videotapes of movies from novels and from plays.

Finally, let us all support Gillard in her urging that we accept the perspectives of our students toward television and use that as a starting point from which to work *with* our students in an exploration of this most dominating medium.

11 Effecting Change in Schools

Mary K. Healy

I'm pleased to be able to speak to you today on the topic of effecting change in schools. At one level, the topic is so impossibly general that I find it difficult to say anything useful about it, especially to an international audience representing countries with quite different school systems and quite different possibilities and problems within those systems. So rather than inducing catatonia with vague ponderosities, I've decided that the central thrust of my discussion of effecting change in schools will center on how I have witnessed change occurring during my own time in education.

While at first glance that route may appear impossibly self-centered if not egomaniacal, I offer this rationale. In my career, I have been extraordinarily fortunate to have been, at three different times, in the right place at the right time as far as participating in efforts to effect change in schools. So I will focus on those three areas or events: (1) how I changed as a novice classroom teacher in response to what was happening in my school; (2) how the beginning and evolution of the Bay Area and National Writing Projects brought about transforming changes in the professional lives of many American teachers; and (3) how the Puente Project has changed the academic and career possibilities for underrepresented Mexican American/Latino students in California who had been systematically excluded from success in schools.

To begin exploring the notion of effecting change in schools, it occurs to me the change comes out of dissonance, that the disturbance of dissonance creates a desire to do something about it. So the linking of dissonance and the desire to change is what fuels the changes we attempt to make. Let me start with a brief and homely example. As an eager young teacher in California, I had the misfortune to teach in a school which was characterized by this pattern of teacher behavior: at the end of each class period during the school day, the teachers would leave their rooms, dash down the hall into the teachers' lounge, take up their cards, and resume their bridge game. I didn't know much about teaching at that point in my career, but I knew there was probably something more to professional behavior than that! What that situation did was propel me out of that school into a search for something better. And, perhaps by pure serendipity, I came to a school which was—to use a nineties word to describe a sixties phenomenon—"restructuring" the organization of the school by moving into team teaching.

Effecting Change by Reducing Teachers' Isolation

The team I was hired to teach on was a four-subject team: English, history, math, and science. We were responsible for the entire day for 150 twelve- and thirteen-year-old pupils. While, like many of our other colleagues in others schools, we were bound somewhat by the curriculum, what we actually did was determined by what was happening in the classroom. Through the opportunity to sit in my colleagues' classes and work on a team from the early stages in my career, I was privileged to be able to watch learning from the students' point of view and able to approximate what it was like to be a student in a classroom. I want to stay on that point for a minute because I think it's tremendously important. As a teacher just beginning her career, to be sitting in the classroom and watching other people teach, and to look and see the effect of that teaching on the pupils, and all of this on a daily basis, brought me right up against the inescapable reality that I could no longer ignore the *effect* of what I was doing in the classroom. I couldn't simply think about planning to get through the period and then think about grading and marking and correcting papers. I had to examine what I was doing; I had to raise questions about what was happening in the classroom. Because of the opportunity daily to watch others teach, I couldn't escape the reality of consequences.

During this team teaching period, I was privileged to meet a British teacher, Pat Jones, who was the head of English in a comprehensive high school in Swindon, England. His department's teachers had decided that they weren't pleased with what was happening in their English classes, so they designed an experiment. One English teacher per week would follow an individual pupil and sit in on the classes and discover what happened to that pupil over the course of a week. The teachers decided to gather this information before they made any further decisions about curriculum or about teaching methods. One of their findings, for example, was that a fifteen-year-old boy went to all his classes for an entire week without once having been spoken to by a teacher. Knowledge of explorations like that reinforced for me that one must continually consider the daily experience of the student in the classroom. What *is* actually happening in the classroom?

So what helped me change and grow as a teacher was to have the opportunity, through the team organization, to look at what was happening to students as they were learning. And, on the basis of what we learned through our observations, we on the team continually negotiated what would happen in our classrooms.

In retrospect, I realized that we teachers often have a quite awful autonomy. We're isolated, we're alone, and yet we have tremendous power. Team teaching allows that power to be shared and worked through, and it forces us to argue convincingly for what we want to do. In isolation we don't have to argue for what we want to do, we simply do what we want. And, of course, there are certain days when we are very happy to do that indeed! But the idea of regularly negotiating what we want to do and regularly having to be explicit about the assumptions behind what we want to do—these are positive constraints which both encourage and facilitate change. In nonteam-teaching situations, how many times are we challenged in our teaching by others? Who would ask us what our assumptions are? And how many times do we have to explain those assumptions?

So I came to learn these things from my team teaching experience, and these realizations made me, as a growing teacher, understand that the asking of questions, the regular negotiation of what curriculum and activities to include, and the continual observations of the pupils to discover how they were experiencing what was happening in the classroom were crucial behaviors. What I also realized was that team teaching offers the gift of time. When we're teaching alone in a classroom, time is inexorable; it is almost impossible to stop and reflect and marshal resources. When we're team teaching, though, we do have this opportunity. One of the major changes I was able to make as a member of a team was to find sufficient time to search on an almost daily basis for the materials that would be interesting and stimulating for my pupils.

Of course, it is difficult to do this, given the present inexorability of curriculum coverage. It's very difficult to stop and "just" read a story aloud. Yet, when pupils are asked what they remember from their classrooms or their teachers, often they will describe what they've read or had read to them. Pupils remember books or stories that they've read and enjoyed. They also remember papers they've written that teachers or others were kind to or appreciated. That's what they remember.

Effecting Change through Teachers Doing What They Teach

The evolution of the Bay Area Writing Project—how did that bring about change in schools? The Bay Area Writing Project, which grew into the National Writing Project, was begun by James Gray and Cap Lavin in 1974 with twenty-five teachers from the San Francisco Bay Area who sat in a room on the University of California, Berkeley, campus for five weeks, writing together and teaching each other. There are two people in this room now who were in that first group. I was there and so was Miles Myers, the executive director of NCTE. We had no idea at that time that we were in any way effecting change. What we knew was that we were tremendously frustrated because the media were proclaiming a national crisis because our students allegedly couldn't write. National magazines were publishing "Why Can't Johnny Write?" stories. The general feeling was that pupils in American schools do not write and were not begin taught to write. So these twenty-five teachers came together to write steadily themselves and to discover what the problem was—to try to explore the problem. What was very different about that first Writing Project Institute was that the major activity during the five weeks was writing and reflection. For the first time in my professional career, I spent an extensive amount of time writing real pieces and then reflecting on the process I had gone through to write them. I shared those reflections with others who were similarly interested and then together we decided how what we were learning applied to our teaching. It was a very rich time and a very frightening time. It was the first time I'd ever read my writing to a group of English teachers. Today, in 1990, we don't think very much of that, but sixteen years ago it was almost revolutionary.

Of course, we never came up with one way to teach writing from that writing and reflection. To this day, I think that one of the biggest misunderstandings about the Bay Area Writing Project is that it's considered by many to be an approach to teaching writing. It's not. The Bay Area Writing Project is a staff development approach, a way for teachers to learn from each other and to grow in their profession. It's a way to help change come about through the interchange of ideas among teachers. Now the Bay Area Writing Project has grown into the 159 sites of the National Writing Project. At all those sites, teachers are writing together and reflecting on their writing and their teaching of writing.

The Bay Area Writing Project and the National Writing Project have brought about a major change in how teachers grow in their professional knowledge through acting as resources for each other. They effected change by demonstrating that when there is a problem in education, and change is needed, bring teachers together, have them *do* their subject together, examine their own processes and reflect on them. Have them read what others are saying about their subject and have them then, from that experience, go back to their own classrooms and experiment and explore. Then come back and share with each other what they learned.

Of course, this makes such sense to us when we hear it now, but it's very important to set this approach in its historical context. In my teaching experience prior to BAWP, teachers were never considered resources for each other. The only "approved" resources for teachers were university professors or, amazing as it seems now, sellers of textbooks. During my first ten years of teaching, I went to innumerable inservice sessions to listen to publishers' representatives talking about why their textbooks were good and how they were based on the latest research. As a wily teacher, I learned to position myself in a room to be out of the sightline of the speaker so I could use that time to respond to papers or read stories or newspapers.

So the Bay Area Writing Project brought about a profound change in the ongoing education of teachers. Its basic premises were that teachers can teach teachers and teachers can research their own practice. From the Writing Project initiative, many different subject area projects developed. Now there is the California Mathematics Project, the California Literature Project, the California Science Project, etc. So, from the model of BAWP, administrators, policymakers, and politicians realized that when teachers got together for an extended period of time, raised questions about their own practice, and pursued those questions collaboratively, change happened in classrooms. In the particular case of writing, students wrote more, they became more involved in and reflective about their own writing processes, and, in consequence, over time their writing improved in significant ways.

One final effect of the Bay Area Writing Project and the National Writing Project is how the work of these projects actually changed the status of the classroom teacher through a broadening of the range of what we can expect of a classroom teacher. In the United States now, we all take for granted that classroom teachers can be hired as consultants for other teachers. In addition, they can also be researchers of their own practice. In fact, the Writing Projects and the National Council of Teachers of English sponsor a growing teacher-researcher movement where teachers, in very systematic, documented ways, are asking questions about what is going on in their own classrooms, carrying out their research projects and publishing their results. Teachers now realize that they will continue to grow as teachers by engaging in this ongoing professional dialogue.

Effecting Change for Underrepresented Students through Involvement of the Community

With this background, then, I next became involved with the Puente Project. (Let me say that I'm blithely skipping a decade at a single bound here!) I will discuss Puente within the larger context of how to effect change for the pupils who are not being served well in our schools—those pupils who have been systematically excluded from the possibility of success in our school systems.

Puente is Spanish for *bridge,* and what the project does is bridge the gulf between the predominantly Anglo culture of the community college and the Mexican American/Latino culture of much of the surrounding community. In order to have the evolution of the Puente Project make sense, I will first mention some demographics, in particular the population figures in California. In the United States, the 1990 census shows that California's population is now roughly 30 million. And 30 percent of those people are either Mexican American or from some other Latin American country. The California public school enrollment is roughly about 4,300,000. Thirty percent of those students are Mexican American/Latino. in the Mexican American/Latino student population, depending upon location in the state, there is from a 40 percent to 60 percent dropout rate. Forty to 60 percent of Hispanic students in the State of California drop out of school! Most of the students drop out of school before the end of the tenth grade (age 15 to 16). Finally, there are roughly 185,000 public school teachers in California but only 6 percent of those teachers are Mexican American/Latino.

So the dilemma for California is that Mexican Americans and Latinos are a fast-growing segment of the population, yet this group also has an equally rapidly increasing high school dropout rate. Clearly the situation is desperate. In the past there have been various approaches which attempted to improve that situation, generally under the heading of multiethnic/multicultural curriculum designs. What that translates into is that in some places, certain Mexican American/Latino writers have been included in the curriculum. But most often this inclusion turns out to be a little stop-gap measure which doesn't get to the heart of the problem. It hasn't worked because little or no time was taken by the proponents to actually look at what happens to these Mexican American/Latino students in the schools.

The Puente Project developed differently. The project began at Chabot College, one of the 107 California community colleges. For the non-Americans in the audience, a community college is one of the three levels in California's tertiary educational system. First, there is the California Community College system, made up of two-year, post-secondary institutions which serve a range of goals for their local communities. I imagine in many ways they are similar to the polytechnics here in New Zealand. At the next level there are the twenty campuses of the California State University, four-year institutions which grant B.A. and M.A. degrees but not doctorates. Finally, there are the nine campuses of University of California, a research institution granting Ph.D. degrees.

One of the many goals of the community college system is to have students transfer after two years of study to complete their undergraduate education at a university. However, the Mexican American/Latino transfer rate to the university system lags way behind that of any other ethnic group. In fact, on some community college campuses in the state, it is nonexistent. So the problem is manifest and growing. The colleges are designed to serve their communities, and yet, even in heavily Mexican American sections of California, the dropout rate of these students is huge.

Enter the Puente Project, founded in 1981 by Patricia McGrath, an English teacher, and Felix Galaviz, a community college counselor and assistant dean. Their work illustrates that to effect change, you must begin in your own situation by taking a long and careful look at what is happening there. What Pat and Felix realized at Chabot was that the Mexican American students who came onto the campus were really the fragile survivors. Most Mexican American students had already dropped out of high school. Those students who did arrive on the campus came for a semester. They found nothing there for them. When Felix and Pat investigated this dropout rate, they discovered three main reasons: (1) the students never had in high school the kinds of writing experiences or the teaching of writing that would enable them to write the papers they had to write at the community college; (2) the students had never received the kinds of academic and career counseling that would enable them to know what to do once they arrive at the community college; and (3) the students had little contact with mentors, with role models in the Mexican American community who had made it through the system and who had gone on to a university, graduated, and initiated successful careers.

So, to deal with these deficiencies in the educational system, McGrath and Galaviz designed an academic and community leadership program which focused on writing, counseling, and mentoring to help students stay in college, learn how to do academic writing and reading, and dramatically change their educational aspirations and their career goals.

Now, in order to understand why the solutions which Galaviz and McGrath developed worked as well as they did, I think it's useful to take a look at the phenomenon of school dropouts. I want to briefly discuss the research that's been done in the United States on dropouts and see whether it resonates for you. Do the same problems, the same kinds of situations happen in your own countries?

In "Empowering Minority Students: A Framework for Intervention," in the *Harvard Educational Review* in 1986, Jim Cummins wrote that when we think about the situation of minority students in schools, we must ask questions like these (and I'm freely paraphrasing his words): To what degree are minority students' language and culture incorporated into the school program? To what degree is the minority community encouraged to participate in school as an integral condition of the students' education? Has the school brought community members into the school and made them a part of the students' education? To what degree does the actual pedagogy in the school promote intrinsic motivation on the part of students to use language actively to create their own meaning? Are these minority students placed in situations where they will see that the use of language helps them learn subjects across the curriculum? Do they, in fact, see language and the language of the schools as a way to give them power in all their curriculum areas? And finally, to what degree are the professionals who are involved in assessing these students advocates for them rather than people who locate the source of the problem in the students themselves?

I think these are crucial questions when we think about solutions to dropout problems. Unless Cummins's points are taken into consideration, I believe it is very difficult to do anything permanent about the dropout problem. Other research on the dropout problem emphasizes the need for mentors, especially for the students in the schools who have little record of previous success. Needed also is provision for sustained, intensive counseling to repair the significant damage that has been done to students through their twelve years of schooling. Another crucial connection urged in the reports on dropouts is that of collaboration between the schools and local businesses to encourage in students a much more detailed sense of what it means to be an educated, successful professional today in our society.

In addition, common to all these reports is a call for schooling for underrepresented students which honors the culture of the student, which encourages family and community participation, which provides a rigorous pedagogy, which emphasizes the generation of personal meaning, includes provision for intensive counseling, and makes links between students and the business and professional world.

What Puente did in its small way in California was to change the power relation. We believe in Puente that nothing will happen for an underserved, underrepresented group in the school unless the power balance changes. How do you change the power balance in the school? Well, what Puente did was link into a team effort the two divisions of the college that affect the student—an academic department, English, and a student services division, counseling. Thus Puente is made up of a team of two people, an English teacher who may be from any ethnic group and a Mexican American/Latino counselor. These two run the program on the campus. Not only do they run the program, they are together in the classroom at the same time. The reason for that is many Mexican American/Latino students have come to school with very little experience of seeing adults doing college-level reading and writing. What the Puente teacher and counselor do on a daily basis is model literacy activities for the pupils in the class. While that may sound very simple and small, it's been extraordinarily important in the success of the project.

By seeing the counselor and the teacher together on a regular basis, and by seeing how they operate when they read and when they talk and when they discuss issues, the students are presented with models of how things could be if they stayed in school and if they were able to continue their education. In addition, there's another crucial part to the Puente model—the mentor. The counselor links the students with mentors from the community and the students go and interview the mentors, who are Mexican American or Latinos who have been successful in business or the professions. The students go out, meet their mentors and talk with them, and then come back to the classroom and write about them.

So Puente is a writing, counseling, mentoring program which includes two consecutive writing courses taught by the same Puente English teacher to the same cohort of selected Puente students. In the first course, the students do a great deal of writing about their meetings with their mentors. This is a crucial component of the program because when the students work in small groups in the classroom, they read to the other students about their meetings with their mentors. Consequently, the students in the classroom benefit from hearing about several different mentors. In a very subtle way, the students are connected regularly to many different models of how Mexican Americans in their own culture have managed to survive the educational system and succeed in business or a profession without abandoning their own cultural identity.

I think it might be useful, at this point, to hear the voices of some Puente students. This first is the voice of a young Puente student who was asked to reflect on what his experiences had been like in the schools and why he felt the way he did about education. He writes:

> I think it starts way back in kindergarten. Either you're taught to win or you're taught to lose. And that's where they start putting you in these little projects. You're special, you're not going to make it, you need help. I think a lot of Chicanos are almost singled out or filtered out of that little factory, the school, because that's what it's modeled after and you're almost like branded. Hey, you're going to fail, you're going to fail, what the hell do you want to go to school for? I think it has a lot to do with the way the system is set up.

And that was the attitude of many of the students who came in a very guarded fashion to Puente and then, after the yearlong program has involved them in a range of rigorous, culturally sensitive writing and reading activities, begin to see that there are real possibilities for growing and for learning in Puente and in other classes in the community college.

Another Puente student illustrates the type of change that can occur over time:

> On the first day of Puente I felt very insecure and I doubted that anyone could ever be able to teach me to write well. But slowly and surely, I started seeing changes in my writing. I started to show my family and friends some of my work for I felt proud about what I had accomplished and I felt like my heart would burst if I did not show some of what I had learned.

One of the keys to Puente's success in effecting change for these students is that it is an accelerated program. I think we have to forget the idea of remediation. It's as simple as that. I think both the concept and the practice of remediation have been the cause of these students' problems in schools. Whatever the remedial approach happens to be, the mere description of a program as remedial often has a powerfully negative effect on both the teachers and students involved. The word immediately limits both the students and the context in which teachers work.

We prefer to think of Puente as an accelerated program. There's nothing very magical about the activities in the program; they are simply writing, writing, writing, and more writing—and a great deal of reading of a range of materials, including those dealing with Mexican American/Latino cultural issues. Finally, there is a great deal of participating in and listening to discussions that arise in the class. The movement of activities in the class can be easily plotted: listening to the issues that come up out of readings and discussions and pursuing those issues in writing and more reading and more discussions. I won't describe the classroom methodology beyond that now because there's a workshop later today where Pat and Felix and I will be demonstrating our approaches. But the key point here is that Puente is an accelerated program for students who have not been successful previously in school reading and writing tasks. Paradoxically, Puente's interpretation of an accelerated program is one that slows things down in the classroom. Instead of coverage of material, Puente teachers and counselors emphasize the two goals of helping students become involved genuinely in writing and in mastering the processes of reading and writing. In other words, when you accelerate, you concentrate on those central goals that the pupils must experience in this safe environment you've created for them. What must the students experience? They must experience that writing is a way to make meaning for themselves. Puente helps them understand, from the inside, that they can help themselves—and their mastery of academic subjects—through their growth in writing and reading skill. The success of Puente's approach depends upon students' understanding that within a year.

In addition, Puente works to help students recognize that writing is an ongoing process which demands collaborative work with others. We want our students to understand that, unlike what many of their other teachers have told them, a good writer is not someone who gets it right the first time. We want them to know, from the writing experiences we encourage, the truth in the words of William Stafford, the American poet, when he describes a writer as someone who has discovered a process to write something that he or she wants to write. When the Puente students understand that, when, over the course of the year they spend in Puente, they develop processes they can use in their various classes, then they are going to be able to be successful in their future college classes, both at the community college and when they transfer to four-year institutions.

The counselor in the Puente Project has two-thirds of the battle because what the counselor must do is teach the students how to maneuver through the education system. The counselor must demonstrate and prove to the students that the educational system on the campus is something that can be learned; it's something that can be used if one understands it. But perhaps most important, the counselors, by their presence and their status on the campus, must demonstrate that Mexican Americans can be successful in the system while at the same time maintaining their cultural identity. I emphasize this last because we in Puente are operating in an educational system that does not always value cultural diversity and that does not always value mastery of more than one language. It's a painful irony to realize that your own educational system does not value the mastery of additional languages. I think it was Claire Woods the other day who, mentioning her recent experiences at an educational symposium in Paris, told how the participants were moving easily from language to language. And from my own experiences since 1982, working in Scandinavia in the summers with Swedish, Finnish, and Norwegian teachers, I have come to both admire their ability in the course of a day's work to use two or three different languages effortlessly and to note the effect of this facility on their attitudes toward their own pupils' language development.

In summary, then, how do we know that the Puente Project has been successful? One, we've learned that the students leave the Puente class with a sense of being writers, that they have developed processes they can use. We've learned that the students do not have to develop into Grade A academic whizzes by the end of that one Puente year. They simply have to learn how to write the way the rest of us who have been more fortunate in our educational experiences do. Two, we've learned that the students can be prepared to handle the bureaucracy of the educational system. Three, we've learned the transforming power of the Puente mentors and the active, engaged Mexican American/Latino community they represent. Four, we've learned that in a year a great many changes can happen in the right context, in a supportive environment. These changes are almost exponential. Pupils go from writing almost nothing to writing confidently and at length.

What is the documentation of Puente's success? The transfer rate of Puente students from community colleges to universities ranges from 40 to 60 percent. These are students who were completely abandoned by the system, and now they're transferring to the universities. And what's even more enriching, I think, for all of us who are in the Project, they're transferring to the universities and coming back as mentors. So the circle continues. The students are coming back as mentors to their own community.

What I hope will happen next in Puente is that these students will come back as teachers. I want them to be teachers so that we have a far better than 6 percent representation of Mexican American/Latino teachers in the schools.

Now, in conclusion, I want to bring in another voice, one who Margaret Gill mentioned several days ago, someone whose presence I very sharply miss here, and that is Jimmy Britton. During his opening address at the IFTE Conference in Sydney, he quoted an American Quaker, Rufus Jones, who in the early days of the twentieth century said: "I pin my hopes to quiet processes, and small circles in which vital and transforming events take place."

So, in terms of effecting change in schools, I think it is important to empower teachers and their colleagues in these small circles to work together, to reach out across the boundaries which institutions often create to find the new solutions to the problems we face. Our object should never be to legislate what others should do, nor to tell others what they should do, nor to write manuals for what others should do. Instead, we encourage change in schools when teachers, working both collaboratively and alone, have extensive and sustained time to reflect on their work, to ask questions, to explore new strategies and approaches, to make new partnerships, and to be supported steadily in these endeavors.

12 Teachers as Agents of Change: A Response to Mary K. Healy

Ruie Jane Pritchard

In her plenary session address, "Effecting Change in Schools," Mary K. Healy gives us home truths about transformation in the teaching of English. The historical account of her personal experiences with team teaching in the sixties, Bay Area and National Writing Project staff development efforts in the seventies and eighties, and the Puente Project from the eighties into the nineties illustrates how the professional soil has been tilled in the twentieth century. However, the educational landscape still holds sediments of nineteenth-century plantings when teaching was considered a short-term job commitment for women on the way to homemaking and for men on the way to more ambitious positions (Holmes Group, 1986, 32). Sometimes, we teachers have to clear the roots before we can change the landscape, and in so doing we must give up some of the comforts of remaining the same. In listening to Mary K.'s address, I found myself responding with "Amens" rather than with note taking; her experience with change speaks to my experience. Therefore, I will relate a few personal stories that parallel the changes that Mary K. illustrates for us, while sharing what I see as common threads across our accounts that contribute to a theory of change in the schools.

Team Teaching

Mary K. Healy tells us that the teachers in her first school were still not enough involved in making the important decisions about education to feel the "dissonance" to do anything about it; they retreated to playing bridge instead. (Coincidentally, Mary K.'s journey was from bridge to *bridge*, which is what the word *Puente* means.)

The educational reform movement introduced team teaching to Mary K.'s career, and freed her from the powerful isolation of her classroom, as well as provided her the opportunity to observe her peers teach. Sitting in her colleagues' classes inspired her to cultivate change: "I could no longer ignore the effect of what I was doing in my own classroom." The experience with team teaching early in her career set up a cycle of teacher growth which characterizes the educational experiences she shares with us in her comments. Interestingly, though Mary K. is obviously an advocate for empowering teachers as agents for restructuring the schools, she does not discount the role of administrators to accomplish lasting change; in her example of team teaching, it is the school authorities who catalyze reform.

I, too, began my career with complete autonomy in my own classroom, but soon moved on to an innovative program of electives, block scheduling, and team teaching. Unlike the writing project which came later in my career, this reform was initiated by administration. Had we teachers been in on the early planning, things might have been different. As it was, we felt that dissonance that spurred us to adjust old methods to a new situation.

In my new school were four teachers and 120 students together in one windowless room for one and a half hours. The building still under construction, noise was a problem; on the first day of class, we had to talk to our students over a class microphone! The challenge to personalize our interactions with students was successfully met, for we devised our own strategies to overcome imposed changes. We preserved the best of the instruction and the relationships that we had enjoyed with our students when we were alone with them in our small, personal, self-contained classrooms. But with the new structure, we necessarily took on the positive experience of having our teaching observed daily by our peers, of planning together, of dividing up the work, of having students work more in groups.

One humbling lesson I learned in those early days of teaching stays with me still: If I organize things well, collect interesting materials, and keep quiet, my students will learn. Effacing myself from my stage as teacher was necessitated by the physical structure of our building. We had only large rooms where we could have 120 students, or we had breakout rooms which held only fifteen. So, if I were in charge of thirty students for an hour and a half for a particular lesson, I had to divide them into at least two groups, one with me in one small discussion room, and the other on its own. At first, because I felt the need to "be there" in that other room, I actually made videotapes of lessons or voice tapes of instructions for those students working without me! Such ego to think that my presence was required in some form! The amazing lessons that I gained from students working without a teacher were convincing enough that I eventually planned things so that students would be working on their own. I provided some structure, but the goals were negotiated, and I encouraged a lot more freedom than I had previously allowed my students. Later, a book called *Writing without Teachers* (1973) appeared. I had already learned from my students that they could have written that book, or perhaps one called *English without Teachers*.

Would we have changed from our comfortable classrooms if we had not been provoked? I, for one, do not think that I would have changed a good thing so early in my career. Now, with having had that planning period and teaching experience shared by four teachers adapting to new ideas, I admit that teaching didn't seem so lonely or difficult at that school as many teachers say it is for them today.

Writing Projects

As a teacher in and then codirector of the Bay Area Writing Project, Mary K. changed in her thinking and teaching as a result of collaborating with her peers, taking risks along with them to share her own writing, exploring alternative ways of doing things. As a codirector of a National Writing Project site for a decade, I, too, witness firsthand the powerful influences such sharing has on the skills and confidences of teachers, myself included. In having our beliefs and practices challenged, even disagreed with, we must search our experience and philosophy and educational theories to justify them or to revise them. We have learned well that teaching behaviors are not random.

Reflecting on Theory

I find that it is more in the daily tasks of teaching than in the library work I do, that I am led to reflect on theory. I believe that most questions about practice, what works and what does not, can be answered on the basis of theory. Let us consider a dialogue that reflective teachers might have:

T1: I had a wonderful lesson today!

T2: Why do you think so?

T1: Because it worked!

T2: What do you mean by *worked?*

What theories might underlie this seemingly simple verb *worked?* A grammar lesson in which students underline subjects and verbs can be said to "work," according to a classroom management theory which says that students working quietly at their desks are well disciplined. But if the goal of the lesson were based on theories of how language is improved, the teacher might feel conflict between her learning theory and her teaching practices. The dissonance will catalyze her to change, either her practices or her theory.

Collaborative Research

Mary K.'s final story is about collaborative efforts in the Puente Project to bring in the community and culture of students who are at risk for continuing in university studies. As the training and research director, she necessarily must see the relationship among research, theory, and practice. She and her colleagues developed a theory of what kind of instruction and guidance Puente students needed to succeed, and implemented it in an innovative program, whose success is borne out in the research conducted on the project. I, too, am now in a position as a teacher educator to implement theories and to study their artifacts in the classroom. Just as classroom teachers are investigating the impact of their own practices on learning, I am experimenting with various research models—some instantiated in research communities and some still struggling to be recognized as legitimate. (Not entirely in jest, my university colleagues note that it is not until after one is tenured that one has the luxury of using nonmainstreamed research methods, of conducting collaborative research, of asking unpopular questions, or of undertaking a long-term study that doesn't yield an immediate line on one's vita.)

A friend who is a scientist explains to me that although it seems that he is working on a small, isolated research question, he keeps in mind the larger dimensions that it addresses. With his colleagues, a larger picture is pieced together. For example, several botanists might be looking into aspects of biological nitrogen fixation in plants. One will look at rhizobium, which makes nitrogen available to the plant for growth; one will look at how infection occurs—how rhizobium gets into the plant; one will look at how the plant limits its growth as a result of infection; one will find out what mechanisms are involved in absorbing nitrogen from bacterium. Together, they will find answers larger than any could achieve alone.

This kind of planned study, where each researcher takes a piece of a larger question and results are published together, is rarer in education, and almost nonexistent in English education, where most researchers work alone and look at discrete questions, unless they happen to be using the same population or setting. In fact, in school settings, the questions classroom teachers ask are often in tension with the questions administration asks. Teachers are often interested in individual development, whereas administrators are interested in school improvement.

As I noted Mary K.'s enthusiasm about the Puente Project, I realized how interesting it would be to work with one school using an "umbrella plan" for change that accomplishes two often-competing goals: schoolwide improvement and individual teacher development. As proposed by John O'Flahavan in an article titled "Emphasizing the Teacher in Teacher Research Communities" (1991), this plan acknowledges that school goals and teacher goals coexist in the teaching-learning context. The school faculty identifies general themes, and individual teachers assume responsibility for in-depth exploration of a facet of the larger problem that they deal with in their own classrooms. For example, a high school may be concerned that its students have trouble with state writing tests. One classroom teacher may investigate how using frequent short writing influences student scores; another may look at the impact of teaching-to-the-test by practicing the specific writing tasks for which the test asks; another may propose and test out adaptations for special-needs students; another may investigate how understanding test prompts influences scores; and another may study the impact of mechanics and grammar instruction; another may survey the entire faculty just to see how much writing is actually done; another may interview students or do case studies on students who do well on the state writing test and those who do not. None of these investigations alone answers the entire question of how and why students in this high school perform a certain way on tests, but together they can offer "a diverse set of solutions to a cluster of related problems."

Individual Growth Is Parallel with Professional Change

As Mary K. relates her own stories of change, the verbs she uses signal her development: As a teacher on a team, although *bound* by the curriculum, she learned to *examine* what she was doing, *raise questions*, and *negotiate* what would happen in the classroom with her team members; as a Bay Area Writing Project participant, she *explored* the problem and *reflected* on her processes of discovery; as a collaborator in the Puente Project, she *takes a long and careful look* at the situation in order to *bridge* the school and the community. Just as this individual professional has broadened the range of what she could expect of herself—first as an effective teacher on a team, then as an informed teacher-consultant for staff development, and currently as teacher-researcher with the Puente Project—so has the English profession evolved. Mary K. points out the growing opportunities in the United States for English teachers to serve as expert consultants to their peers, and to research and reflect on their own teaching: "Teachers now realize that they will continue to grow as teachers by engaging in an ongoing professional dialogue."

In looking at the three professional experiences that Mary K. describes for us, consider: Why does she feel that they have worked? At one level, all three contexts have in common implications for classroom practices. On another level, these applications are likely to share assumptions about the teaching-learning relationship. On still another level, these assumptions might all participate in a common theory about how change is effected in schools. In her experiences, Mary K. has illustrated three main tenets of a theory of how change is effected:

- Change occurs when teachers experience dissonance between theory and practice, between ends and means, between individual goals and schoolwide goals, or when conflict or uncertainty catalyzes it.
- Change occurs when teachers are collaborators with their peers and the larger community, acting as resources for each other.
- Change occurs when teachers are reflective practitioners learning along with their students.

In linking practical experiences from three areas of her professional life, Mary K. has offered us a theory about effecting change in the schools. The theory gives us a perspective that allows us to investigate why something works so we can continually redefine and renew ourselves—that is, change. Our unexamined assumptions can potentially stifle our growth. As Ann Berthoff says in her article "Teacher as Researcher":

> ... theory saves us from too much particularity. Teachers have to be pragmatic; they have to be down to earth, but being down to earth without knowing the theoretical coordinates for the landscape is a good way to lose your sense of direction. (1987, p. 32)

Berthoff adds that the theoretical questions arising out of teacher practices also help the rest of the English profession to rethink some of the claims it continues to make about teaching and learning. In her own process of discovery, Mary K. Healy has modeled for us how teachers, working with each other, with educational leaders, and with their larger communities, can be the agents of profound change by challenging and researching practices and the theories in which they are grounded. This creates a rich topsoil for the education landscapes of the twenty-first century.

References

Berthoff, A. (1987). The teacher as researcher. In Goswami, D., & Stillman, P. (Eds.), *Reclaiming the classroom: Teacher research as an agency for change.* (pp. 28–39). Upper Montclair, NJ: Boynton/Cook.

The Holmes Group. (1986). *Tomorrow's teachers: A report of the Holmes Group.* East Lansing, MI: The Holmes Group.

O'Flahavan, J. (Aug.–Sept. 1991). Emphasizing the teacher in teacher research communities. *Reading Today.* Newark, NJ: International Reading Association.

III Waita (Song)

Classroom Practices

After each of the morning plenary sessions, participants at the IFTE Conference attended workshops and paper presentations designed to stimulate open discussions and exploration. This section of *Global Voices* provides you with a sense of the dialogue generated by these smaller-group sessions. Meant to be read as a diptych, these essays are paired by topic—the first essay being a response to a session attended by the writer, the second essay being the original presenter's reply to the attendee's response. Most of the response essays follow a format that includes (1) General Concept; (2) Classroom Application; (3) Limitations for Application; and (4) Forecast/Projection for Instructional Impact so that you will be able to read around in this section and locate the instructional ideas quickly. We urge you to read both essays in each pair because the dialogue reflects the spirit the participants developed during this six-day interaction.

The topics represented in these dialogues deal with some pretty sticky issues. Not the least of these concerns is that of curriculum and politics. Questions during these discussions include the following: Who controls the curriculum? Is a "national curriculum" the way to solve the problems of education? Who sets the standards for the curriculum? The first two pairs of essays take on this issue with verve and examine the national curriculum movement both in New Zealand and in the United Kingdom. Reviewed by educators from outside these countries, the dialogue is rich and raises some knotty points worth global attention. *National curriculum* and *national standards,* terms being bandied intellectually and politically in cultures around the work, have significant implications; the choices that nations make regarding "guidelines" such as these will have enormous impact on educational systems, local cultures, and classroom instruction. It is worth reading and considering these first two pairs of essays before making a commitment to any kind of national control; we can learn a great deal from the New Zealand and Great Britain voices of experience.

Focusing the political lens on classroom instruction, the paired essays which follow the curriculum discussions explore issues related to ESL instruction; the whole language history, vision, and impact; reader-response activities and the questions which naturally accompany this pedagogy and philosophy; and writing instruction. Undergirding each of these pairs are issues of diversity, classroom hierarchy, dominant cultures, and power; and if we deconstruct them, we see the existence of political stances that each of them contains. As Carole Edelsky reminds us in her work, all of our instructional decisions are based on a philosophy, a belief system about human beings, a political view that drives our decisions. The political views of the authors in this text reflect genuine struggles with ways of minimizing classroom hierarchies so that learners take responsibility for their own thinking and learning, thereby not relying on the teacher as the sole purveyor of knowledge; ways of honoring readers as participants in the process of literature instruction—participants who bring with them biases and perspectives that are enriched as well as circumscribed by their own cultures, experiences, and language; ways of building on children's differences as gifts, rather than as stigmas or disadvantages; ways of hearing and supporting students' voices, accepting students' abilities as differences, not weaknesses; and ways of supporting, not overregulating, teachers who are striving to cope with issues of diversity in their classrooms.

To distill these essays here so as to describe their implications for instruction is to distort the richness of the dialogue, to detract from the integrity of the voices. However, we assure you that if you dip into these conversations, you will find instructional ideas—ideas guided by principles which honor students' voices in the classroom, acknowledge cultural biases, demonstrate the value of ethnographic research in the classroom, and honor the diversity which has vast implications for instructional and curricular decisions.

13 Cultural Interpretations of Language Acquisition/ The Culture of Power: ESL Traditions, Mayan Resistance

An exploration presented by Janet Giltrow and Edward R. Colhoun of cultural attitudes toward learning and using additional languages.

Response by Wendy Strachan

General Concept

Those of us concerned with teaching ESL students know that these students confront and deal with an array of issues, only some of which seem directly related to the actual learning of language. As teachers, we try to assist them in dealing with cultural differences, with conflicts between parental and school expectations, and with peer relations. We hope to reduce their sense of separateness by teaching them about our institutions and ways of proceeding as well as our language. We sense that we are transmitting new values and new cultural norms along with language, but our focus is on enabling them to become linguistically proficient and to function confidently in the new sociolinguistic setting. Our success in this endeavor feels like a "good thing." We have helped and enabled the learner to survive in a new sociolinguistic environment. If the learner also acquires cultural knowledge, it seems generally that that is desirable, a means by which he or she can become more readily accepted and assimilated into the mainstream culture. The research presented by Janet Giltrow and Edward Colhoun, however, caused me to question the assumptions underlying that view. They propose a reexamination of ESL pedagogy, based on their extended encounters with Guatemalan Mayans learning English in Vancouver, B.C., Canada.

In 1987, Giltrow and Colhoun began holding regular meetings with a group of more than forty Guatemalan Mayan refugees living in Vancouver. A large percentage of them spoke one of three mutually unintelligible Mayan tongues, most knew some Spanish (half of them were literate in Spanish), but only three were literate in their Mayan tongue. The intent of the ESL class was to meet these refugees' linguistic survival needs, but in fact, they themselves considered that they had a very restricted need for English. They were able to depend on their common knowledge of Spanish and when necessary drew on bilingual interpreters. Their limited need meant that their motivation to learn was also limited. They were aware that merely learning English without at the same time acquiring education or training would not result in the better-paying jobs promised by the agencies promoting ESL classes.

Without the conviction that acquiring English would give them access to participation in the world they wanted to enter, the Mayans chose to hold onto their own, much more adequate language. Their own language enabled them to achieve their own cultural purposes; it also held meanings that go, as Giltrow and Colhoun put it, "beyond communicative practice. For our informants, use of Mayan languages supersedes even blood ties as determinants of ethnic identity."

The beliefs and attitudes which the Mayans brought to the ESL experience became fully articulated as they questioned the methods by which they were being taught English, methods which contrasted in important ways with the approaches they took to learning and preserving their own literate language. In the process of learning English, the Mayans discovered the importance of error in our culture. Their use of English was evaluated according to their deviance from a prescribed standard. They wondered, says Giltrow, "What was this system which had captured them and their speech for purposes of ranking, scoring, and screening?" In learning English, they were expected to follow sequences of grammar exercises. They questioned the purpose of these exercises, the purpose of placing priority on certain forms, and the pattern of authority which led teachers to choose and assign what was to be learned and then to assess and designate the "level" which had been reached.

Rejecting this endeavor as unrewarding, the Mayans pursued independent study of their own literature and language. That the Mayan language they were learning has no practical utility was not disincentive to them to learning it. They learned without pedagogy. They simply met together to talk as their ancestors had talked, following an apprenticeship model in which information and understanding was freely exchanged, and it was assumed that the learners could eventually become the teachers and enjoy their status.

Classroom Application

Giltrow and Colhoun specifically restrained themselves from making any curricular or pedagogical suggestions on the basis of what they learned. After examining the culture and traditions out of which much ESL teaching proceeds, they commented that "Every language behavior which research reveals or constructs is eligible to become a unit of experience in the learner's classroom life. It ceases to be the language user's instrument of comprehension or inference and becomes instead the institution's instrument of measurement, capable of detaining the learner and his or her lifetime." Giltrow and Colhoun were thus unwilling to follow a similar practice.

ESL teachers, however, must and do make choices about teaching methods. They also want to teach in ways which avoid the sense of powerlessness and futility which overtook the Mayan students. I felt that this research implied principles and strategies which would permit successful work with adult learners.

In the first place, teachers need to know what value students assign to the language learning and to be aware of the contexts in which students expect to use it. Rather than make assumptions about needs on the basis of entrance tests, teachers might assemble information in a variety of media: film, photographs, news items, magazine articles, advertisements, and so on—about the value and contexts of use—and present this as subject matter through which to teach the language. Students then will teach the teachers what they want to know and why. They will use the language purposefully from the outset. Over two or three class periods, they will indicate what they hope to gain from the class and what use they have for English in their daily lives.

Teachers will then respond seriously to what they learn from the students and construct the curriculum accordingly. In this way, students will influence what they learn. Classes can also be organized less by level than by interest and activity; thus, they can be grounded in purposes which require language but are not purely linguistic. Students individually, in pairs, or in small groups might elect, for instance, to teach the class about something particularly interesting or important to them. To do so, they would need to acquire the necessary vocabulary and sentence structures. The teacher's role is to assist them to "language" what they know and wish to share. The teacher-student relationship in such a situation is likely to be reciprocal rather than unidirectional. The teacher gains new insights and knowledge—the student learns the language.

As important as enabling students to influence what they learn is, secondly, involving them in decisions about the forms and purposes of evaluation. They need to decide whether screening and measuring techniques serve their learning purposes and freely elect to be tested. Much testing is simply a means of restricting access. It rarely helps students determine what they want or need to learn next, or to recognize what they have learned. In contrast, inviting students to become aware of their own processes and to articulate what they are doing and learning enables them to evaluate themselves and their progress. In consultation with the teacher, they can use that information to effect their own learning, rather than be operated on by what the teacher alone determines. Students may simply need enough language to get by in certain situations. They will want to pay less attention to accuracy and more attention to meaning and communication. They will not want, nor do they probably need, to be evaluated, for instance, on their conventional use of possessives or pronoun references. The responsive teacher will focus her attention at first on whether she "gets the idea" of what the student is trying to communicate. She will help the students work toward and not from refinements of particulars in the language.

Limitations for Application

Implementing approaches of the kind described above would certainly call on the teacher's ingenuity and flexibility. She would need to be able to work with groups and individuals, to set up partnerships, buddy systems, and mentoring relationships. The authority of the teacher in such a class would lie in what she knows of the language, not in her power to authorize what shall be learned by the student.

Some students, accustomed to formal teacher-student relationships, might resist such nonhierarchical learning situations. They remember from their experience as children that teachers make all teaching decisions and are the arbiters of learning success or failure. Since conventional methods of instruction offer that kind of teacher direction, students will have no difficulty locating such courses and, of course, need to be free to make that choice. There is only choice, however, where alternatives are available. As ESL teachers, we need to offer alternatives. We are rightly becoming wary of our assumptions about the unproblematic nature of language acquisition. We realize that learning English is not a simple matter of being a "good thing" for everyone and have tended to be naive about the cultural and colonial implications of teaching our language.

Consulting students about their learning, encouraging awareness of their own processes, developing skills in self-evaluation, establishing collaborative and cooperative structures in the classroom—these are strategies which increasingly we see being advocated and successfully practiced in many learning contexts, both inside and outside of schools. They seem particularly appropriate for adult learners in ESL classes.

Instructional Impact

Adults who decide to enroll in an ESL class have already discovered the disadvantages of not being able to speak the language. The inadequacy they feel need not be compounded by instruction that renders their own knowledge, purposes, and needs irrelevant. I think the Mayans' response to ESL instruction illustrates most compellingly that adults learn languages for many different reasons and that those diverse reasons must be articulated and respected. When working with children in ESL classes, we attach educational objectives to the language learning. When we work with adults, educational objectives may be presumptuous as well as inappropriate.

An approach to instruction which values and responds to what the learner determines as important seems simply sensible. In a time when societies are increasingly multicultural and multilingual, it seems not only sensible but also essential to make room for different purposes as well as different voices.

Reply by Janet Giltrow

Wendy Strachan's summary of our presentation captures very well the essential findings of our research—although in my first reading of the review I felt that she may have minimized the hard, even brutal political edge of the life experience the Mayans brought with them to Vancouver. Our Mayan associates had experienced torture and persecution, endured the ruin of their homes, witnessed the murder of family and friends. And they kept close to their hearts not only their personal experiences of oppression but also their ancestors' experience of colonial subjugation over centuries of imperial exploitation. The Mayans' political sensibilities were charged with meanings that flowed into their interpretation of life in Canada—including life in the ESL classroom.

But my second reading of Strachan's response showed me that she had indeed captured the political dimension of our account, and translated our commentary into a vision of classroom life which cancelled the authoritarian practices that all too easily reminded the Mayans of colonial oppression. I am struck by her suggestion that "we must consult students we are teaching and teach with their *consent*" (emphasis added). That principle of consent illuminates the activities she proposes: discussing language and its uses in our culture ("news items, magazine articles, advertisements"); investigating students' beliefs about language (and languages) and the values they assign to language; offering students the opportunity to "elect" to have their grammatical competence tested. And her vision of classroom reciprocity—free exchange, mutual instruction—not only develops logically from her analysis and proposals but also mirrors our firsthand experience with our Mayan associates: in our meetings, we instructed one another, initiated one another into our respective languages.

Yet, despite this evidence of the feasibility of Strachan's applications of our research, I am haunted by lingering doubt. As Dr. Strachan reports, we offered no suggestions for pedagogy, reluctant to convert our research into yet another classroom system. The conventional classroom—conservative, hierarchical, error-based—is a powerful force in our culture, and a powerful agent of our culture's beliefs about language. And innovation so often ends up being recruited to its service. While I am convinced that Strachan's classroom would be in fact the humane, dignified, mutually enriching place she describes, I am nevertheless doubtful about the capacity of our educational institutions to let go of language learning as an instrument of normalization. Perhaps I am too much a hostage of postcolonial guilt to develop a vision of change.

I am grateful for Wendy Strachan's sensitive and creative reception of our presentation. I wish I could say "*we* are grateful," but I cannot; my cherished colleague and coauthor, Ed Colhoun, died suddenly in November 1990. To him goes all credit for addressing our research project with the kindly spirit and scholarly expertise which opened doors to Mayan experience in Canada. In turn, the "Different Voices" conference in Auckland addressed *him* with its philosophy that respected all tongues. He told me, only a week before he died, that the Auckland meeting was a golden moment in his life.

14 Sources of the Whole Language Movement

A review presented by Robert E. Shafer of the historical research which formed the basis of the "whole language" movement.

Response by Patsy M. Ginns

In his paper "Sources of the Whole Language Movement: What's Old and What's New?" Robert Shafer defines a clear relationship between the current-day whole language movement in the United States and other English-speaking nations and educational movements from the past. He cites others, as well, who are currently writing of this connection, among them Yetta Goodman in her paper "Roots of the Whole Language Movement," published in 1989.

Shafer confirms Goodman's reference to Comenius in that children learn by associating new concepts with that which they already know, a view seen to be consistent with today's grass-roots, whole language approach. Both Shafer and Goodman speak of the practices of teachers meeting together to discuss among themselves the issues concerned with how children use language and go about learning.

Because Shafer's paper is historical in nature, I will present an overview of its content, along with the importance it plays in our understanding of the whole language movement. Shafer relates the underlying philosophies of the movement to a number of educational theorists and draws a particular connecting thread to the progressive movement and the work of John Dewey.

Shafer links his definition of whole language, in part, to that of Altwerger, Edelsky, and Flores (1987), who picture it as a "framework" more than a method. They cite conventional practices found in whole language classrooms but note that none is essential. They note "meaning-making" and the broad associated connotations of language, rather than confined practices that can be "skill-mastered." In particular, Dr. Shafer quotes from Altwerger, et al., noting that the whole language approach proposes the fostering of "skilled language users," not those who "learn language skills" (p. 148).

In reference to Cremin, Shafer notes the philosophy that the fostering of democratic government necessitates the common people's becoming an enlightened body, one dedicated to improving their own lot in life; thus the term *progressivism* came into vogue. Shafer presents the thesis that the current-day whole language movement is simply a modern outcropping of progressive education—in fact, that it is a refinement of it which incorporates the expanding body of research which has come to bear on the subject of how children learn.

Shafer cites Dewey's "purposeful learning" and makes connection with a number of tenets that are included with the current whole language approach, such as cultivation of individuality, free activity, learning through experience, living for the current experience, and acquiring knowledge for coping with a changing world. From William Heard Kilpatrick to Ken Goodman, Shafer traces the concept of the "whole child," in contrast to the concept of isolated skill building. He sees progressive education as supposedly dying in the 1950s and being supplanted by, first, basic education and then "Open Education," which he deems another face of progressivism.

From this point, Shafer traces the background of the whole language movement through the British school system, where it seemed to fare somewhat better than in the United States, making, thus, a more direct connection with the current approach. In the English primary schools during this span of approximately forty years, teachers have allowed students' input and structured activities much nearer to their interests than was being done in America. They were integrating the curriculum and applying a program more nearly whole in concept and philosophy.

In America, in contrast, when the so-called "open education" approach was introduced, schools opened their classroom spaces, not their methods or curricula; thus the movement was doomed from the start as teachers promptly "plugged" the openings and went on teaching the same way they had always taught. Obviously, the main tenets of the approach were not made clear to the teachers and administrators, who either did not feel comfortable in implementing the new approach or were not given sufficient evidence of its basic educational philosophy to be convinced that it was an effective improvement over the methods they had been accustomed to using.

Shafer goes on to review the era in American education—whose characteristics are still in evidence today—when the basal readers reigned supreme, with teachers following manuals which accompany textbook series. Often the next day's lesson is merely "... turn the page and do the exercise you find there." In the fifties, the concept of individualized reading programs became popular, and Shafer cites, too, the work done by Jeanette Veatch in her forty years of leadership in this form of education.

However, since those who advocated progressivism did not have access to the current research, Shafer does not see whole language as a direct outgrowth of the progressive movement. Only now, he contends, could all the earlier philosophies and modern research have come together to bear one educational theory and practice. Indeed, he envisions a new age of progressivism in America, one that is at once more practical and more thoroughly based in an improved understanding of how children develop and how they learn, yet at the same time being a "descendant" of the progressive educational movements of the past.

Discussion which followed Shafer's presentation focused attention on the current grass-roots movement and its origin and spread in America. Attention was drawn to the S.M.I.L.E. organization in Arizona and how it began and grew, with classroom teachers coming together of their own accord to share, research, plan, and collaborate in an effort to improve the way they teach and the way in which children can learn. "Whole Language" was the term applied to the outgrowth of this grass-roots effort.

Reply by Robert E. Shafer

After reading Patsy Ginn's review of my New Zealand paper, I note the need to attempt a clarification of several points which may not have emerged in quite the way I intended them to in my paper.

As to the relationship between whole language and the progressive education, it may well be that further discussion of the matter may be unproductive. It is probably not a subject which many will find challenging or even interesting and, indeed, it would seem to have little to say to a teacher facing a classroom of children on Monday morning. Nevertheless, if one believes as I do that every classroom practice represents a theory, whether one recognizes it or not, then one is obligated to at least recognize the theoretical aspects since they may ultimately determine how the practice plays itself out in the classroom.

There is not enough space for an extended analysis here but suffice it to say that Yetta Goodman and I seem to see in the whole language theorists' statements (so far) a clear relationship to the progressive education movement of the 1920s, thirties, and forties in the United States and in certain parts of the United Kingdom, particularly the basic theory underlying the development of the British primary schools. This connection seems clear because of the emphasis in both movements on basing the learning experiences within the classroom primarily on the child's interests and developmental characteristics and on the child's concern for solving real or, as the whole language theorists would say, "authentic" problems. Further, there is the concentration of both movements on the integration of subject matter and on developing the child's creative abilities, especially in writing and in making a response to reading literature.

What the whole language theorists are calling "authenticity" is clearly linked to Dewey's concept of "experience" as developed first in his experimental schools at Chicago and Columbia. Children in those schools were not to sit quietly in rows, reading, writing, and reciting when called upon by the teacher but were to be "active learners," moving freely about in the classroom, actively engaged in "projects" whose bases were questions the children themselves had formulated with the assistance of the teacher. These "inquiries" were genuine concerns of the children arising from what Charles Pierce had called the "persistent irritations of doubt." Dewey drew freely from the work of Pierce, William James, and other advocates of the philosophy of "pragmatism" in developing his philosophy of education.

Dewey explained his philosophy in a variety of books and articles written over his lengthy career. In *Experience and Education* (1938), *Democracy and Education* (1916), and *Art as Experience* (1934), he noted the importance of the concept of "experience" and its meaning and relevance to educators. In *How We Think* (1933), he described how teachers can place children in the role of scientists or social scientists in the classroom as they proceed through similar steps in solving "authentic" problems that scientists use in their everyday work. Although the Progressive Education movement was well known in the twenties, thirties, and forties as a worldwide movement, and Dewey was recognized as its unquestioned leader, after his death in 1950, few teachers and teacher educators read his books. Interest in Dewey's work has largely been kept alive by a small group of educators interested more in scholarly historical studies than in applications to current educational theory. The "accountability" and "back-to-basics" movements which began in the late sixties swept away the intellectual traditions of Progressivism and have left teachers with only their instincts and observations of children recognizing that there is something basically right about what the whole language advocates are saying—that the recognition of children as active, involved learners engaged in "authentic" tasks, reading real books, and writing for their own purposes works out better for them than the imposition of subject matter set-out-to-be-learned in a "learning system" put together by editors in New York, Boston, or Orlando.

Of course, "individualized reading," as it first appeared in the works of Jeanette Veatch and others in the 1950s, was an outcropping of Progressive Education. Theoretically, it was based on the Progressives' concern for interest and experience and on Willard Olson's research into child growth and development at the University of Michigan from which the principle of "self-selection" emerged. Children were to select their own books to read on the basis of their own school experiences and interests in learning to read. But teachers must know a vast array of children's books in order to make the program work. Alas! Many teachers did not and therefore could not. So much for the widespread application of individualized reading.

There were other similar revolutions against the all-encompassing basal readers, such as "language experience" and "key word vocabulary," which were also aspects of Progressivism but for one reason or another were also difficult to apply wholesale to American classrooms. These were in tune with teachers' instincts and observations of children's learning and therefore provided a backdrop for "whole language" to emerge in the early 1980s and to catch on in wholly unimagined ways throughout the decade, just as Progressive Education had done fifty years before.

What made it possible for whole language to emerge was something totally unrelated to classroom teaching or Progressive Education. What the whole language theorists knew that the Progressives did not was that more than thirty years of child language research had supplied incontrovertible evidence that the concepts underlying whole language were in fact supported by the ways children learn language in the first place. The explosion of research in child language was greatly influenced, if not actually triggered, by Noam Chomsky in his *Syntactic Structures* in 1957 and his later *Aspects of a Theory of Syntax* (1965) as well as his review of B. F. Skinner's *Verbal Behavior* (1957) in *Language* (1959). The review thoroughly discredited Skinner's view of child language acquisition as a behavioristic process of operant conditioning. Chomsky's characterizing of the child as a "creative language user" developing his or her own grammar through a variety of stages and by means of varied interactions with caregivers laid the groundwork for hundreds of studies which were largely unknown to educators until the later 1970s and early 1980s, when the Linguistics and

Reading Committee of the International Reading Association and the Joint NCTE/IRA Committee on Child Language focused attention on the classroom applications of child language research. The work of the linguist M. A. K. Halliday was foundational in these efforts in that Halliday clearly showed that children learn to use language by attempting to use it in situations requiring genuine communication to satisfy their needs. Practicing artificial bits in artificial situations does not result in learning the various functions of language.

The fact that some whole language theorists do not recognize that elements of Progressive Education existing in the residual memory of many teachers and teacher educators have formed a backdrop for the development of whole language theory and practice is perhaps unfortunate but it will certainly not prove fatal to the movement. What is to be hoped is that current practitioners will look back as well as ahead in the development of their day-to-day work with children so that their efforts will be enriched by the work of a Hughes Mearns and a Lou LaBrant and many like them from the Progressive end. Anyone would hope, also, as Patsy Ginns suggests in her review, that current theory would join both the new and the old, creating a new era altogether—one which builds on the creative energies and gifts of children as language users and the creative abilities of teachers to provide for them. It is already happening!

References

Altwerger, B., Edelsky, C., & Flores, B. (1987). Whole language: What's new? *Reading Teacher,* 41(2), 144–154.

Goodman, Y. (1989). Roots of the whole language movement. *Elementary School Journal,* 90(2), 113–127.

15 The National Curriculum for English in the United Kingdom: The Case Against

An argument presented by Winifred Crombie against the National Curriculum, including comments on the relevance of the argument in other parts of the world and on issues relating to bilingualism and cultural diversity.

Response by Joan (Mittelstaedt) Steiner

General Concept

Crombie's case against The National Curriculum for English in the United Kingdom centered on the treatment of *bilingualism* and *cultural diversity*. According to Crombie, the National Curriculum documents imply what is "essentially a transitional view of bilingualism—one which fails to recognize the need to ensure that a child does not become less proficient in his or her home language/s as he or she becomes more proficient in that of the dominant culture." References to reading "from a range of cultures" were originally placed in *attainment targets* (which were assessable); however, the government later placed these references in *programmes of study* (which are *not* assessable). Crombie stated: "It is unsurprising that the Commission for Racial Equality is not prepared to accept the official view that the change is insignificant."

Crombie's succeeding arguments against the National Curriculum were couched in the facts that 70 percent of the world's population is at least bilingual, and 23 percent of children educated within Inner London speak a language other than, or in addition to, English at home. She also noted that in many parts of the world, there has been a move away from the national planning of education, thereby empowering decisions at a more local level.

Crombie also addressed other issues related to the National Curriculum: lack of an adequate research base or consultation procedure; assumption of a linear model of cognitive development; confusion relating to the connection between attainment targets, programmes of study and assessment; limited and ethnocentric view of the English language and "Standard English"; almost total neglect of gender-related issues.

Problems/Difficulties

The National Curriculum is testing-central and subject oriented, according to Crombie. Teachers were not represented in the development of the curriculum. The government hurried the writing of it; the work was done with neither time nor money allotments. Furthermore, there is no assessment of the National Curriculum. Teachers were involved in name only. The agenda was established in advance, and teacher input was not valued. Crombie stated that the Curriculum sought to avoid conflict; yet in striving for that ideal, it has undermined education.

Forecasts/Implications

Issues that arise from the National Curriculum center on educational philosophy. Crombie questioned whose curriculum and whose culture is represented in the Curriculum. No one seems to be questioning *good* and *relevant* in relationship to the Curriculum. Bilingualism is not explored and in fact is seen as a weakness. The Curriculum, which suppresses cultural issues, distinguishes between language and cognitive development.

Crombie posed several questions: Is one curriculum for all? Is our culture one culture? Is a general curriculum molding all students into one culture? What are the political advantages of that? Crombie emphasized that there is no celebration of diversity in the National Curriculum. As a result of the National Curriculum, local control levels are greater; however, attainment of targets is paramount, not students' well being.

Reply by Winifred Crombie

Since I delivered my paper on the National Curriculum for English in the U.K., I have left England to live and work at Waikato University in New Zealand where I am now director of the University of Waikato Language Institute. I left England partly because I was concerned about what was happening to the education system. I do not regret leaving and I am, if anything, more outraged by the National Curriculum exercise in the U.K. than I was a year ago. What particularly concerns me now is the fact that the New Zealand government seems determined to follow the U.K. National Curriculum model in designing its own common curriculum. This is particularly unfortunate because New Zealand is, like the U.K., a country which has a wealth of different languages and cultures. It is also, of course, a country which has an official Maori/English bilingual policy and one which is learning to place a high value on the reassertion of Maori language and culture.

There are, however, two factors which might prevent New Zealand from producing a National Curriculum which is as unenlightened as that of the U.K. First, the draft version of a *National Languages Policy* for New Zealand is an excellent document which demonstrates a commitment to respect for the languages and cultures of all of New Zealand's people. Inevitably, this document will be taken into account in the construction of a National Curriculum. Secondly, although the National Curriculum documents may not take account of all of the consultation that has taken place in the past, there has at least been consultation. I hope these factors will prevent a repetition of the situation in the U.K. I shall certainly attempt to have some influence—however small—on the outcome and, in that attempt, I shall be helped by one of New Zealand's leading educators, Charmaine Pountney, who is now principal and dean of the School of Education at Waikato University. Charmaine's excellent work with the multilingual and multicultural community of Auckland Girls' Grammar during her time as principal is well known here in New Zealand. It is a measure of the genuine concern for schooling in this country that she, rather than a lifelong academic, has been appointed dean of education at Waikato University. It is this respect for the importance of teaching that may finally save New Zealand's education system from the dangers of a national curriculum exercise modelled on that of the U.K.

16 Scented Gardens for the Bland: Curriculum, Culture, and Controversy in the Proposed New Syllabus for Senior English in New Zealand Secondary Schools

An exploration presented by Jenny Buist and Vince Catherwood of language and literature within the English curriculum and the ways in which ideas of culture and identity were developed in the curriculum.

Response by Nancy S. Thompson

This session, presented by Jenny Buist and Vince Catherwood (and including speakers Paul Howe, Stuart Middleton, Elody Rathgen, and Margaret Gill), focused on ideas of culture and identity, and the ways in which they were developed, in the language and literature sections of New Zealand's proposed national English syllabus for the last two years of secondary school. Jenny Buist, vice president of NZATE, and HOD English/Wellington East Girls' College, was a member of this Forms Six and Seven English Syllabus Committee. Vince Catherwood was the original chair of the group charged with developing the syllabus. After a major governmental reorganization of the New Zealand Department of Education, he continues in the new New Zealand Ministry of Education as Curriculum Functions Manager.

General Concept

Taking off from the title of Janet Frame's book *Scented Gardens for the Blind* (1982), which explores a multiplicity of sensory possibilities, Buist and Catherwood suggested that if the conservative critics have their way, the proposed curriculum will be edited into blandness. At the time of the conference, we were presented with copies of the fifth draft coming out of several years of development. Already some of its shining points had been "blanded." However, what I saw was still forward looking and exciting, especially in three controversial areas that I want to discuss: biculturalism, media studies, and gender equity.

First, a little background about a national syllabus in New Zealand and how it is developed. New Zealand has traditionally had a national curriculum. This new syllabus presents broad, centralized guidelines, and it seems to me *attitudes,* that reflect the best knowledge we have of curriculum development. Though a national curriculum is by nature centralized, this one takes advantage of decentralization by leaving interpretation and specific teaching practices to the individual teacher, or groups of teachers, in schools. The NZ curriculum writers suggest that, in groups of teachers, much can be learned by each teaching from his or her strength within the general curriculum guidelines and sharing those creative teaching ideas with others.

Planning of the syllabus for senior English has been under way since the mid-1980s. The members of the Syllabus Committee represented a broad cross-section of interests: the Department of Education, the secondary teaching profession, the universities, the teachers' colleges, the polytechnics, employer and employee organizations, boards of governors, the young people themselves, the media, and the community. In August 1990 when we saw the draft, it was momentarily being considered by government groups that presenters felt were having trouble approving some of the more progressive ideas.

Since the time the committee was appointed, radical changes in the NZ government have altered the structure of education. The committee, which was set up under the former Department of Education, has been disbanded. Now, several curriculum project groups in different parts of the country are contracted, without government support, to continue the development. The group in the Christchurch area is headed by Elody Rathgen and the one in Auckland by Isobel Rose and Phil Coogan. The next draft of the syllabus, number six, has yet to be handed over to the new Ministry of Education. The presenters hoped that the progressive ideas would not be overcome by a small, inappropriate number of dissenters.

Some of the general underpinnings of the syllabus include a holistic view of language, a knowledge of how learning occurs, and use of the competencies and interests of the students in the classroom.

The biculturalism of the curriculum—including literature by and about Maori culture and study of the Maori language—emanates from the strong movement in New Zealand to recognize the 1850 Treaty of Waitangi, which honors the place of the Maori as a major force in New Zealand culture and ensures their rights. The session speakers, especially Stuart Middleton, who has worked on the syllabus throughout the process, were incensed that mention of the treaty has been struck from the present draft and the commitment to bilingualism has been severely watered down. Also, the media production section has come under attack because of the resources of technology and inservice training that would be necessary.

Application

The syllabus does not prescribe specific texts, or even teaching practices, but suggests an overall structure and attitudes and seeks to set up guidelines for making specific choices. I am limiting my discussion here to the three controversial areas I listed above.

Biculturalism

The only author's name mentioned is Shakespeare (as the plays "speak powerfully to the students of today because their message is universal and timeless"). The syllabus strongly urges the use of New Zealand literature representing both the Maori and the Pakeha (the British/European) culture thrusts in New Zealand society. In the language section, the syllabus proposes a comparative study of Maori and English as a basis for descriptive study of how language works. One of the controversies has been, "Why so much focus on Maori as a second language for school study when there are numerous South Pacific languages emerging in New Zealand schools?" Linguist Stuart Middleton defended Maori as the second major language force in the country and explained that other languages could take their lead from the Maori language used in this way. (Incidentally, I met several young Pakeha people in my travel throughout the country who took great pride in learning the Maori language in school.)

The cultural thrust was felt in the conference program itself, which incorporated Maori cultural protocol, a practice in NZ for many conferences and other public gatherings. Our conference opened with a *powhiri,* a ceremony greeting guests and getting the conference under way; and throughout the conference the presence of Maori culture was felt, from the daily plenary sessions, where everyone sat on floor mats as in a Maori meeting house, to the ending *hui*, where representatives from each country spoke from the floor, in addition to any other individuals who wished to speak. These Maori conventions, though controversial to some, gave the Auckland conference its unique personality; they allowed guests to participate in a strong experience of another culture. The Maori were represented throughout the conference by speakers and other programs and as a cultural presence in the Maori-influenced design of the artworks covering the walls of our meeting hall.

As I thought about the bicultural situation in New Zealand, I couldn't help making comparisons with the United States. In New Zealand, the indigenous Maori people comprise about 15 percent of the total population. Through awareness and celebration of the Treaty of Waitangi and through other activist thrusts, the Maori are fighting to make their cultural and political presence felt more strongly in the country. One comparison that immediately comes to mind is the African American-influenced culture in the United States, especially in the South, where 30–40 percent of the population is African American. Though their mother tongues do not exist here, the English they speak *does* echo their African languages. In particular, students' study of what is sometimes called Black English would clarify that "mistakes" like the use of the "be" verb are really "correct" uses of language, which might help relieve the stigma toward Black English. More recognition, understanding, and appreciation of our African heritage could help reenfranchise young African Americans and enrich others as well.

The United States is such a large and diverse country that recognition of other cultures will need to be accomplished on a regional basis. In some regions, the American Indian culture—perhaps in some ways a more direct comparison with New Zealand because it is indigenous—is more prominent. There, those indigenous cultures could become the cultural sounding board. In the West and Southwest, the Hispanic culture is strongly felt. New York City and other large cities offer a polyphony of languages and cultures—*all* could be considered *resources* to enrich our culture and education and help us overcome our lack of exposure to other languages.

Media Studies

Media Studies is also a controversial area of the proposed syllabus. As its introduction suggests, this senior secondary syllabus builds from the junior secondary syllabus for Forms 3–5 that was adopted in 1983. One of the innovations in that syllabus was Charmaine Pountney's reformulation of the communication skills. In addition to perception and production of traditional verbal language, she adds visual and kinesthetic modes:

Production	Reception
Speaking	Listening
Writing	Reading
Moving	Watching
Shaping	Viewing

Moving refers to "using facial expressions, gestures, and movement in situations that range from everyday conversations to live theatre while *watching* is the receptive equivalent." The production mode of *shaping* is "using visual effects in writing and in media such as posters, models, television and cinema," while its receptive mode, *viewing*, "calls for a developing awareness of these visual effects" (Shafer, p. 17).

This view helps us see the language in which we carry on our cultural business as an expanded language that no longer consists only of verbal language. Now, our students can generate computer graphics to insert into their verbal texts, or they can use graphics and sound as easily as giving speech in verbal language only. One has only to observe business reports to understand our growing dependence on visual information. Though we sometimes despair at what we think are the disadvantages of young people's diet of visual images, the new media undeniably offer a rich array of communication messages that can add to (rather than detract from) our traditional use of verbal language. I applaud New Zealand's forward-looking recognition of electronic communication media and hope we can adopt such attitudes more widely.

Gender Equity

Speaker Jenny Buist stressed the desire of the Syllabus Committee that gender equity not be confined to one section of the syllabus, but that "equity objectives underpin *all* the aims of this syllabus." The committee's thrust, in Jenny's words, is "toward an *anti*-sexist curriculum, not just *non*-sexist." The introduction to the syllabus states that it "affirms the voices of women and girls alongside those of men and boys." New Zealand has a strong women's past and a very energetic group of women writers presently at work. The new syllabus urges that women's voices and their skills be valued and respected. This kind of direct encouragement opens the way for more women authors in NZ's classroom study, and such statements in curricula in the U.S. and other countries can help provide the needed support for breaking from the traditional, white-male-oriented canon.

Limitations for Application

The Forms Six and Seven Syllabus has received enormous positive response from educators in general and strong agreement among teachers. However, the highly political process the syllabus is having to go through before its approval is eroding the innovative positions New Zealand educators are taking on controversial topics like those above. Stuart Middleton asked, "Are we to toss out one hundred years of good curriculum development in New Zealand?" With fewer financial resources, government has turned over much of the decision making for schools to volunteer community boards in each area.

Representing the Maori voice, Paul Howe expressed a sense of urgency: If Pakeha people do not take on the responsibility to preserve the Maori language, then it will continue to decline because of the natural forces against this minority voice. He testified that he had had to re-learn what being Maori means and had to understand the meaning of the Treaty of Waitangi. Howe reported that the other Maori members of the committee were not present because they reject the watered-down biculturalism of the present draft. The Maori generally expressed reservations about the present draft of the syllabus because the weakened focus on Maori culture and language could have a negative effect. Elody Rathgen voiced the general fear of dishonoring the Maori because of inadequate knowledge.

At the time of the conference, the media section was also under consideration for revision. Elody Rathgen predicted that the media *production* aspirations would have to be minimized because of the need for many more technical and inservice teaching resources that are not economically feasible. Instead, she thought, emphasis would be changed to *projections* by teachers and students of how production *might be* planned and produced.

Though there was no discussion of resistance to the gender-equity statements in the syllabus, we all know how difficult it is to break out of the traditional pattern of male-author-dominated texts for study.

Forecast/Projection

If such an innovative national syllabus cannot get through the political process in a smaller country like New Zealand, I doubt if one would have much hope of being approved and adopted in larger and even more diverse countries. However, with leadership like New Zealand's, ideas are planted and catch hold in pockets everywhere. Even though the NZ Syllabus is, according to their standards, somewhat watered down in this fifth draft, I believe that it still lives up to the innovative, risk-taking tradition of New Zealand curriculum development.

Though we do not know yet if this national syllabus will be adopted, much of interest is happening in New Zealand education, some of it influenced by the Maori (and other South Pacific) language and culture groups. Many of the ideas can be adapted for the diverse cultural situations arising now in all English-speaking countries. Since New Zealand gave us the whole language consciousness that underpins much of our own recent curriculum development in the United States, perhaps we can look to them for leadership toward a whole culture mind-set in the polycultural world we now inhabit. Kudos to New Zealand.

Reply by Jenny Buist

Since August 1990, there have been a number of significant developments which have affected the whole structure of education in New Zealand. The status of the various drafts of the Forms Six and Seven English Syllabus has been shaken by the fallout from proposed changes to national curricula and assessment procedures currently under way.

At the time of the International Conference, draft 5 of the syllabus had been circulated to all schools for response. Though most of those involved with the syllabus viewed this draft as a laundered version, as Nancy Thompson describes, the response to it from teachers was largely positive. Elody Rathgen, contracted to the Ministry of Education to assess these responses and take them into account in producing a sixth draft, worked with a team of teachers throughout 1990 on this task.

In October 1990, right in the middle of Elody's rewriting process, a national election brought about a change of government for New Zealand, and a new minister of education, Dr. Lockwood Smith.

Within weeks, Dr. Smith had put all English syllabus work on hold. He issued statements to the effect that he wanted senior students "studying English, not perusing some social agenda," and that the attempt to make teachers "social engineers" was over.

Dr. Smith called a meeting in December 1990, to which a range of people were invited to consider the draft syllabus produced under the leadership of Elody Rathgen. None of the people invited to this meeting had been involved in any aspect of the syllabus development prior to this point; indeed, Elody herself was not invited to be present.

An outcome of this meeting was that in May 1991, Roger Robinson, professor of English at Victoria University of Wellington, who had been present at the December meeting, was contracted by the Ministry of Education to rewrite the Christchurch draft. This move was approved by the minister. The consultancy group with which Professor Robinson was to work included two of the most vocal opponents of the equity provisions in previous syllabus drafts.

The first Robinson draft syllabus duly appeared in September 1991, and was circulated to all schools for comment. The concerns of many English teachers about this draft are summarised in part of the NZATE (New Zealand Association for the Teaching of English) submission in response to it, as follows:

> Our concerns are the following:
> (i) that there are no statements in the draft syllabus affirming a commitment to the Treaty of Waitangi;
> (ii) that there is no recognition in the draft syllabus of the equal status of Maori and European culture in this country, and the need to reflect this equality in programmes of learning;
> (iii) that there is no recognition in the draft syllabus of the equal status of literature by women and by men, and the need to reflect this equality in programmes of learning;
> (iv) that both biculturalism and gender issues are trivialised in the draft syllabus by being relegated to the status of "topical issues" and "pre-occupations" in the introduction;
> (v) that statements from previous drafts recognising and affirming diversity of peoples, languages and cultures, have been weakened or removed from this draft.
>
> All of these concerns point to the fact that the philosophical stance of previous drafts has undergone major shifts in the process which has produced that September draft. Teachers of English in New Zealand have endorsed an earlier draft of the syllabus which was circulated to all schools.

> That the outcome of that consultative process has been ignored in the production of this draft syllabus leads us to seriously question whether the primary aim of this draft is to enhance students' "capacity to use language and respond to language" as stated in the introduction.

At the time of writing, we await a new Robinson draft, which is to take into account the responses received.

The issues remain the same. Along with concerns about biculturalism, gender equity, language study, New Zealand literature, female and male writers, and the development of the individual's relationship with her or his world, is the parallel issue of appropriate processes of curriculum development in this country.

We need a New Zealand curriculum appropriate for the needs of our students, based on the best of current classroom practice. Therefore it is vital that teachers with knowledge, skills, professional involvement, and curriculum development experience are involved in syllabus development. The history of the development of the Forms Six and Seven English Syllabus thus far raises vital questions about whether the excellent track record New Zealand has so far held in this respect is valued by those in power.

Dr. Smith, current minister of education, has set in motion the production of new curriculum statements for all "basic" subjects under the title of the Achievement Initiative. In New Zealand it is the minister of education who holds the legislative power to approve national syllabi for primary and secondary schools. The relationship between the Forms Six and Seven English Syllabus and a new comprehensive curriculum statement for English in primary and secondary schools is not yet clear.

We await the outcome.

17 The Errors of Our Expectations: An Ethnographic Study of Basic and Honors College Writers

A description presented by Deborah James and P. B. Parris of what happens to ethnographic research in a classroom when the teacher being observed is a colleague.

Response by Ann Buhman Renninger

General Concept

Deborah James asked the questions: "How are college freshmen who enter the University already in special categories designated Honors or Developmental, introduced into and included or excluded from membership in the academic community? What are the critical factors in which Basic Writers succeed and fail in college?"

In an attempt to answer these questions, James conducted an ethnographic study of two college writing classes: an Honors and a Basic Writing class. Data were collected in the form of notes based on her observations of Peggy Parris's Honors writing class; a journal in which Parris made entries after each class meeting; and notes based on her observations of her own Basic Writing class.

Teaching Points/Activities

Parris and her class were an appropriate selection for the research project because she has an established reputation as a strong, confident writing teacher who teaches clearly defined process writing, is teaching this course for the second time, and truly sees her own writing, like that of her students, as always in process.

Problems/Difficulties

The ethnographic research process involved some difficulties inherent in the methodology and the class selection.

James describes as "hallucination that a participant observation study would unfold neatly." Although both James and Parris held one another in high personal and professional regard and began the study with a high trust level, Parris admitted to a brief period of "paranoid panic" concerning suspicions as to why James was really in her classroom. Said James, "My presence in the classroom causes real anxiety for colleagues."

Another area of concern was that James found herself "hamstrung by her inability to reciprocate." What she offered Parris in return (working with students, responding to papers), Parris had no need of, so James did not feel she could ask Parris for what she needed. For example, she needed more detailed notes for her research study, but she felt it would be presumptuous to ask.

Because James was a teacher, she was outside normal class activity in her observations. The only elaborated insider's view to which she had consistent access was the teacher's. Likewise, James's view was also skewed toward the teacher's view when she tried to be an observer in her own class.

Although the intent of sharing response/observation journals with one another was to form the context for rich reflection and refinement of ideas, both Parris and James felt freed when they decided not to share the journals.

Forecast/Implications

The Errors of Parris's Expectations

1. Honors students were not more highly motivated and more sophisticated in their thinking than were the mainstream freshmen.

2. Instead of James's mirroring what Parris was doing, Parris found that, "thanks to the stimulation provided by the study, I was doing it for myself. I became conscious of my strengths and painfully aware of my inadequacies. What eased the pain was being able to read Deborah James's own teaching journal and hear the echoes of doubt and frustration that I now know other teachers also feel. I suspect that the hope of reaching all students equally well and the

inevitable frustration at finding that some of our expectations are in error, move us to seek new ways to do a better job."

The Errors of James's Expectations

1. Honors students are *not* near cousins of graduate students in English. What they do know is how to deal with teachers, while Basic Writers hold "a firm belief that talking to authorities about extenuating circumstances is like telling the Auckland sky we can't have rain today." Another enabling belief of Basic Writers includes that of magical realism—a *hope* that if they can somehow work harder and longer, they will meet deadlines—a hope that dies only at the eleventh hour. When Basic students miss a deadline, teachers are less tolerant than they are of Honors students, sure that this is a sign of academic weakness. Basic students cannot "buy credit" with their previous classroom performance.

2. What was deemed important for Honors students was to be introduced to professional historians and scientists, and to practice writing like members of that profession. Meanwhile, Basic Writing students were to learn what the professors expected of them and to practice writing that communicated that idea to the audience. This "difference is illustrative of a more pervasive difference in academic initiation between the groups," says James.

Two months into her study, James reflects in her journals on how we speak and present ourselves to the two groups:

> The assumption of all of us seems to be that these students [Basic Writers] must "hang on" till graduation: that the academic beast is even now trying to rid itself of infestation by these lesser beings. There is little sense, I think, either in what/how students talk about their own lives or in how they are spoken to—that is visionary or speaks with any confidence about an expected future in which they will function fully as really, truly, college educated.

James further states, "This survivalist mentality of Basic Writers and those who help them may increase their lack of confidence and their sense that this is an impossible task. I only want to suggest that those empowered to assist any marginalized group in their efforts to find a place within the mainstream, should think carefully about how their own positioning (choosing to teach Basic Writers rather than Honors Writers, for example, and therefore placing oneself at the edge of the profession) may unconsciously affect the view of the university that a teacher communicates to his or her students."

Deborah James learned that there is a need to examine the rhetoric of writing classes at different levels in the University because the format of how writing instruction is delivered communicates expectations to the students receiving that instruction. We may sometimes be saying things through those forms which would surprise and distress us.

When doing this kind of collaborative research, the participants need to address issues of professional equity and find some means of accommodating any differences. The researchers also must be sensitive to context—university and class settings as well as varying teaching and research styles. These issues are inherent to classroom-based inquiry.

Reply by Deborah James and P. B. Parris

General Concept

James

My presentation, "The Researcher's View," covered two areas. First, it introduced the preliminary findings of my comparisons of Basic and Honors writing students derived from two participant-observation studies. Both studies focused on how the university teaches students their "place." The second half of my presentation analyzed the flaws in the Honors writing study, considering the questions they raised about how to appropriately conduct ethnographic research and analyzing the errors I, as researcher, made because of some unexamined, unarticulated expectations.

Parris

My portion of the presentation was entitled "Observations of the Observed." It surveyed my first experience with being a participant-observer in an ethnographic study; my purpose in the study was to test my own perceptions of how Honors freshmen differed from mainstream and Basic first-year composition students, with an eye to improve my own teaching. The study was also my first experience with being observed in the classroom for an entire semester. A third first: I had never kept a teaching journal—nor any other sort of journal—that was intended for eyes other than my own, and I'm ordinarily a very private person.

Teaching Points/Activities

James

Parris agreed to have me observe in her classroom for the whole semester, during which time I kept observation notes and interviewed students in their peer editing groups. In addition, both of us kept journals in which we regularly recorded our reactions to the class as it unfolded. I read her journal entries each week and responded in my journal to her observations as well.

Parris

Deborah James is a fine teacher whom I respect; she has fourteen years' experience working successfully with Basic Writers and has a background in ethnographic study. She is also a valued colleague and friend. I doubt I would have undertaken the study with anyone else. She came into my classroom each day and made her presence as noninvasive as possible, sitting out of my direct line of sight; as the semester went along, her warm manner toward the students and me helped to build the level of trust necessary for a productive classroom atmosphere—and for an ethnographic study.

Problems/Difficulties

James

In analyzing the Honors study to make comparisons of Honors and Basic Writers, I discovered that there were problems in (1) the design of the study and (2) my collaboration with Peggy Parris. In designing the study, I had assumed that at least some of the Honors students would themselves be eager and willing co-researchers. I failed to offer appropriate inducements to engage them as student informants or adequate reciprocation for their assistance. I also failed to provide a mechanism for consistent access to student views in the class. Both of these errors were exacerbated by the errors I made in my collaboration with Parris. I assumed that she also saw herself as a co-researcher. Only after the project was begun, did I see that because she was participating in this project primarily because we were friends and colleagues, she saw herself as the object of research much more than as a researcher. When I became aware of that, I felt constrained not to make the demands of her that I would have otherwise. For example, I did not ask for greater detail in her journal because she was already giving me precious time by keeping it in the first place. We also did not consistently exchange views of the class as the class proceeded. Finally, I discovered that even though we were friends and have great respect for each other, because our interaction in this project became defined as "researcher" and "researched," my initial presence in the classroom created more tension than I had anticipated, and to lessen that anxiety, I limited the types of observations I could make.

Parris

After the study was completed, I was able to read James's own teaching journal from that period. It eased my sense of inadequacy, as recorded in the entries in my journal, to hear the echoes of doubt and frustration in hers. I now understand that all teachers feel some of these same emotions. We want to reach all of our students and help them make positive changes, but those lofty desires are too often thwarted. Yet it is when we find our expectations in error that we are motivated to look for new ways to become better teachers.

Forecasts/Implications

James

Even though the second study was flawed, I learned a good deal about differences in how the University initiates Honors vs. Basic Writing students. Those insights have begun reshaping my teaching of Basic Writing. In addition, they will form the basis of my next participant-observation study. Furthermore, I am beginning to look at the two teaching journals to report on comparisons between "process" writing teachers. Though flawed, this was a rewarding experience that I will repeat as soon as I can.

Parris

I recently reread the journal that I kept during the study. How differently it reads now from this distance in time compared to when I was in the middle/muddle of observing and being observed. But I can see where I was developing a clearer picture of myself as a teacher and my students' reactions to particular assignments and activities. Looking back at each class period through writing made me more aware of what I was doing, more conscious of what was working and what was not. I saw as I never could before how it is that I communicate my expectation to my students and how that shapes their responses. I learned that I have a personal, largely unconscious rhythm to my classes that I have evolved over the years; I was made aware of how I pace the tasks in each class period, the cumulative tasks for each paper, the paper due dates throughout the term. That awareness has helped me to better adjust to differing student needs in the classes that I have taught since. I know that I have grown from the experience of the study, and my teaching has changed as a result of watching myself watch my students as Deborah James watched us all.

"Would you do it again?" someone asked at our presentation in Auckland. Yes, I believe I would—if Deborah James were to ask me.

18 Organizing a Whole Language Program through the Use of a Loose-Leaf Notebook

A presentation by Stella D. Holmes of instructional techniques successful in integrating reading, writing, speaking, listening, and thinking skills in all grades.

Response by Merle Yvonne Williams-Price

General Concept

Stella Holmes thinks that the most significant function of school is to encourage and *motivate* students to strive throughout their school tenure to become efficient, self-directed, independent thinkers in every academic area. She believes that the whole language movement allows teachers to challenge their students to pursue their academic goals and intellectual pursuits. In the whole language setting students are eager to select books, read aloud, participate in related language activities, and share their own writing without reservation. One of the basic techniques for organizing such a variety of activities is to have students create a loose-leaf notebook which serves as a portfolio to showcase students' work.

In approaching reading, listening, thinking, speaking, and writing, Stella Holmes emphasized a series of relevant activities and strategies that can reflect a step-by-step process for implementing a whole language philosophy.

Classroom Application

Stella Holmes reinforced the value of the Whole Language Movement by explaining that this philosophy encourages the teaching concepts, merging strategies and topics that were, in the past, never seen as related by some teachers.

Currently, students in whole language classrooms are excited about reading myths, folktales, hero tales, and poetry. These types of literature have exposed students to vocabulary and style that often will later appear in their own writings.

Because there is more time for students to listen, talk, read, think, and write in such a program, workbooks, dittos, and worksheets are unnecessary. There are numerous and unending strategies that may be incorporated without relying on isolated skill-building activities.

Ms. Holmes discussed activities such as the following:

- students reading short stories and other original tradebook texts
- students writing answers in personal notebooks, rather than in workbooks
- students experiencing the interaction of reading, speaking, listening, writing, and thinking as a major component of the classwork
- students sharing, displaying, and publishing their work

Limitations for Applications

The implementation of a whole language philosophy evolves gradually through stages. It is important that the teacher proceed and implement the process slowly, making necessary changes as the program develops.

In order to support this change, the teacher needs to join supportive organizations and read professional literature for the exchange of information and discussion of the philosophy and practice of whole language. Such activities are critical because there are risks and uncertainties, and because the teacher may have to produce specific test data, files, and student progress to justify the effectiveness of the program.

Forecast/Projection for Instructional Impact

The whole language movement has brought much excitement, inspiration, and unlimited creativity to the classroom because the instructional philosophy supports the integration of reading, listening, thinking, speaking, and writing and makes schoolwork more purposeful. This plan is in sharp contrast with past teaching practices that have focused on skills, especially writing in isolated settings. Because such an approach underscores the importance of "real world" quality in student work, I believe that we are just beginning to feel the impact of this grass-roots movement. Teachers recognize its power for their students, for their classrooms, and for the future.

Reply by Stella D. Holmes

Because educators of all kinds attend conferences, presenters can become so anxious that they fail to discuss their projects fully; they often omit the most pertinent and significant component: Objectives. Therefore I considered it crucial to address this issue before commencing this workshop.

The participants were told that at the conclusion of the session, each person would be able to (1) relate and link *whole language* to the communication skills: listening, thinking, speaking, reading, and writing; and (2) organize a *whole language* lesson through the utilization of creative teaching practices: process writing, cooperative learning, giving oral presentations.

The following are areas of concern I tried to address in the workshop so that participants would see the interrelated parts of a whole language program.

Program Credibility and Believability

This is an area that had to be explained in detail. There were educators from all parts of the world, so it was of utmost importance to provide the participants with enough materials and different strategies to convince them that the program can become a reality.

This strategy worked: Participants were eager to share and relate similar experiences when they realized the approach was practical, realistic, and could be implemented by anyone. The loose-leaf notebook, for example, is merely a concept which could be realised as a simple folder, a binder, or even fold-over construction paper.

Explaining the Process

This task became easier because there was a detailed table of contents for each participant displayed on the overhead projector and fully discussed as we proceeded to describe and explain how each activity from the table of contents could be used in a classroom setting for middle or high school. Some of the components from the syllabus could be modified for the elementary grades.

Color-Coding

Students in this program learn to organize their work sequentially through the coding process. The following list reflects a sample of the color-coding students have utilized in the past:

- Reading/Literature Core: Blue
- Organization or Course of Study Plan: Gray
- Listening: Yellow
- Thinking: Green
- Writing: Lavender
- Speaking: Pink

This was only one strategy that we utilized to organize the notebook. The color-coding system could be replaced easily with numbers or alphabets. I am quite sure there are many other plans that work just as effectively as the one that was presented. The idea is to develop a plan, experiment with the students, and make changes when there is a need to adjust the management plan.

Assessment

The ratings: Superior, Above Average, Fair, and Needs More Training encourage students to work harder and to present work that is organized, completed, and fairly neat. They take pride in seeing their quarterly work packaged, labeled, and organized. This system is in sharp contrast to the loose-leaf, day-to-day work that is sent home from most traditional classrooms. This system is an innovative way to profile students' progress.

Student Collaboration

Cooperative grouping and learning are strategies employed, conducted, and organized by students. Students share in brainstorming, sharing ideas, listening, and thinking. These activities can be interjected within the context of each teacher's daily lesson as a major component of the program.

The review that was written by Merle Price is an accurate report of what happens whenever that activity is presented in most cooperative learning situations. My goal was to address the basic concerns of a *whole language* classroom and demonstrate them in the workshop; I believe that the participants were able to leave with ideas and concepts that could be implemented in a classroom setting with a minimum of planning, vision, and collaboration. Merle Price's response indicates that I was successful.

19 Teaching Resistance

An account presented by Catherine Beavis of the attempts of a group of Victorian teachers to translate new insights about reading into classroom practice.

Response by Nancy B. Lester

General Concept

Going beyond the reader-response school of literary criticism, this workshop focused on promoting alternative interpretations of texts based on theories of social and cultural construction. The purpose of such kinds of readings is to encourage teachers and their students to question, critique, and reflect on how texts and their own readings of such texts are shaped by powerful social and cultural views of the world, like racism and sexism.

While this workshop described using this approach to reading and responding to literature with secondary students, it could and probably should be part of how students learn to read when they begin to learn to read. Obviously, the setting or the classroom context would reflect a collaborative spirit, with small and whole groups talking with each other and sharing ideas and critiques together.

Classroom Application

It became clear, as those of us who participated in the workshop worked on an actual text, that we were living the theory in action. Our individual and sometimes collective views of the world were clearly reflected in our responses to the texts we read. As we shared further, our discussions inevitably turned toward pedagogy, and to how we might begin a dialogue with colleagues and students about teaching resistance. Although there was not complete agreement, some consensus that emerged reflected the necessity of allowing learners to respond and react to texts without prior attempts to teach resistance.

Having such "raw" responses first would allow a collaborative critique of new texts (our responses), where we could ask why we came to such-and-such an interpretation or what made us view a scene or character the way we did. Continuing discussions of this nature could engender more critical stances as teachers and learners grow more comfortable and accustomed to deconstructing the social and cultural influences on their responses to literature.

What is needed to try this out is an interesting and provocative piece of literature; students who want to read with each other and talk with each other about their readings (i.e., students who respect each other's knowledge and expertise, not to mention points of view); teachers who are willing to offer their interpretation/critique alongside those of the students (not impose their own); and teachers who are also prepared to provoke their own and their students' assumptions about how and why we respond to literary texts in the way we do.

Limitations for Application

The greatest problem would seem to be that of change: i.e., assisting teachers and learners in moving away from efferent or new criticism readings of texts. These approaches to the teaching of literature are pervasive and taken completely for granted in schools around the world. They, themselves, need to be subjected to a teaching-resistance regime.

Both students and teachers need also, as a result, to learn to become comfortable with less teacher-directed questions and with dialogues which may not result in either consensus or even conclusion.

Forecasts/Projection for Instructional Impact

There is no question that teaching resistance must be the future direction for the teaching of literature. The theory of the social construction of reality is cropping up not only in literary studies, but in fields as diverse as paleontology, anthropology, mathematics, and history. If we are truly sincere in saying that our goal is to grow learners who are critical thinkers and negotiators, then teaching resistance is a process of learning by which to do so. Learning resistance, however, is not easy, nor valued in schools. This will be the real challenge of the future.

Reply by Catherine Beavis

Recent developments in literary theory, going beyond reader response to more deconstructionist approaches, confront teachers in secondary schools with a significant challenge to the ways in which literature and response to texts are characteristically taught. Central to this theory are issues of perspectives which demand we reconceptualise our notions of what reading entails. These perspectives include the question of where meaning arises or resides: a view of texts as artifacts; a view of both texts and reading as socially constructed activities, and a view of readers as consumers whom the text works to position in particular ways, to serve particular ends.

What are the implications of this for the ways we work with students on texts? In Australia, as elsewhere, these notions have begun to appear in senior secondary curricula in English and literature. Exciting course materials have been developed which have gained widespread popularity. Bronwyn Mellors, Annettee Patterson, and Marnie O'Neill in particular, have produced a series of booklets through Chalkface Press which allow students to explore texts from this point of view. Through short stories, poems, even Shakespearian tragedy, these booklets challenge students to look at texts afresh and to question their assumptions about reading, and their own role as readers.

But is this a theory for accomplished readers only? Is it useful also for students lower down the school? Does it presuppose a level of conceptual sophistication, or can it be helpful also to young people learning to respond to texts, in school terms, at junior secondary level and below? And what place is there for the personal pleasure readers gain from their engagements with texts? My hunch was that these perspectives could be used at junior levels, and with students who were not proficient readers, if we could make the materials sufficiently interesting and find appropriate teaching strategies. Accordingly, with the help of two Victorian country teachers, Jan Rammage and Jenny Cassidy, their classes and colleagues, I set out to develop a set of resources that would translate the theory for the junior secondary classroom. Bronwyn Mellors's admirable *Making Stories* (1984) and *Changing Stories* (1984) led the way.

A particular concern was for the needs of students who did not much like either reading or school. At a theoretical level the social agenda of rendering texts' assumptions and ideologies visible suggested that this approach could also work in the interests of marginalized students. A key question was whether teaching in this way might help students who find reading inhospitable to make more sense of what they were doing, and of what was put in front of them.

So this was the project: to develop materials which enacted the new theories in a practical way for Australian students at the junior secondary level. I wanted to produce local "multicultural" materials for "ordinary" students and for students who felt school and reading had little of value to offer them. To do this, I sought out local and relatively unknown stories, poems, letters, and cartoons, many of them written by young people, with an emphasis frequently on their experience as migrants or as teenagers with a foot in two worlds. To meet my concern that reading be seen as pleasurable as well as relevant, I tried to find texts that also offered a measure of aesthetic satisfaction to me, if no one else!

But the agenda which soon overtook the development of materials was the way in which the attempt to design such resources increasingly confronted me with assumptions and questions about the whole enterprise, and about literary response. A journey thus began in my own thinking back and forth between literary theory, classroom practicalities, and the private and social worlds each individual inhabits and constructs. It was out of this context that the workshop "Teaching Resistance" arose.

The title, "Teaching Resistance," refers to a process of working with texts in such a way that students become aware of underlying attitudes and assumptions, which the text positions them to uncritically accept. Becoming "resistant" entails recognising these assumptions, seeing how the reader is invited to share them, and critically assessing whether one does indeed wish to embrace them. It is an approach which recognises that there will properly be a number of readings within the class for any one text. As each reader makes his or her own reading, shaped powerfully both by social and personal experience and the text itself, the teacher needs to anticipate and plan for this diversity. Private readings need to be nurtured alongside those versions which the text itself and the dominant culture each seeks to privilege.

As Nancy Lester points out, to teach this way presupposes a collaborative classroom environment where students feel safe to explore ideas in small groups and as a whole. I wanted to use the workshop to try out the activities we had developed in an international context, but also to use the occasion to tease out a number of issues which continuously arose in the course of thinking and planning in the area. I had anticipated that we would explore such issues through work on specific materials, but that the bulk of our time would be spent designing and evaluating classroom activities. These would centre particularly on strategies which allowed for multiple readings and exercises which might serve to highlight both the constructedness and the ideology of the pieces I chose. For this purpose I brought in two local short stories, each concerned with the experience of migrant communities and young people in urban Australia, as seen through Anglo-Celtic eyes.

What happened, in fact, was much as Nancy described. Very rapidly we have begun to explore these approaches with students. At the upper secondary and tertiary levels the strategies have helped students become more powerful readers of texts, of the world, and of themselves. How to make these strengths available to students in lower grades, or at least to prepare them for the experience, remains a worthy challenge to pursue.

20 New Zealand Book-Based Resources: Positive Female Role Models, Maori Perspective

Booklists and information presented by Noeline Wright about New Zealand books for use in libraries and classrooms.

Response by P. B. Parris

General Concept

In accordance with New Zealand's new multicultural curriculum and as a reflection of current feminist concerns, Noeline Wright has developed a booklist of fiction for secondary school courses in English literature. The list also offers resources to teachers in this country who may be looking for ways to introduce students at any level to the people of New Zealand, Maori and Pakeha (those of European descent), and/or to positive depictions of women and girls.

In addition to listing over ninety fiction works by more than forty New Zealand authors, Ms. Wright further divides some of the books into shorter lists of those with a predominantly Maori perspective; those about teenage relationships; and those with fantasy, time travel, and sci-fi themes. She also appends a list of nonfiction works for historical and social background to the fiction and concludes with a collection of related resource publications for classroom teachers.

Classroom Application

In the workshop, Ms. Wright discussed some of the techniques which she has found useful in involving her students in the study of the fiction on her list. She utilizes a three-level approach: Level 1 involves a literal retelling of what the text says; level 2 requires some interpretation on the part of the reader; and level 3 moves on to an analysis of the wider implications of the work. Among the handouts provided at the workshop were assignments suggesting activities that carry the students through the first two levels to prepare them for classroom discussion at the third. Here, for example, are twelve activities, of which a student must complete the first and any five of the others:

1. Write a plot summary.
2. Create a skeleton book summary (an ingenious drawing of a human skeleton with lines in the bones for plot, characters, setting, and so forth).
3. Make a character star for one of the main characters. (Put the name of the character in the centre and words describing the qualities and the personality of the character radiating out.)
4. Draw a map showing places mentioned in the novel.
5. Create an original design for the front cover of the novel.
6. Imagine what you would like to say if you were able to write to the author of the novel. Write that letter.
7. If the author of your novel is well known, you may be able to find out something about her life. Do some research. Imagine you are introducing the author to an audience she is going to address. Write your introduction using the material from your research.
8. Write a poem that relates somehow to the novel (on a similar theme or from the point of view of one of the characters).
9. In the novel find twelve words of which you do not know the meaning. Use a dictionary to find the correct meaning for the word as it is used in the novel. List the words and meanings.
10. Create a poster which captures your response to the novel. From magazines cut out pictures and words which relate to your experience of the novel. Arrange them in a suitable design and glue them on. Make sure the name of the novel is featured somewhere on the poster.
11. Write an interview with one of the main characters in the novel. Write out the interviewer's questions and the answer given by the character. Choose someone from the class to help you record the interview on tape.
12. Some other imaginative activity you design yourself.

Ms. Wright has herself designed a number of other imaginative activities for her literature students, including an assignment directly related to growing up in New Zealand in relationship to Maori culture. Though too lengthy to quote here, the activity sheet, it seems to me, could readily be adapted to suit any multicultural setting in this country (see below).

Limitations for Application

The only problem I can foresee in applying to our own classrooms what was presented in Ms. Wright's workshop is the difficulty of getting copies of the works on her booklist. She admitted herself that she had been unable to locate sufficient copies of some of the titles for one entire class to read the same novel at the same time, so she had allowed students to select from those available, after which each gave an oral report to the rest of the class.

Unfortunately, New Zealand titles are very scarce in this country. Some of the better-known novels—Keri Hulmes's *The Bone People* and the works of Patricia Grace and Janet Frame, for instance—are available in paperback, however, and offer us amazing historical and contemporary insights into Maori culture.

Forecasts/Projections for Instructional Impact

First, let me admit my embarrassment at my own ignorance and naiveté about the country of New Zealand and the culture of its native people. Until the joyfully enlightening IFTE Conference, I had spent my literate life reading American and Anglo-European work and thought myself an educated person. What I learned in Auckland is how little I really know, and I suspect from my conversations with other attendees, I am not alone in that. If we are to prepare our students to live in a world connected instantly by satellite television and Fax machines, a world that is becoming increasingly dominated by the economics of the Pacific Rim, then we need to turn our attention to the literatures of those countries and cultures, large and small, that make up the other hemisphere of our planet.

Closer to home, what Noeline Wright and her colleagues in New Zealand have begun doing to implement that new multicultural curriculum should stand as an example to those of us who teach English in the United States, where we have so many rich and varied cultures to draw upon, including that of our own Native Americans. Ms. Wright's assignment sheet, "Growing Up in New Zealand," which I mentioned earlier, may be a place to start, adapting it to whatever cultural minority our students may come from or already be acquainted with. It could just as readily be adapted to "Growing Up Female/Male," as a way of looking at gender issues.

As I said before, the material presented in the workshop has application beyond secondary school. I have recently modified some of it for use in a graduate seminar on contemporary world literature.

Reply by Noeline Wright

General Concept

The workshop grew out of a number of considerations. Firstly, English teachers have to read a lot to keep up; secondly, many New Zealand novelists write wonderful teen fiction (e.g., Margaret Mahy, Maurice Gee, Gaelyn Gordon); thirdly, issues of biculturalism and gender are important in our society; and lastly, NZ fiction is a hobby of mine—particularly novels applicable to secondary school students.

Reading the books and compiling the booklist was therefore relatively straightforward, since NZ writers, especially in the last decade, have been prolific. Subdividing the list into groups of texts focusing on specific themes was intended to show teachers ways of using a number of books to cater to the following:

- acknowledging different stages of language development within classes
- providing for different social, cultural, intellectual backgrounds within classes
- encouraging students to read a wide range of literature
- encouraging students to make their own responses
- encouraging learning rather than teaching
- providing students with many opportunities to increase competence and confidence in language

In classrooms where there is a wide mixed-ability range, ethnic variety, and gender mix, using mixed sets of texts can be important for teachers to consider. Once teachers use more than one text at a time in a classroom, their role must change from pedagogue to facilitator. Using activities such as I have supplied from various schools in our region can enhance that role change. And even when teachers use one novel at a time, teachers can easily adopt a facilitator role by incorporating a variety of student-centered activities in the unit of work to allow students time to speak, listen, reflect, respond, be creative, and deepen their understanding.

Classroom Application

While English teachers intend students to move from the literal interpretation to the analytical levels in the way programmes are organised, a three-level guide, as such, is a discussion tool aimed to deepen students' understanding and familiarity with a text. I included a sample of a three-level guide on Patricia Grace's novel *Potiki*, plus a summary of how to create and use one with a pyramid discussion technique. The wad of sample units and suggested activities were included because teachers are always hungry for practical ideas they can adapt for their own needs, activities that still cover the elements of fiction—style, character, theme, plot, setting—but in less traditional ways. In NZ secondary schools, three Language Aims provide the core of our approach:

1. To increase each student's ability to understand language and use it effectively
2. To extend each student's imaginative and emotional responsiveness through language
3. To extend each student's awareness of ideas and values through language

Therefore, I saw the activities as samples of what some teachers have organised for their classes, with the view that all ideas are infinitely variable and can be applied to a whole variety of different texts and can be used in different combinations to fulfill those aims. The sample of activities that Peggy Parris lists from the workshop is a case in point. For instance:

1. They could be arranged under headings (e.g., style, plot, etc.). Students would have to choose one item from each group.
2. Single items could be used as a teaching focus—e.g.,
   (a) Character star: What things help us decide what a character is like?

   How does a novel show us?

   What things in our own experiences can affect our view of character?

   (1) Questions for discussion groups; report back.

   (2) Create stars.

   (3) Such a close analysis could provide the model for students to develop an in-depth piece of writing on a character with the diagram as a start point.

(b) Letter to author: provides focus for lesson on letter-writing formats; allows groups to discuss what sorts of things should be included; gives opportunity for letter-writing practice. Sophisticated version could require students to write letter to author *as a character*, using language the character would use. This adds character analysis to the task and shows how well a student can understand the character and aspects of work, use language effectively in specific ways, and sustain a sense of style.

Limits of Application

Obviously, the biggest problem in *directly* applying the workshop materials is the availability of NZ texts to students outside NZ. However, if teachers viewed the workshop as providing a framework for approaching novels, then it is infinitely applicable and, because the conference was about "different voices," it was entirely appropriate for my session to focus on NZ works. In fact, many of the strategies and activities are appropriate for studying poetry, drama, and short stories. There is no reason why anyone should be prevented from using my "model" as a basis for creating a text list of local works for use by other teachers, or even as a reading list for students to dip into.

I'd like to close with a statement from the New Zealand *English, Forms 3–5 Statement of Aims:*

> Literature
>
> Through literature, students can encounter language in its most complex and varied forms. By exploring these complexities, students can come to know the thoughts, emotions, and experiences of people beyond the circle of their immediate knowledge. An experience of life through literature is of great value, for with it can come an imaginative insight into other people's lives, an extension of the individual's own awareness and a development of that empathy which is part of the civilising and humanising tradition of literature.
>
> The ability to experience and to respond to literature should be developed so that it may become for the student both a source of pleasure and a way of extending experience and understanding. (1983, p. 21)

21 Cultural Bonding through Literature

A discussion presented by Claire Lacattiva of the significance of folktale literature as a cultural bonding agent.

Response by Helga M. Lewis

General Concept

This session developed the concept of cultural bonding through literature by using folktales, including myths and fairy tales, to foster greater understanding of different backgrounds and heritages. Folktales, mainly stories of ordinary people overcoming odds, were shown to have global recognition and understanding. This kind of literature is one that can be successfully used with any age group—young child to young adult—to promote understanding of one's own and of other cultural backgrounds.

Classroom Application

Claire Lacattiva spoke of many ways folktales could be taught in a meaningful way to promote cultural understanding.

1. Have students read and compare different versions of folktales, also modernized versions. This gives a sense of how writing has changed with the course of history. Also, reading diversely brings students to the realization that there are surface changes, according to culture, but the common thread, the human condition, pervades and provides a bond throughout history.

2. Encourage students to tell old familiar favorites and create new tales. Many folktales come from oral history. Practice of the art of storytelling will enhance their appreciation, develop listening and speaking skills, and, most important, bridge past and present—bringing the child to his original roots and ancestry.

3. Folktales, especially myths, can lead to the discovery of word origins and literary allusions. (Dr. Lacattiva gave the example of Echo and Pandora's Box.)

4. Folktales lend themselves to dramatization—puppets, pantomime, and creative dramatics. Drama helps students think and feel the way others think and feel.

5. Have students write new, creative endings for fairy tales. Modern versions of fairy tales are also great fun—also making up an original "pourquoi" tale, such as "Why the Rabbit Has Long Ears."

6. Oral history and the origins of folktales could be studied to discover how stories were originally communicated and how they came to be written down. This fosters literary appreciation and stimulates interest, especially in upper grades.

7. Oral history could be studied firsthand, also, as students and family members tell stories of days gone by—stories handed down to them or experienced by them. Have students interview the storytellers about the origins of the tales they tell. This serves to cross not only culture but generations—grandparents, parents, and child.

8. Have students compare and contrast the similarity in characters and themes of folktales from around the world. They will learn, for example, that the Jackal of India, the Weasel of Africa, and Brer Rabbit of the United States have common characteristics. This demonstrates the global interrelatedness of people.

Limitations

There are no serious limits to the use of this genre in the elementary grades.

Forecasts/Projections for Instructional Impact

In the future, even more so than the present, it will be important to understand our heritage so that our children know where they came from and where they are going. Only though understanding the past can they begin to understand the present and then plan for the ever-changing future. No matter what place they occupy in time, there will always be odds to overcome, and it should be reassuring to know, from whatever culture they come, that their folk history is full of such victories.

Reply by Claire Lacattiva

It is important that our schools prepare our children for global citizenship. Essential to meeting the needs for the future is a broad understanding of all people of the world regarding themselves and others. What better way to understand who we are than to look at who we were. Folk literature can do just this. Therein lies the core of my presentation "Cultural Bonding through Literature." It is very gratifying to hear my ideas being endorsed by teachers such as Ms. Lewis, who speaks enthusiastically about the instructional impact of folk literature in the classroom.

Teacher efforts to promote children's feelings of commitment to self and to the group are dependent upon promoting understanding of their own similarities and differences as well as those of others. When diversity is due to cultural background, the task of the teacher is compounded because of deeply rooted differences in values, attitudes, and philosophies which are entrenched in the child's roots. How then can we best bridge these differences and bond youngsters from different ethnic, racial, and cultural backgrounds so as to foster their acceptance of the universality of people as different strands of a common cloth? It is through language, the basic vehicle in reaching the mind and heart of another, that I believe the answers lie. Whether it be written or oral, it is through language and social intercourse that understanding among people is made possible. We need only look at the writings of people to understand them and the mores of their cultural heritage. Folk literature, or what is sometimes referred to as traditional literature, is particularly significant insofar as it is the oral tradition of a people, expressing as it does, their hopes, dreams, fears, and desires. The tales, myths, and legends that have been told from person to person and handed down over the years have much to tell about ourselves and others. Because of their universality, they are a vital resource for creating a shared background information without which it is impossible to relate to people of other cultures effectively.

There are many opportunities for cultural meshing afforded by the use of folk literature—both in mono- and multicultural classrooms. Ms. Lewis's discussion and description of some of the teaching strategies suggested in my presentation are both vivid and accurate, and they are enhanced by being assimilated through the eyes of the practitioner. I am pleased to hear Ms. Lewis' enthusiasm and successful use of my suggested teaching strategies, and it is my hope that others will follow her lead. Success is dependent upon several factors. It is critical to remember that to be an effective catalyst in this bonding process, the teacher must herself truly believe in the individual worth of each child and be attuned and alert to the many "different voices" she may hear. A set of suggested guidelines for effective teacher use of folk literature is available upon request from the author.

22 Responding to Writing: Findings of a Recent Research Project

A description presented by David Philips of responding techniques used in assisting pupils' writing.

Response by Dennise M. Bartelo

General Concept

The focus of this research, conducted by Ann O'Rourke and David Philips, was to identify effective classroom teaching strategies of successful teachers' approaches to process writing across the grades with children ages seven through sixteen. This fifteen-month continuous observational study of twenty-five primary and secondary teachers, funded by the New Zealand Council for Educational Research, Ministry of Education, sought to establish a tradition of writing research comparable to the wealth of studies on writing in the United States. Successful teachers were defined as those who were positive to students, demonstrated respect for cultural differences, had knowledge of process and writing development, and used supportive evaluation techniques.

Teaching Points

At the primary school level (ages 5–10), the researchers found a consistency in views and approaches toward the teaching of writing. Teachers believed writing to be an integral component of language and stressed concern for children's development of competence and confidence as writers. The sharing of writing occurred at all stages of the writing process. Writing was a daily activity in all of the classes. The classrooms presented a purposeful and print-rich environment for writing. Organization of space and seating arrangements in the classrooms demonstrated recognition of individual and collaborative needs in writing process. The four types of conferencing observed were roving, group, peer, and individual conferences.

At the intermediate school level (ages 11–12), teachers considered the preparation of writing a vital part of the process. The modelling of the writing process and the development of audience-specific writing were frequently occurring practices. Roving conferences were most often used to help less confident and less skillful writers. Teachers provided constant oral as well as written feedback to students about their writing. Teachers' assessment of student writing was descriptive in nature and focused on the strengths of the writer.

At the secondary level (13–18 years of age), the responsibility for teaching writing fell mainly to the English teacher. Writing process was used, and emphasis was on writing in a variety of styles. Teachers viewed the drafting stage as the foundation of writing. Much writing at this level involved responding to literature, with little freedom for individual choice of topic. Clear guidelines were given to students for specific writing tasks. Some teachers used journals and writing workshops. Individual conferences were seen as important avenues for the teaching of spelling, punctuation, grammar, and mechanics.

Problems/Difficulties in Teaching Writing

At the primary level, teachers expressed concern about allowing students total freedom in the selection of topics in writing. Teachers worried about modelling the writing process excessively to the extent that this would have an impact on students' voice and spontaneity in writing. Another concern was an overemphasis on creative and imaginative writing.

At the intermediate level, none of the teachers allowed for total freedom of choice in the selection of topics for writing. The secondary-level teachers felt restricted by school policies and examination standards in the teaching of writing. They expressed concern over a lack of time to conference with students about their writing as well as the time needed to teach occupational skills.

Summary

Writing was an integral and daily part of the school curriculum. Teachers were seen as facilitators in this process approach to teaching. No strict syllabus or set time existed for lesson content throughout the schools. Private areas for writing were present in the classrooms as well as flexible seating arrangements to encourage collaborative writing strategies. One-on-one individualized teaching was the dominant mode of instruction. Peer conferences tended to fade away at the secondary level as well as the freedom to select topics in writing. The format for the publication of writing varied and less variety occurred at the secondary level. Teachers viewed conferencing as the time when most of their teaching of writing was done. There appeared to be a general lack of writing-across-the-curriculum policies in the schools.

Implications

Students are more likely to experience consistency and continuity in the approach toward the teaching of writing at the primary rather than at the secondary level. Further research is needed on investigating the problems that occur in the transition from teacher to teacher and classroom to school in teacher expectations of students' writing. The constraint of exams at the secondary level needs to be reviewed and more attention given to the role of writing as a tool for learning across the curriculum.

Response by Bertadean Baker

General Concept

Ann O'Rourke and David Philips observed fifteen teachers in the primary schools and found that there was remarkable consistency in their views of and approaches to writing. They saw writing as an integral component of language and in teaching writing, and emphasized its association with both oral language and reading activities.

The following goals were considered important for all writing activities:

- establishing an environment in which pupils can develop confidence in writing
- developing a writing programme based upon children's own interests and knowledge
- providing daily opportunities to write
- encouraging pupils to think clearly, express themselves fluently, and communicate effectively with regard to meaning, purpose, and audience

- enabling children to develop confidence in expressing their own voice and thus to "own" their writing
- developing awareness of the need for self-evaluation, proofreading, and editing
- experimenting with a variety of genres or forms and increasing confidence in handling these
- using writing for a variety of purposes and integrating it into all aspects of the curriculum

Teaching Points/Activities

Ideas and Topics

Topics were drawn from experience, personal and shared reading, thematic studies, and knowledge of local and current events. The teacher supported the students by assisting with the generation of ideas and occasionally choosing topics or themes for the whole class to write on.

Prewriting Activities

The following writing activities were used to generate ideas: discussions, brainstorming, reading drama and role-playing activities, visual and audio stimuli. Prewriting activities were focused on aspects of writing such as purpose, audience, gender, presentation, publication, and the skills and conventions of writing, including proofreading and editing.

Modeling

Modeling the process was considered to be more important than the product. Story outlines and sequencing of ideas and language conventions were demonstrated. Extracts from established writers, examples of good sentences or phrases from other students' writing, outline of layouts, cards, and charts were used as models for children's writing.

Drafting

Drafting was used as a means of getting ideas down on paper and for clarifying meaning through revision. Some techniques for drafting include the use of scrap paper, writing in pencil on every other line, with problem words circled in pen.

Proofreading

Proofreading was a helpful procedure for correcting spelling and elementary grammar and punctuation. Self-proofing and checking with a peer before checking with the teacher were also good procedures.

Conference Techniques

Four kinds of conferences were employed throughout the primary grades: roving conferences, when the teacher went to pupils around the classroom who seemed to need help most; group conferences, when children with similar needs were helped together; peer conferences, when children helped each other; and individual conferences, when the teacher and the pupil met on a regular basis for a semiformal dialogue on aspects of the pupil's writing.

Publication

Audience

The children were made aware of the audience for whom they were writing in order to clarify their ideas and to give purpose to their writing.

Sharing

Sharing served as an important vehicle for obtaining feedback for the writer. Pupils exchanged comments and writings. Ideas and reactions were shared by students in order to obtain help or to indicate what they were doing. Daily sharing sessions were used to read stories in draft or published form.

Editing

Before a piece of writing could be published, the pupil proceeded through several stages of checking the copy—self-editing, peer editing, conferencing with the teacher, and production of a second draft—in order to remove as many errors as possible. The teacher's responsibility was to edit the students' papers while at the same time ensuring that the students' voices in the writing were still audible.

Publication Formats

Several formats were used for publication: journals, writing folders, charts and posters, mobiles, wall displays, magazines and newspapers, cards, big books, scrapbooks, and projects. Teachers encouraged students to prepare presentations carefully so that they matched the purpose and the intended audience.

Evaluation

Teachers in the primary classes preferred to see themselves as facilitators rather than interventionists. Help was given when a child seemed to be in difficulty or during conferencing time with the child. Most teachers considered the individual conference to be the time when most teaching was done. Individual needs were targeted, and the assistance focused upon clarifying ideas and intentions, language usage, and the diagnosis of strengths and weaknesses.

Problems/Difficulties in Teaching Writing

The following concerns about the teaching of writing were shared by all teachers:

- total freedom in the selection of all topics, excessive writing, and overintervention could lead to a loss of spontaneity and individual voice in writing
- overemphasis on creative and imaginative writing could delete the fostering of skills related to factual or expository writing
- lack of time necessary to conduct conferences
- need for schools to develop writing-across-the-curriculum policies, to view writing as a schoolwide activity for learning which is the responsibility of all teachers to develop, not just English teachers

Forecasts/Implications

Philips and O'Rourke found that it is time for stronger emphasis upon writing across the curriculum, and as a consequence, for teacher courses to give more attention to the valuable role that writing plays in learning.

They also stated that further research is needed in the relationship to the teaching and learning of writing when pupils transfer from teacher to teacher, class to class, school to school, and from one sector of the education system to another.

Reply by David Philips

Research On Writing in New Zealand

Dennise Bartelo makes the observation that *Responding Effectively to Pupils' Writing* "sought to establish a tradition of writing research comparable to the wealth of studies in writing in the United States." Although New Zealand has an enviable reputation for its literacy programmes, very little research on writing has been carried out in New Zealand. However, there is a high level of interest in effective teaching techniques; hence the focus of this research study. The researchers hoped that it would extend the work which had already been discussed in *A Month's Writing in Four Classrooms,* which looked at the teaching of writing across the curriculum, and *Writing Performance in New Zealand Schools,* which reported the results of New Zealand 12- and 15-year-olds' writing as part of the IEA Written Composition Study.

It was also hoped that interest in this study would encourage further research on writing in New Zealand. This need is still strong as, apart from a few graduate dissertations, very little research on writing is currently being carried out in New Zealand. Although a handful of New Zealanders have been fortunate enough to study research on writing and successful writing programmes in the United States, the research base is still relatively insignificant and is likely to remain so without a major commitment to funding and support.

What Is a Successful Teacher of Writing?

Dennise Bartelo points out that the study identified "effective classroom teaching strategies of successful teachers' approaches to process writing across the grades." The researchers decided to examine teachers who were regarded as successful teachers of writing. During the 1980s a New Zealand version of the Bay Area Writing Project was developed, and it was considered important to include the results of New Zealand research on writing as part of the local projects which were run throughout the country. As earlier studies of the teaching of writing had focused upon what could be called "normal" or "average" practice, we felt that it was absolutely essential to focus upon successful teachers of writing. There seemed little point in describing what a random sample of teachers did (this was done in the IEA study), since the aim of the study was to help improve the teaching and learning of writing, not simply to reinforce current practices irrespective of their type of proven usefulness.

Various people were consulted in order to arrive at about sixty-five teachers, and other procedures were applied to make the final selection. We did not have a series of objectively measurable criteria on which to select these teachers; rather a careful assessment was made using intensive interviews, classroom observations, and samples of pupils' writing. The researchers also relied on their own knowledge of successful teaching practices, and it is undoubtedly true that we were influenced heavily by approaches which emphasised the various stages involved in the writing process. We developed our own indicators of sound writing teaching, rather than applying overseas models, but were particularly interested in teachers who used a range of techniques for responding to their pupils' writing at various stages ranging from drafting to the presentation of the final, "published" version.

Systemwide Focus

Bartelo describes the results of the study in three clusters, reflecting the principal divisions of the New Zealand school system (primary, intermediate, and secondary). Our study deliberately looked at teachers across the main levels of the New Zealand education system. We could have done a detailed study of two or three teachers, perhaps the same school, or of ten teachers at the same level but from a variety of schools across the country. However, because the participants in the New Zealand writing projects came from the primary (children aged 5 to 11), intermediate (11–13) and secondary (13–18) sectors, we selected teachers for close observation who came from each of these sectors. We also made sure that five clusters of teachers who taught students of roughly the same age were included so that any conclusions reached by the researchers would have some generalisability and would not be based simply on the methods used by one or two teachers. We also ensured that pupils in these classes represented the wide range of ethnic groups in New Zealand.

Aspects Observed

Bartelo provides a very succinct summary of the findings from the study. These aspects of the teaching of writing in particular were closely observed:

- teachers' views of or approaches to writing—interpretation of the writing process, the strengths of an approach emphasising the writing process, concerns about this approach
- classroom management—environment, room layout, seating and groupings, student/student and student/teacher relationships
- the writing process—objectives set, choice of ideas and topics, prewriting activities, modelling practices, drafting, proofreading, conferencing, audience awareness, sharing, editing for publication, choice of formats
- evaluation and feedback—objectives set, oral feedback, written feedback, use of marks and grades, records and checklists
- intervention and assistance—general principles, spelling, punctuation, grammar, voice, and ownership

There is not room here to describe all the results of the study (see O'Rourke and Philips). We believe that the practices observed in the classrooms of the effective teachers can be successfully adopted by all primary language teachers and secondary teachers of English, as well as teachers who use writing across the curriculum. These approaches are discussed in more detail in *The Word Process* (Carruthers et al.). This book is designed as a handbook for teachers of writing, and is based largely on the writing project approach, including a chapter on the teacher as a researcher.

Recognising Individual and Collective Needs

Bartelo observes that "organization of space and seating arrangements in the classrooms demonstrated recognition of individual and collaborative needs." New Zealand primary teachers place a strong emphasis upon the identification of individual needs and the provision of programmes which meet the needs of particular groups of students. This is not reflected just in seating arrangements. Support is provided for varied learning styles and modes of interaction when pupils feel more comfortable with them. Successful teachers of writing are sensitive to the needs of Maori and Pacific Island children (who form nearly a quarter of all pupils in New Zealand primary schools) and actively promote awareness and acceptance of different cultures in their classrooms. Many also make a conscious effort to give girls as much attention as boys, giving rewards in order to boost their confidence.

A little more detail about types of conference also seems appropriate. Conferencing, in various forms, was often observed. Roving conferences occurred daily, when the teacher went round pupils who seemed to need most help, particularly to less confident writers (often Maori and Pacific Island children, and those learning English as a second language), briefly offering assistance and support. Group conferences were used to help students with similar needs, and were common at the junior and middle school levels, though were confined to group project work at the intermediate level. Peer conferences, with children reading each other's writing and commenting upon it, or proofreading, were an integral part of each class, as were individual conferences, when the teacher and pupil met on a regular basis for a semiformal dialogue on aspects of the pupil's writing.

All levels recognised the importance of small-group or one-to-one discussion for children learning English as a second language, or who were less proficient at writing. During these sessions, emphasis was placed upon the pupil's ownership of the writing, so the thrust tended to be positive, with questions and comments designed to allow pupils to describe what they were doing in their own writing and to have time to respond to the teacher's remarks. Some pupils preferred to have their peers within listening distance when conferencing with the teacher, so that others could make comments, and this practice was actively adopted in many classrooms, especially with Maori and Pacific Island students.

Also, at all levels, whole-class language teaching was rare; spelling, punctuation, and grammar tended to be dealt with on an individual basis, either in small groups or one-to-one. Each teacher was aware of the need to preserve the individual voice of pupils, with writing seen as a means for them to convey personal ideas and their own experience in their own style. All of the primary and secondary teachers in this study acknowledged and respected the point of view of each child in their class, irrespective of cultural background.

Evaluation of Pupils' Writing

Dennise Bartelo makes little reference to evaluation in her summary, although this was one of the main themes of the research. The evaluation of pupils' writing was generally considered to be an integral part of the writing process, although its purpose varied from level to level. In the junior classes (first three years of the primary school), its main purpose at the draft stage was to assist in clarifying the message and form of the writing. At the prepublication stage, its function was to enable pupils to take responsibility for their writing through proofreading and to foster skills of commenting on the writing of their peers. In the middle school, objectives were set for specific tasks, and for individual pupils; these were sometimes arrived at through discussion with the pupil—not just predetermined by the teacher—and took into account individual strengths and weaknesses.

At the intermediate level, evaluation was either largely oral, taking place during conference time, or followed criteria specified in the school's language scheme, or was part of a well-developed policy, as in two schools where specific objectives were set for each piece of teacher-initiated writing. These were carefully communicated to the pupils, who were frequently involved in determining them. Assessment was seen as an integral part of the learning process, not something appended to it.

At the secondary level, a comprehensive set of objectives in each case had to be met by the students, although at the junior high school level, in particular, the objectives were often worked out collaboratively by the teacher and students. Criteria were made known by the teachers, and formal assessment was frequent, particularly at the senior high school level.

Research Implications of the Study

Bartelo observes that "further research is needed on investigating the problems that occur in the transition from teacher to teacher and classroom to school in teacher expectations of students' writing." She also states that "the role of writing as a tool for learning across the curriculum" needs more attention. While our study revealed a high degree of consistency across all levels in the approaches used by teachers of writing, though more so at the primary level, there were differences in emphasis from teacher to teacher. Some liked modelling writing by writing at the same time as their pupils; others did not. Some responded to pupils' drafts, while others preferred to retain their comments until the "final" copy was completed. The degree of conferencing of different types varied from classroom to classroom, and some teachers made more extensive comments on their pupils' writing than did others. More research is required on the causes and effectiveness of different preferences in the teaching and learning of writing.

Perhaps the most important conclusion we can make is that a consistent policy for the teaching of writing is required both within schools (see Philips 1991) and across schools. Such a policy would need to be soundly based on research. New Zealand has a highly mobile population, and a National Curriculum is currently being developed, so it is essential that a reasonable degree of consistency (given the small population of 3,500,000) is maintained between schools and regions if pupils are to develop their writing to a high level, and to learn more effectively through writing across the curriculum. In this way, research findings such as those explored in *Responding Effectively to Pupils' Writing* can be incorporated into policy developments, teaching resources, and classroom writing programmes.

References

Carruthers, A., Philips, D., Rathgen, E., & Scanlan, P. (1991). *The word process*. Auckland, Longman Paul.

Lamb, H. (1989). *Writing performance in New Zealand schools*. Wellington: Department of Education.

O'Rourke, A., & Philips, D. (1989). *Responding effectively to pupils' writing*. Wellington: New Zealand Council for Educational Research.

Philips, D. (1985). *A month's writing in four classrooms*. Wellington: New Zealand Council for Educational Research.

Philips, D. (1991). Reviewing a school's writing programme. *Reading Forum, 1*, 3–9.

23 Humane Literacy: Literary Competence and the Ways of Knowing

A distinction presented by Sheridan Blau of "personal literacy" from "textual literacy" and "cultural literacy."

Response by Carole Bencich

General Concept

Reading is also text production. It includes revision and interpretation of something other than the text. Given this understanding, authentic literacy must begin in personal literacy.

In a one-hour session, Sheridan Blau discussed the differences among textual literacy (Scholes, *Textual Power*, 1985), cultural literacy (Hirsch, *Cultural Literacy*, 1987), and personal literacy. If textual literacy means "knowing how," and cultural literacy means "knowing about," personal literacy means simply "knowing . . ." Blau identified six dimensions of personal literacy:

1. Capacity for sustained focused attention
2. Willingness to suspend closure—to entertain problems rather than avoid them
3. Willingness to take risks—to predict and be wrong, to respond honestly, to offer variant readings
4. Tolerance for failure: willingness to reread and reread again
5. Tolerance for ambiguity, paradox, and uncertainty
6. Intellectual generosity and ego-permeability: willingness to change mind, to appreciate alternative visions, and to engage in methodological believing as well as doubting.

Classroom Application

By acknowledging the dimensions of personal literacy, we can lead students into cultural literacy and textual literacy. Commenting that "most of the ways we engage in text with students puts them off from text," Blau demonstrated his meaning by asking participants to respond to four frequently anthologized poems, a lesser-known poem, a cartoon strip, and an ambiguous quotation. Many of us had taught the four well-known poems, and therefore had some preconceived ideas about what they "meant." Reading John Morris's "For Julia in the Deep Water" provoked varying tentative responses in a process which contrasted with our assured readings of the more familiar poems.

To demonstrate the difference between how students and expert teachers of literature encounter difficult texts, Blau asked us to interpret a difficult passage from Thoreau ("Sometimes we are inclined to classify the once-and-a-half-witted with the half-witted because we appreciate only a third part of their wit") and to raise our hands as soon as we had produced what we would regard as a satisfactory reading. Timing us with a stopwatch, he noted that it took most English teachers several rereadings and perhaps a couple of minutes of attention before they were satisfied that they understood this passage clearly. He told of giving the same passage to a group of college-prep high school students, however, and finding that they didn't look at the passage for more than a few seconds before they decided that they couldn't make any sense of it and that they weren't qualified to interpret it. He conjectured that the response of the high school students to the Thoreau passage doesn't indicate that the passage was actually too difficult for them, but that they have never learned how to operate by themselves as readers of texts that at first glance seem too difficult for them. He hypothesized, furthermore, that the students had been taught to be incompetent readers by teaching practices that restrict teachers to teaching only those texts that the teacher already knows very well. Blau argued that when we teach only familiar and comfortable (to us) literature, we forget the process of meaning making which students must undertake in order to understand what they read. We forget that by always being knowledgeable and comfortable with the literature we teach, we are demonstrating that reading is easy and quick once you know how to do it—an idea that is neither true nor helpful to students.

To further involve us, Blau used a two-page reading from *Sudden Fiction* (1986), an anthology of very short stories edited by Shapard and Thomas.

Participants paired off to share the oral reading of David Ordan's "Any Minute Mom Should Come Blasting through the Door." Everyone took part in this, and the room resonated with the cacophony of some fifteen concurrent readings. "Something happens when you read together," Blau said. And indeed, I was aware not only of my own experience of apprehending the story, but of the nuance provided by my partner as he read aloud.

After a brief whole-group sharing of favorite lines, words, or chunks of text, Blau next invited us to do "jump in reading," with a second oral reading of the story done a sentence or paragraph at a time by individuals on a spontaneous basis. He started the reading, inviting one of us to jump in and continue any time a reader stopped. I was unfamiliar with jump in reading. It not only gave a second exposure to the story, but it gave the added dimension of oral performance by a series of readers, all of whom were nominally familiar with the story's meanings.

Next Blau asked us to do "text rendering," that is, to select a line from the story and write about it. I selected the closing line of the story, "Is that really how you want to remember your mother?" a question which puzzled me. After about two minutes of writing and thinking, I realized, "Of course. Sexuality. What it always comes down to." I wrote this without reading back through the two-page story, and with assurance I would not have to read it out loud to the group or even share it with my paired reading partner. It felt okay to have my personal insight to the story, one which would not be compared or tested in any way. That feeling of ownership is denied students when they are expected to come up with appropriate answers to predetermined questions about a text.

Then, Blau asked us to write a bit, telling how what we wrote about the story reflected ourselves. Again within the privacy of my own reflection, I realized the source of my insight: I was a parent and also someone who had lost a spouse, and this had informed my reading of a story about the sudden death of a boy's mother. This metacognitive awareness was just as valuable to me as the previous "figuring out" of meaning. Both techniques had encouraged my involvement by allowing me to choose the focus for my attention.

I was amazed at how quickly (about 20 minutes) this whole sequence was accomplished, compared to the rich dividend in private and collaborative construction of meaning which resulted. Participants eagerly volunteered their insights, and the range of meaning was astounding. Blau confirmed my intuitions about the use of this technique with young people: "The kinds of things you want students to get, they get. And *more!*" In addition, he said that he always learned something new about the text each time he used it with a group. I liked this potential for turning teachers and students into co-learners, and for eliminating the need for traditional, single-viewed readings of a text.

Summing up, Blau recommended assignments which encourage dealing with ambiguity, which invite reading as a process, and which promote affiliation, or the ability to work in groups. "Literacy is measured by the ability to accept contradictions," he said, repeating that, in literature, "the only lines worth talking about are the ones you don't understand."

Limitations for Application

The still-popular practice of using prescriptive meanings for literary texts serves neither student nor teacher. It distances students from literature by making them feel ignorant or incapable when they repeatedly make "incorrect" readings of text. It reinforces the notion that reading is "magic," and that textual meaning resides *outside* the world of the student. At the same time, it inhibits teachers from using contemporary literature in class, and from venturing to share with students their own interpretations of ambiguous passages. What it promotes is a one-eyed view of a limited body of work—the so-called "canon" which is honored more in theory than in practice. Students learn the names, authors, and "facts" of a few "great" literary works, but fail to connect with literature in any personally significant way.

This emphasis on correct readings of canonical literary works creates barriers between textual, cultural, and personal literacy—barriers which many students cannot overcome. Nevertheless, many public voices continue to insist on adherence to a narrowly defined cultural literacy, even where it is achieved at the expense of personal literacy. In their zeal to promote exposure to the same cultural meanings for all students, advocates often fail to acknowledge the power of individual experience to shape response.

Forecasts/Projections for Instructional Impact

Reader-response methods empower students and teachers alike to construct meaning. The implications of this assertion for promoting thinking are obvious. Just as important are the implications for leading students to their own confident experiences with literature and for bridging the gap between personal and cultural literacy.

A humane literacy which begins by honoring individual ways of knowing would promote literary competence for all students. By including different voices in the cultural conversation, it would promote an active, living cultural heritage, one to be pursued by students rather than impressed upon them.

Reply by Sheridan Blau

Carole Bencich has presented the broad outlines of the conceptual framework and demonstration lesson that I introduced to the participants in my session at the 1991 IFTE Conference in New Zealand, and she has reflected helpfully on the implications of my work. I appreciate her perceptive and illuminating account of my presentation and will try not to repeat her points as I use my opportunity to reply by elaborating briefly on one dimension of the theory I proposed and on its applications to classroom practice.

The key term I have introduced to our discourse about literary pedagogy through the conceptual framework of "humane literacy" is the term "personal literacy," a kind of literacy I identify with what I call "enabling knowledge," and that I distinguish from two other related literacies or ways of knowing "textual literacy" (pretty much what Scholes calls "textual power") or "procedural knowledge," and cultural literacy (cf. E. D. Hirsch) or "informational knowledge."

In my presentation I define personal literacy by describing its opposition through a series of anecdotes based on observations of students and teachers in secondary school and college classrooms. The burden of my stories is that conventional teaching methods foreground the right reading of texts—which students sometimes regard as the teacher's authoritative reading, but which is more likely the standard reading, which is to say the reading authorized by such sources as standard introductions (or *Cliffs Notes*), the critical tradition, or, most likely, the college professors of the teacher. That is to say, literary study, insofar as it is directed (as Jim Marshall and Don Zancanella have shown it to be) toward providing students with authoritative readings of canonical texts, does not entail authentic reading and the construction of meaning by students, but puts students in the role of being receivers of somebody else's authoritative reading.

Yet, as Louise Rosenblatt says, to accept somebody else's interpretation of a literary text as your own is like having somebody else eat your dinner for you. I would take that conceit a step further and argue that taking somebody else's reading as your own as the main diet of a literary education is like having somebody else eat your dinner for you so often that your gastric juices no longer operate as they might and you become incapable of eating and digesting for yourself.

It is especially interesting to me that Rosenblatt employs a metaphor of eating to adumbrate the nature of unauthentic literary knowledge, because I think she is talking about precisely the same kind of false knowledge that Milton associated (in a structurally opposite metaphor) with eating of the fruit of the tree of knowledge, where, through eating or gulping down knowledge, as it were, in one bite (as opposed to producing it gradually and in stages through one's own learning), one gains only false knowledge, the kind of knowledge that leaves the knower bereft of his sense of himself as a being capable of growth and deprived of his capacity (while under the influence of his false knowledge) of further growth. False knowledge is precisely that: knowledge that prevents further learning. This is surely the kind of knowledge that teachers exhibit, when, afraid to test the knowledge they derive from college lectures or other authoritative but external sources, they seek to pass that knowledge directly on to their students rather than explore with students the meanings of texts and thereby construct knowledge anew in a community of learners. Such teachers suffer the effects of false knowledge and seek to reproduce it in their students.

Consider the two principal lessons that students learn about reading and texts from instructors who see it as their business to transmit literary culture by passing on to their students conventional and authoritative readings. Their students learn, first, that texts have determinable meanings which teachers can tell you; and second, that competent readers can discern those meanings almost at once as they read a text—i.e., that such meanings are immediately apprehended by good readers. Thus students of literature in conventional literature classes come to see the act of reading much the way the most inexperienced writers see the act of writing: not as something that takes place in a messy construction site where meaning is built through a recursive process of vision and revision, but as a neat act of intellectual magic or mystery whereby those who know the secret can construct finished texts in one pass, as if the Declaration of Independence could be written in one continuous act of freewriting. Students who see the writing process as such a single draft enterprise, as Shaughnessy has reported, tend to look at a manuscript produced by a famous writer and, noting all the crossed out passages and reworking of the text, conclude that "this guy doesn't know how to write," reasoning that if he knew, he wouldn't make so many "mistakes."

The construct of reading learned by students in conventional English classes is, I would argue, often the same. Seeing teachers produce only authoritative readings in class (which is to say, not produce them at all, but merely transmit previously produced readings), students conclude that truly competent readers arrive at readings such as teachers present in one reading—the one modelled in class. What students never see is the authentic reading process in which the teacher, reading a new or unfamiliar text, experiences all the perils of misreading, frustration, feelings of inadequacy, and so on that usually attend the unassisted reading of a difficult text. Even literary scholars who may themselves be credited with having produced and published authoritative readings rarely demonstrate their real reading processes to students. Students see only the products of those processes, the way readers see only final drafts which are the products of many revisions in a long and messy process. How often will even the brilliant teacher who is offering deft interpretations and original penetrating insights into a literary work pause to mention to students that such insightful reading as the teacher is displaying with this particular text is the product of dozens, perhaps hundreds, of readings (and reading about the text) over a career as a professional reader?

What students are most likely to learn from conventional literature instruction then, aside from hearsay knowledge about what certain texts are supposed to mean, is that they themselves are incapable of being readers, which is to say, of producing such meanings as their teachers produce, apparently without effort. That is to say, students learn from literary instruction (even from many of their most literate teachers) that, until and unless they complete some advanced specialized program of study in literature (or acquire a Ph.D.), they themselves are incapable of reading the very texts they are being taught. And if that is what students learn from the study of literature, then one must conclude that the study of literature constitutes instruction in illiteracy or something we can call "counter-literacy" or, for those students who learn how to mimic their teachers effectively, perhaps "pseudo-literacy."

The antidote to pseudo-literacy or counter-literacy is what I have called personal literacy or enabling knowledge—the kind of knowledge that enables students to become autonomous, engaged readers of difficult literary texts. And it is a literacy to which instruction itself will be obstructive, until teachers provide students with the sort of literary experiences that will enable their students to acquire a set of attributes that appear to be the marks of proficient readers and that more nearly resemble character traits than what we ordinarily identify as literary skills. These traits are the dimensions of personal literacy—tolerance of failure, capacity for sustained focused attention, and so on that I listed on my handout at the conference and that Carole Bencich has reprinted in her review.

The question then is exactly what model of instruction is best suited to promoting personal literacy in students. The answer is any mode of instruction that focuses on the process of reading and rereading and that puts greater emphasis on the quality of a reader's experience in transactions with a literary text than on any body of knowledge about a text. More specifically, we can promote personal literacy with a variety of assignments, such as those I modelled as part of my presentation at the IFTE Conference. These assignments can be classified usefully under the following headings:

1. Assignments that focus on the changes in a reader's response to and understanding of a text through a series of rereadings. This can involve students in keeping logs or double-entry journals which record changes in their understanding from reading to reading and then asking them to write about those changes.

2. Assignments that foreground and honor the problems that readers encounter and feel unable to solve as they read, acknowledging that it is in recognizing problems that readers grow in their understanding of texts. These assignments should also invite collaboration between students in pairs and groups as they work on problems and recognize the value of problem recognition as a key to advances in understanding.

3. Writing assignments addressed to significant unresolved problems, rather than problems with known answers.

4. Writing assignments that encourage students to elaborate problems in interpretation and open up possibilities for interpretation, rather than advancing a thesis which would shut down interpretation.

5. Assignments that focus on differences in the way various students read, interpret, and respond to the same text—honoring those differences and attempting to account for their sources without necessarily seeking to develop a consensus or normative reading.

6. "Pants-down reading," a term coined in my Writing Project for a lesson in which a teacher and a class work collaboratively on reading and interpreting a poem (usually canonical) that none of them has seen before.

The assignments listed above, like the teaching strategies I demonstrated in my presentation in New Zealand, are all informed by the same two related perspectives and premises which are foundational for the model of literacy that I have been proposing. First, they are designed to promote in students intellectual and attitudinal attributes that are prerequisites for the task of reading difficult texts—attributes that collectively constitute what I have called "personal literacy." Second, they acknowledge and invite students to recognize the degree to which reading is an act of text construction or meaning making, much like writing; entailing the same processes of drafting and re-drafting, of vision and re-vision; subject to the same perils and frustrations in the process; and to the same dividends from negotiating meaning with others by testing, revising, and sharing meaning within a community of readers and writers.

References

Shapard, R., & Thomas, J. (Eds.). (1986). *Sudden fiction: American short-short stories.* Salt Lake City: Gibbs Smith.

Thoreau, H. D. (1979). Walden. *Norton Anthology of American Literature* (3rd ed., vol. 1, p. 1803). New York: Norton.

24 Building on Students' Strengths: Voices in the Writing Class

An exploration presented by William Boswell, Ann Beer, and Jane Ledwell-Brown of the view that students become effective writers only if their voices and expertise are valued in the writing classroom.

Response by Marian Bryan

General Concept

"We believe that in the past we have underestimated the students that we teach. Only when we value their different voices, build upon the knowledge and expertise that they bring to the classroom with them, and encourage collaboration among them, can the writing of our students become truly effective."

Thus was established the theme of a two-hour workshop in which the presenter explained the Effective Written Communication (EWC) course offered at McGill University Centre for the Study and Teaching of Writing. The centre is in the process of publishing a book for writers which is based on the course. One goal of the McGill writing program is to guide each student to discover that he or she possesses valuable resources and experiences from which to draw interesting and dynamic writing material. Several assumptions underlie the McGill approach to writing classes. One is the belief that each person can be the "expert"—the informer on some topic. The second assumption is that written language is usually from a "position of strength" in that writers know more than their readers about a particular subject. Usually, we are writing to inform, persuade, clarify or describe. The McGill group maintains that school is one of the few places where students write from a "position of weakness" in that they know less than their reader (teacher).

The third assumption is that students must be committed to each piece of writing; in order to achieve this commitment, the student must be involved in the selection of the topic, the theme, and its direction or development. The fourth assumption is that writing is a social activity.

Therefore, the class is run as a workshop and students work in small groups.

The goals of the McGill teachers are: (1) to help students discover and trust their own resources and thus confirm themselves as writers; (2) to help students develop strategies to improve their writing; (3) to provide students with a wide range of audiences and genuine purposes for writing; and (4) to respond to students' writing as fellow writers, interested readers, and compassionate editors.

Classroom Application

William Boswell outlined several typical classroom writing assignments which help students to realize their own resources as assets. Usually, students have four formal assignments; within each, they work through a complete process, generating ideas, sharing, organizing. With each succeeding assignment, students are expected to refine their writing, building upon what they have previously learned. One project is the "expert's paper" wherein students are asked to describe for fellow students a subject in which they are "experts." Evidently, this assignment is valuable from the standpoint that students must reflect upon the fact that they do indeed possess rich knowledge and information about a particular sport, hobby, geographic location, or some facet of cultural or ethnic background which would inform and be of interest to others.

This concept sounds simple, and most teachers of writing may say, "Sure, I do this every day." However, we participated in an exercise in the workshop which impressed me with just how dynamic the McGill technique can be. Mr. Boswell asked us to list as many topics as we could in which we were informed or knowledgeable. Often, one's first reaction is to think—"it is presumptuous to claim I'm an 'expert' in something." I began my list by first thinking professionally and wrote—using the computer to compose and edit (I realize that several colleagues avoid computers and still write first drafts in longhand). Then, after a pause, I decided to have fun with some more "esoteric skills" and wrote: (1) growing asparagus ferns, (2) cooking shrimp créole, (3) baking pumpkin bread, (4) finding petrified shark's teeth on the beach.

In about five minutes, our teachers asked us to team with another class member and share our list. Each partner marked two choices he or she would like to know more about and then wrote a series of questions about the topic. My partner was a man from Australia, and he starred my shark item and asked: How do you know where to look? How do they get there? What does "petrified" mean, exactly? What do you do with them when found? Is this a solitary or shared interest? How big are these teeth? Do they decay? How did you get interested in this? Do sharks, in general, interest you? Are some beaches more "fruitful" than others? If so, why?

When I got his questions back, I could hardly wait to start writing: "The best place to look for shark's teeth is on Topsail Beach, a slender barrier island north of Wilmington, North Carolina. One must have a sharp eye to spy the small, shiny, black teeth from the m...."

"STOP!" said our instructor. "Due to time constraints, we cannot finish your writing now."

I understood we had to move on in the workshop, but I wanted to continue writing. I was also eager to read my partner's answers to my questions on how he teaches poetry writing. The only way this "lesson plan" would be different in a classroom is that I would have written responses to the questions, finished my essay, and again shared with my partner. I could tell from my own enthusiasm how motivational this method could be.

Next, we were asked to respond to our experience. Some of the reactions were: "stimulated intriguing conversation," "no restriction," "conversation with partner gave opportunity to explore, think out ideas," "capitalized on own ideas," "questions 'framed' or outlined paper nicely," "excellent pre-writing activity," "near-writing to far-writing," and "expressive to transactional." I wrote, "excitement, immediate involvement."

A second assignment which builds on student strengths is the "How It Works" paper. Groups of four or five students collaborate in writing one paper, describing for a younger audience how something such as a light bulb or a bank actually works. In this assignment the group must develop a "sense of audience," cooperate, negotiate, and come to a consensus on how to explain or describe something simply and effectively to a ten-year-old child, for example.

"Letters of application" is another practical and personal writing assignment which requires self-analysis, organization, personal commitment, and involvement. In addition to developing writing skills, this assignment has immediate application when students are seeking scholarships, jobs, or graduate school entry.

One assignment which has been most successful at McGill has been the "burning issue" paper. Students write a paper dealing with a topic that is of great concern to them. To be most effective, the topic must be specific and personal rather than broad and general. One student wrote a moving paper discussing his personal involvement in the Israeli-Palestinian conflict during the time he lived on the West Bank. In our workshop, we experienced a taste of how a teacher would approach the "expert" paper, but all major assignments would include similar elements of idea generation, sharing, organizing, and refining.

Journal writing is a key component of the EWC course and is the foundation for all the other writing that takes place. Mr. Boswell models journal writing in his classes by sharing his journal entries upon occasion. No student is required to share his or her journal writing, but all students are invited to share in class. Usually, students freewrite in class and do journal writing at home. Students also keep logs. A log is self-reflective and describes the process of producing a piece of writing. A student is required to analyze the activities and thought processes he or she is going through in writing a piece. Students are informing themselves of some of their writing strengths and weaknesses through review and reflection in their logs.

Instructional Impact

One of the most important points Mr. Boswell made was that teachers at all levels must realize that writing is *developmental*. Therefore, they do not grade each paper from the beginning of the semester and then *average* the grades at the end. This practice makes no sense and refutes the fact that growth and learning have occurred during the course. The more sensible procedure would be to grade writing near the end of the semester when a student can demonstrate what he or she has learned during the course.

The presenter's point is well taken. In many conventional writing projects from elementary grades forward, a teacher makes a writing assignment, perhaps reviews the student's outline or rough draft, reads the final copy, and assigns a grade. These marks are then averaged for a final grade in the class. There is little process involved and often little interaction with peers or teacher in the formative stages of a paper. If learning takes place, it is in the *content* being explored (which is rarely personal) rather than in the process of communicating through writing.

I am an elementary teacher and can use these workshop ideas with my students with few adjustments, and I assume any teacher from elementary through graduate school could use variations of this writing format.

Possible Limitations

Conceivably, the greatest hesitation in using this approach comes from the area of evaluation. Teachers may ask, "How does one motivate students to write to the best of their ability if grades are not assigned from the beginning?" Two facets of the McGill program address this important question. One, most students will be intimately involved in the process if they are writing from personal experiences and beliefs. Two, the peer groups have a built-in encouraging, motivational component and, no doubt, exert subtle pressure to perform. If a student does not participate fully in the writing assignments, journaling, logs, editing, and group sessions, then this concern can be the basis for early conferences with the teacher and some one-on-one problem-solving and goal-setting sessions.

Future

Rapidly gaining acceptance in schools in Canada, the U.S., Great Britain, New Zealand, Australia, and other English-speaking areas, this writing approach is process oriented and corresponds with most of the tenets of the National Writing Project. This approach to writing seems particularly important to use with "English as a second language" students so their personal experiences and cultural orientation can be fully valued and shared within the classroom. In an age when communication and information processing are increasingly central to an individual's successful negotiations in society, we must continue to examine and improve methods of assisting young people to clearly and effectively express written thoughts, feelings, and ideas.

Reply by William Boswell

To begin with, I would like to emphasize that the session reviewed by Marian Bryan was the result of collaboration on three levels. First, my colleagues Ann Beer and Jane Ledwell-Brown worked with me in preparing the material and organizing the presentation; unfortunately, however, they could not be at the conference in person.

In addition, all the Effective Written Communication (EWC) teachers and our director, Patrick Dias, were collaborators whether they realize it or not. There are about twenty of us, and most of us are part time. We come to the EWC program from a variety of backgrounds such as business, public relations, theatre, journalism, and public school teaching. (I, for example, recently retired after teaching secondary school English for almost thirty years.) Thus we not only build on student expertise; we also bring our own different experiences to our teaching. We meet every other week to share ideas, discuss common concerns, and consider possible modifications and improvements to the program.

Finally, the students. Since I began teaching EWC, I have learned to listen to their different voices and have gained tremendously from the fresh viewpoints they bring to the classroom with them.

Having said that, however, I should also point out that even though our program is a collaborative one, we are all free to be flexible in our own class. Thus, in this response, I speak with an individual voice as well.

It was a rewarding experience reading Marian Bryan's review. I have presented at a number of previous conferences, but this is the first time I have discovered in detail how at least one participant felt about what I had to say. What struck me was that she seemed to become really engaged when she was writing instead of listening—all teachers take note! I could feel her enthusiasm when she was describing how she gathered shark's teeth and I could feel her disappointment when I interrupted what the participants were doing and prevented them from completing their writing. There is a good object lesson here, I feel. Too often, we teachers interrupt what our students are engaged in in order to impose our own agenda.

In responding to Bryan's review, I would like to make two clarifications and develop a few ideas that I did not have time to deal with during the workshop. What I meant when I was talking about writing from a position of weakness (assumption #2) was that, more often than not, students in schools are required to do silly things (writing to someone who knows more) and that schools are the only place where this occurs (when we write in our everyday lives, we know more than our readers, a possible exception being when we write to request information). What we at McGill try to do then is turn matters around and create writing situations in which the students write from a position of strength and/or knowledge and address real readers.

The four writing assignments that Marian Bryan describes are by no means the only ones we use but are ones that seem, at the moment at least, to work well for me. Other teachers have variations of these or use different ones altogether. We also like to try out new things in the classroom and talk about them in our Friday meetings. What the assignments have in common, however, is that they are based on the *writer's* experience and grow out of the *writer's* concerns and needs.

As Marian Bryan states in her review, during the workshop I stressed the importance of journal writing and gave the obvious reasons—for example, getting into the writing habit, increasing fluency, and clarifying thinking. The more I teach the EWC course, the more I realize how important it is to the writer to write in the expressive mode, about matters that are of interest to the writer. What is more exciting to me is the fact that my students seem to be increasingly willing to explore new territory and take greater risks (writing poetry, working through a personal problem). The journal is safe—it is theirs to write in as they wish, my only ground rule being that they write often and regularly. The journal, more than anything else, helps to confirm the student as a writer and, perhaps more important, as an individual with interesting and valuable things to say. I'll let the students speak for themselves:

> The journal is discovery.... It is a chance to write with a real voice, one that is not tempered by an inner critic or an outside reader.

Or:

> Hey, Bill, this writing stuff really expands the mind. I'm impressed.

How the teacher responds to the students' writing is crucial to the success of using journals in the classroom. I respond as often as I can, and as a reader, *not* as a teacher. I talk about my own experiences, my own feelings, and ask questions about the writing I have just read. Above all, I try to be honest.

Several semesters ago, I started to write, too, and share my writing with the students. I had often heard that a teacher of writing should be a writer, but I never realized until I tried it myself how valuable an experience it can be. I have discovered, for example, that there are times when I do not want to write; I have also discovered that it takes me a page of writing to find out what I really want to say. In addition to serving as a model, then, the teacher-writer can become a better teacher as a result of experiencing what the students are living through. Finally, I have discovered that writing with the students has made me want to write more so that I am now writing poems and stories for myself.

I agree with what Bryan says about evaluation, which is always problematic in a course such as ours. What we do is to try and make evaluation part of the learning—the students are given criteria early in the semester which are discussed in detail and referred to as the course progresses. We are constantly giving feedback—through responses in journals, comments (either on tape or written) about assignments, in conferences. In addition, the students are part of the evaluation process—as assessors of their own work and by responding to the work of others.

I also agree with Bryan's comments at the end of the review. A course such as ours, I feel, deals with the reality of our increasingly multicultural classes. It values differences, builds on the knowledge and experience of each student, and provides opportunity for these to be shared. In addition, there is no doubt that second-language students gain from having to write regularly and frequently in nonthreatening situations. Bryan talks about today's students negotiating successfully in society—they are encouraged to do that in the EWC classes as well by being made responsible for their own learning, establishing goals for themselves, and deciding with the teacher how these might best be met.

The clients of EWC are students in faculties such as engineering and management, and our mandate is to help them become more effective communicators. In order to do this, we provide them with a variety of writing situations which we try to make as real as possible, discuss matters such as purpose and audience, and show them a number of strategies from which they can choose depending on the particular writing task. However, as the title of the book that McGill's Centre for Writing is publishing—*Writing for Ourselves/Writing for Others*—suggests, there is a by-product of the EWC program that in the long run may be even more important. When the students use writing as a means of exploring their own feelings and their own thinking, they can discover who they are and gain confidence as a result.

I spoke earlier about confirming the students as both writers and as people who are worthy of recognition. If we can do this, then, it seems to me everything else follows. I will close with, once again, listening to a student's voice:

> Also, writing about things, emotions, reactions helped me gain confidence in my opinions in the sense that, after rereading what I had written I would say to myself, "Hey, I know a lot more about this than I thought I did!" And this added confidence has helped me in expressing myself more coherently and fluently.

IV Poroporoaki (Farewell)

Global Futures

We close our global conversation by leaning forward, toward our 1995 rendezvous with New York City. We do not think forward only; we lurch back and forth in time to properly understand who we are and what we might become. We point toward the realization of McLuhan's global village, which we approximate with our sojourner encampments every five years. Those cyclical moments have enlivened the wires that network us. We talk to each other, work with each other, visit each other, and read each other with a frequency that is ever accelerated.

Three village-minded English teachers speak for our communion. One lyrically, yet penetratingly, tours us rearward to the brave days of Dartmouth, when first we gathered. One situates us at the moral core of Auckland's meeting and makes us understand our hosts' intentions and the commitments which informed that assemblage. One leads us forward to our future settlement in cosmos city, where we will see eternity in a grain of sand, can experience the world's diversity on one subway token.

In the first recollection, Natalie White circles around our international gatherings, settling on the metaphoric moments of the five-year intersections of Dartmouth, York, Sydney, Ottawa, and Auckland. She asks us to clear away some of the monolithic notions about Dartmouth to help us hear all of the voices who spoke there. She remembers the splintering as well as the splendor, the bickering as well as the beauty.

Elody Rathgen speaks more directly to the moral issues that centered on our Auckland gathering. She continues the praise of the "metabody," which is more than the sum of the individuals who compose it. She understands participants' uneasiness with new rites and others' language, and expresses her own disease in attaching religion so closely to schooling. She shows us that our feeling marginalized, disquieted is just what we need to experience in order to understand what we have allowed the cultural others of our various societies to live with daily.

John Mayher, the next convener of IFTE, brings us a final word about our future. To do this, he explains our past and helps us fully understand the need for such global connection. He sets the tone for the diversity that will greet us and will inform our future sojourn in New York.

25 Voices and Visions

Natalie White

I BELIEVE THAT
the first response to literature is to accept it
the next may be to value it
the next may be a desire to make it
but that the most valuable response, and the one
against which I will judge my teaching, is the
acceptance of values, discovered in literature, to help
in the business of living.
—Peter Smart of New Zealand; Friday, August 22,
  meeting of our working party, Third International
  Conference, Sydney, 1980

The remembered voice of Peter Smart appropriately begins this overview of the international movement in our profession. Intuitions about the vision which may have inspired him to write the credo above one night at the Third International Conference on the Teaching of English in Sydney may inform us more than a decade later. A passionate member of my working party in the Commission on Literature, Peter, sleepless one night, had written this on a sheet of paper. As we were wont to do, our group slept either on poems or problems—feeling the pressure of our profession, the importance of our collaboration, the need for the timeless inspiration that is the gift of poetry in its may forms. This piece of paper, its message and its writer have been much in mind during the decade since, a decade in which I chronicled the Dartmouth seminar and the subsequent internationals which it spawned. A classroom teacher, I did so in order to learn the workable centers of the seminar, then following the connections and the insights back into the art of pedagogy which we still too frequently see as mere craft. But that is another story. It is fitting here to begin with the words of a gifted teacher, an ancestor of some importance, someone to be remembered, whose life is to be celebrated.

Soon after the Sydney conference, those of us who had become Peter's friends were saddened by his sudden death. Recalling his words, his meanings as points of departure in a venture into the past bring his voice forward into the concert led by his colleagues and fellow New Zealanders. "The business of living" has changed. The world in 1980 stood in need of connection; the values discovered in literature and in the English classroom which were of urgent importance then are even more so today. In our international meetings, teachers become part of international lines of communication, collaboration. Other cultures, other literatures, and the visions inherent within them challenge the contradictions inherent in all cultural systems. We find answers and questions in the literature of all the world. The ideas and ideals in songs and stories, the values of cultures other than our own expand horizons and may even correct our misconceptions, our unconscious wrongs. This is the central task of literature and those who teach it, while the practical "business of living" evolves to a newer age. In international work English teachers may yet reach beyond Babel, to open the full spectrum of the rainbow for the illumination of humanity. Values, visions, connections, change—centers in the past—are potential inspirations for a better future.

The international movement in the teaching of English is the province of the teacher. The International Federation of Teachers of English, as Garth Boomer so aptly says, need not take a top-down structure. Teachers are—and can be—increasingly full participants, desirable leaders, distinguished by the directness of experience, the understanding drawn from the tension of teaching. A participant in Sydney, a presenter in Ottawa, in Auckland, and a secondary teacher of seventeen years, I have taken the rich legacies from these internationals into my classroom, into my teaching, enriching my students' worlds as well as my own. The urgency of international connections is metaphor and symbol in "The Thin, Red Line." Here it is more linear and direct—but no less urgent.

American teachers now take the role of the chorus in the preparation for the next international. We become the *nostoi*, follow a path to a homecoming which may contain the best of the democratic processes at Dartmouth. The seminar, bringing NCTE and MLA together, considered the question "What Is English?" Discourse there was to develop as many Dartmouths as there were participants. The central question, "What Is English?" had as many answers. While centers abide in Dixon's book and others, too much is unknown, too much will be lost if we do not hear our ancestor voices. If we do not know the past, how can we cast our frail ship toward the future? Former executive secretary of NCTE, Jim Squire was in Auckland, a quiet, democratic participant. The voices of John Dixon, Jimmy Britton, Merron Chorny were not among us there, yet in the subtleties of our interactions, the presence of their visions was indeed verifiable. Because of absence of real awareness of past internationals, I spent more than a decade following a trail from Dartmouth through subsequent conferences. Errors and misunderstandings in the record are abundant, as are methodological and philosophical centers.

The Dartmouth Seminar: A Beginning

The story of our past begins with another journey in time and place, but with a division rather than a connection. Wayne O'Neil's epic journey to Dartmouth through Mesa Verde, Caco Canyon, Bandeleir prophetically wound through Boston, Montreal, Ontario, Michigan, Wisconsin, Illinois, Missouri, Oklahoma, Texas. O'Neil reached perhaps blindly for ancestor visions in "ancient, white, desolate cities." Reacting against "the present squalor the American Indian has been subjected to . . . " he was, in many ways, trying to connect with a past, trying to hear voices. Others had similar feelings. The one to make it all practical was Paul Olson, chair of the Study Group on Myth and Translation, who had grown up on a Sioux reservation, who was to spend some time at the seminar camping away from the all-too-civilized barbs over brandy in the evening. Companions on his pilgrim journey, such as Barbara Hardy and Cap Lavin, collaborated on facets of the Study Group findings. Their monograph, old as it is, still is worthwhile and practical.

Different voices resounded in minds and journeys toward Dartmouth. But at the seminar, many possessed an easy and divisive certainty. Knowing in their own minds the answer to the central question "What Is English?" some felt they had only to expose the glorious wares tucked in their baggage, collect a few converts, emerge as winners of big pieces of the pie. But others also heard the voices, knew the differences, had the visions which we have so bitterly won as English teachers.

Yet their voices were not heard, their answers were not known. In America, shortly after Dartmouth, cities burned, strife tore us one from the other. Teachers spanned the gaping hole. In the twenty-five years since Dartmouth, the insights of the seminar which returned to the circling winds have successfully made their way into the full consciousness of the classroom teacher. No one directly sought what O'Neil, himself part of the cultural-linguistic revolution, envisioned in those dwellings, in the pueblos, on the reservations. O'Neil was angry, justly so. The profession in America characteristically did not ask why, but trudged blindly onward, hoping for consensus around the next bend in the road. We recognized import in what he wrote but went no further—this cognitive potential lay fallow for twenty years.

Returning to O'Neil's essay was to set me onto a different road to Auckland—a road like his journey to Dartmouth, a labyrinth which revealed aspects of our international past. I was to come to know Dartmouth, Sydney, Ottawa, to experience Auckland in a different way. Voices newly heard carried echoes of the past, of triumph and tragedy, of gain and loss. Questions came more readily than answers. Not knowing it, I was embarking on a journey, a quest which perhaps was not to answer "What Is English?" but, rather, compelled by the many students I've taught, to decide "*Why* English Is." One benefit of the personal growth paradigm is that it correctly answers this question.

This essay delves into international traditions and reforms from the Dartmouth Seminar forward. The story line begun at the Dartmouth Seminar, continued in York and Vancouver, achieved a fertile state of "rising action" in the re-founding of the International Federation of Teachers of English. The drama thus set on its course was to be, rather than a pageant of players or a parade of pedagogues, a resounding chorus of teacher-voices malleable, dynamic in response to each other and the many realities of the classroom.

The Sydney International

In Sydney, celebrants at the Third International considered the theme for their act in the drama "The Issues of the Eighties." And issues there were in that decade, all too many of them. We were misunderstanding measurability and suffering its misapplications, forces for censorship were growing and organizing, there were too many needs, too many impacted children. There was too little time, too little money—and a vision of teaching and learning that wouldn't go away. Coming as I did from a district in which I was required to note the "reading level" of each student in my grade book and foster or facilitate only "at level" texts, the shock of freedom of inquiry, open questioning, and discourse at the University of Sydney caused nothing less than a transformation. For the first time, I saw the limits in politics and processes which never took power over me again.

And of the players and the roles they played in Sydney, of the interludes, so much was of meaning and moment. Scan the cast, take a taste of the text and context:

> Into the Commission on Research, enter Aristophanes with . . . a chorus of frogs. A clipping of their parody:
>
> "Pardon me, good croakers, but can you tell me what makes for good croaking?"
> "It is a gift," said one.
> "It comes from inner contemplation," said another.
> "It is a political act," said another.
> "It is an art."
> "It can be taught in four years if I design the course."
> "It can come only to those who are whole frogs."
> "It is the prerogative of the true frogs amongst us only."
> "It is mandatory."
> "It is the most basic of basics."

What delight to have been a "fly-on-the-wall" narrator, to have seen the frog chorus of researchers as they hammered out this dialogue—the most refreshingly honest, creative "essay" into imagination and truth I've known an otherwise stolid group to produce.

In a more serious vein, one small group determined that the conference had to conclude something about the "Issues of the Eighties." They worked out a resolution to address the kind of realities teachers saw: "WHEREAS there exists a need to force a dialogue between the language of literature and the languages of media, the need for research on language and media. BE IT RESOLVED that the Eighties should be a period when the profession considers children's language in its private context (family, peers, personal narratives) and in its tension with public languages (press, television, radio) . . . That literature in the eighties should be truly international. . . ."[1] The little but resolute body turned then to teacher power, a resounding theme in Australia, "That teachers must publish their insights outside the conventional publishing routes. . . ." The conclusion of this resolution, given the resounding chorus of a vote in acclamation by the hundreds at the final plenary session was: "The issue of the Eighties is language and cultural power." That issue and the tensions this group presented in their resolution are still with us and will no doubt emerge again in our international discourse. The powers of the media have intensified, as have the questions classroom teachers must ask and answer. No longer have we the luxury of addressing these questions in the comfort of mere nationhood. Issues are increasingly world-class. As some have said, what has been forgotten returns to the circling winds. Perhaps the voice of the wind, fair or foul, should enter among those which inspire our action.

The Ottawa International

At the Fourth International, Ian Pringle set the center of the conference firmly in an all-too-accurate memory of the tensions at the Dartmouth Seminar. The Ottawa conference, the Fourth International, considered "Issues Which Divide Us." Honestly, directly looking at our divisions strangely bonded us. Starting with our differences brought us into the human family. Twenty years it had been since the divisions at Dartmouth. It was time to consider both minds and memories. The stunning achievement of the Canadians was that they carried us to a new level of internationalism. While there had been fifty-one at Dartmouth, the assembled members of the Ottawa conference numbered one thousand one hundred and fifty. They represented thirty-two nationals: Nigeria, Guyana, Kenya, Tanzania, India, Israel. Only with work and dedication will we assemble such ambassadors again.

A comment there by Harold Rosen encapsulates the kind of teacher discourse occasioned in Canada: "We begin by telling stories and end by telling the truth." This was the meaning of our moments together. Edward Kamau Brathwaite enchanted us with poetry and vision, like the line he read from "Cricket": "Poetry is a history, an archeology of metaphor." Moffett and Dixon both spoke of the necessity of both personal and social growth. Gatherings and groupings there were never national—the larger world-view was in progress.

In limited time and space, one center must be unearthed, one session John Dixon, Jim Squire, and others who had been at Dartmouth gathered. Most of the players in the International Assembly were present. John Mayher spoke as I had never heard him, collapsing idea into idea. He said the personal growth model is still the best metaphor for the teaching of English and the growth perspective is yet the most certain way to develop the social consciousness of the individual. While the Dartmouth perspective may not have won some of the elders of English pedagogy (the academic world is, after all, head-shaped), it did win their graduate students. He declared that transactions must be mutual, inside out and outside in. Taking a similar integrity to consideration of text, he asserted that not literature but myth is the core of this growth model, that literature leads to the externals of the text, mythos to its vital center. Mayher will, perhaps, take such a center to the planning of the next international.

The Fifth International in New Zealand was to open the stage to a flurry of "Different Voices." All were changed, both by the voices and the visions. Reactions to the accents of difference ran the full spectrum—positive, negative, and degrees in between. The past was present. Some came expecting a classical drama—others desired a "happening." None found what they predicted. Writing the scenario for the next international becomes more important to American teachers now; in its next stage, the drama returns to our shores.

The teacher, the individual student and growth, both personal and sociocultural, center our international traditions and cast forth continuing international reform and the revision to which each international has contributed. The past is always present but it is often misremembered. The Dartmouth Seminar has been softened by the patina of ensuing years. In actuality, the seminar had been a place of irreparable divisions, of argument, strife, and even tears. One participant was welcomed with the comment "*Who* invited you?" Meltdown occurred one dark day. The cerebral Seminar almost ended before its time—in an international division never to be forgotten by its participants. While one did leave in anger, others muddled through the month. There were many silences for a while.

Venturing to the Fifth International, this teacher had to follow patterns in the past. I had to return to questions raised, insights garnered in 1980. In some ways, I had to look at Arnhem Land rather than Australia. I had to be in schools, with teachers, talk to kids in hallways. I had to walk with a different nature. Like O'Neil's circuitous path, mine led to a center. Like the center of the labyrinth of old—a center in the human soul, a thin, red line continuing throughout time, across cultures. My labyrinthine pathway to Aotearoa led me first to the University of Sydney, where the international continuum began for me. I visited memories, did formal and informal interviews, heard many teacher stories, talked to students in the schools. Ken Watson (University of Sydney) and Syd Smythe (Scotland) were major contributors. From there, to Adelaide and other agendas: asking Garth Boomer about the vision of his reconvening of IFTE, the *why* of international meetings. What had we accomplished during the eighties—and why? What remained to be done? What vistas were opening in English education in Australia? What were the new directions for insightful people like Claire Woods? What answers, what questions centered teacher energies? What were the initiatives taken by Peter Moss in the decade of the eighties? To Melbourne then, where I unexpectedly found a woman's way of knowing in the work of Margaret Gill, Sr. Kathleen Hill, and others whose energies and insights have inspired me over time. Then to Tasmania, where ancestor voices cannot be stilled. Taking questions to David Mallick, who had chaired the Commission on Literature in Sydney, I found few answers. Taking long quiet walks on the shore, hearing silences, voices long ago obliterated gave me their gentle truth, took me back to echoes of Wayne O'Neil's dismay over Dartmouth. The world has not welcomed many of the differences we hunger for today, knowing full well we have lost our center.

International Reformation

Tensions unacknowledged set one against the other have continued the delicate balance of our international meetings, according to Garth Boomer, re-founding chair of the International Federation of Teachers of English. Boomer speaks of tensions directly, honestly, forcefully—his words revealing the scenario as it was lived, as it continues to be, rather than as it was idealized or dreamt. His rationale as founding chair of IFTE was nothing less than setting "a new paradigm for international conferences." He saw it as a way for nations to pool "riches and resources" in dialogue. IFTE was to become, in his vision, "an amplifier of voices, a way of continuing conversations" begun at Dartmouth, bringing them forward "to meet the needs of teachers and students, in real classrooms, all too real social situations, many facing similar problems."

Rather than the exclusive nature of the Dartmouth Seminar, Boomer envisioned an IFTE "inclusive of all voices in all countries," especially, increasing the voice of the teacher, addressing even uncomfortable issues like multiculturalism. Boomer had spoken elsewhere, compellingly, of that which Harold Rosen has called the continuation of politics by other means, of the need to go beyond progressivism—since such an orientation has produced mere rhetoric rather than change. Even though Australia is still "pushing the wagons out," a frontier country, he admits their progressivism has yielded little. He goes beyond progressivism. IFTE, a federation rather than an exclusive club, was to be nothing less than "member countries having extended dialogue" rather than a parade of vanities, a litany of leaders. Boomer's vision is yet to be fully achieved: "We have to inject generosity into dialogue, share, abandon our parochiality." Otherwise, he notes, a conference becomes mere ritual, "a recitation of scriptures" in a "religious enclave."

Beginning to break out of "the more precious club mentality" in Sydney, 1980, was not easy. To more fully hear the voices, see the visions—even those obscured by the chaos, the conflict in the classroom—"more teachers must be involved" in our international gatherings. Boomer says we must accord more dignity to the teacher in these international gatherings, and in their publications. Looking as exemplar to law "which has, from its inception been based on cases," we must similarly base education, "developing a literature of cases," affirming the teacher as action researcher, making the academic mere "explicator of those texts."

One further aspect of the dialogue Boomer envisions is "the connection of dialogue with subtlety." A person becomes a more subtle thinker by exposure to "different thoughts." Negotiation occurs: "By listening and attending and responding you move toward the language and the understanding of the other." What Boomer and Australia gave the international movement was first evident in the Sydney conference, a construct of careful design, intended, like all subsequent meetings, to reflect "a federation rather than an exclusive club" or steering committee. The Sydney conference was to assemble "a perverse lot," to become a different kind of gathering, ideally, placing "the toxic alongside the brilliant." Boomer wished at all costs to avoid IFTE conferences becoming a series of pallid sessions with each conferee "seeking their favorite soap." Commitment, he felt, would force real alliance and exchange. Thus, Sydney was to become a confluence of alliances in a federation loose enough to allow formation of its own splinter group led by Merron Chorny of Canada.

In issue-related forums "complexities" and "the problematic" would naturally emerge, generating important dialogue, facilitating urgent thought across international boundaries. Boomer had felt that commitment, alliances along the lines of issues in education might force participants to "go deep, build linkages, continue associations through correspondence, continuing the dialogue." Boomer termed the organism that is IFTE a "metabody": sharing quests through discourse, it shares thought, then action and essence, reflecting synchronicity, sharing meaning. As the discourse, the exchanges collide in thought, they are forged, sometimes uncomfortably, into ideas, taking on a power they would not have had in isolation. The model is a good one, an urgent one to IFTE national, their teachers and children.

Boomer's associate, Claire Woods, was to add an important parallel to his remarks. In her presentation for IFTE in Auckland, she recalled Tillie Olson's *Silences,* saying we must not only hear different voices, but must hear the silences as well, coming as they do from class, from gender, from race. We must extend our thoughts into their potential and bring them to articulation. She called for the English teacher to be "vulnerable to the lifeblood of other cultures and languages." Increasingly, we are.

Afterword: Moving beyond Babel

Our international work will take us beyond Babel. The potential of such movement toward meaning, understanding, and wisdom is as limitless as the minds of teachers of English in all the world. At the close of the ceremonies in Auckland we celebrated voices in song, in story, in the profound accents of the assembled participants. As the convenor of the next international, John Mayher was given a myth-gift, a basket. Three baskets of knowledge were Tane's[2]: one contained peace, goodness, and love; another, prayer, incantation, and ritual; the third, works of earth and stone, agriculture and war. The teachers who assemble at the next international will mediate the contents of the basket given to Mayher. While the convenors of the New York international hold the basket, teachers from the Americas and all the world will contribute contents. Consider what you will bring. Hearing the circling winds, the ancestor voices, we move together toward the millennium.

Bruce Chatwin places a grain of sand we can turn into a pearl in *The Songlines*. Discussing the many meanings of Babel, he opens the insight of "the ancient Jews—sandwiched as they were between bullying empires" casting forth the idea of the state as Leviathan. He closes his small meditation on Babel with one culture's understanding which advises our considerations for the next international:

> They were, perhaps, the first people to understand that the Tower was chaos, that order was chaos, and that language—the gift of tongues which Jahweh breathed into the mouth of Adam—has a rebellious and wayward vitality compared to which the foundations of the Pyramid are as dust. (1987, p. 189)

Not just Adam's, it is Eve's. Not just language, but the power which connects, also constructs. We merely have to claim our province, work our centers—together in our differing voices and visions founding a better world.

Notes

1. It would be irresponsible of me not to say at this point that work is to be done in this area—the kind of work only teachers would do. During the reconvening of IFTE, one matter considered important was the nomination of

stories for inclusion in an international anthology. Once nominations were made within a nation, the children themselves would take the power of voting for the best, the most representative. Some member countries' English teacher organizations have been reluctant to venture forth since publications lists are for teachers, not students, since the venture would be cumbersome, the profits might be small. Because of this understandable reluctance, the work of looking into the how, the why has never been done. Yet to have such a resource would be an asset.

2. God of forests, he who separated the primordial parents Rangi from Papa, sky from earth.

26 Different Voices, Aotearoa 1990: The Memories and the Messages

Elody Rathgen

It is now the start of 1992. Seventeen months have passed since the conclusion of "Different Voices, Aotearoa 1990." What are my memories of that time? What new perspectives on English teaching did I gain from that international meeting? How has it influenced my teaching? What are the consequences of it for my students?

For us in New Zealand the whole thing had been going on for three or four years prior to 1990. We were handed the responsibility for IFTE's fifth conference by Ian Pringle in Ottawa in 1986. The timing was significant; 1990 marked ten years' existence for the New Zealand Association for the Teaching of English, which had been born out of the Third International Conference held in Sydney in 1980.

Nineteen ninety was also a milestone (perhaps a millstone?) for New Zealand as a nation. New Zealand had become a Crown Colony in 1840. The Treaty of Waitangi established this fact, and guaranteed protection and rights for the Maori people of Aotearoa as well. But 150 years on, in spite of becoming an independent, democratic nation with a comparatively good standard of living, New Zealand still had as much to attend to in the area of equity as it had to celebrate. Rangatiratanga, tribal control of tribal resources guaranteed to Maori people under the treaty, has not been honoured by successive governments.

Issues of equity—racial, cultural, sexual, class, and gender—have featured prominently in the concerns of the NZATE from its beginning. The association has policy on most of these issues and members do their best in taking them into account in their classroom practice. Out of this background the theme for the conference readily emerged: "Different Voices." Those responsible for the vision behind the conference were thinking in a deeper and more challenging way than simple acknowledgement of different voices. Accepting the challenge that those committed to biculturalism have faced, the conference organisers realised that equity means not just recognition or acceptance of different; it means change in power structure, reallocation of time and money, reviewing approaches to languages, reconsidering the content and methodology of our teaching.

In the midst of these issues the matter of South African delegates' participation came up. It caused a great deal of pain to the New Zealanders and obviously to colleagues from other countries. Rugby is the biggest sport in New Zealand. We are (or have been and will be again!) the world leaders in this sport. Maori colleagues and those Pakeha English teachers who worked with them had fought for many years against rugby contracts with South Africa. We had watched Maori players go to South Africa dubbed "honorary whites." We had watched teams go with Maori players excluded from selection. We saw, and participated in, one of the most significant protest movements, riots and violence in New Zealand's history as a result of one government's decision to invite a racist rugby team here. We asked our friends in South Africa what advice they had for us. They said, please keep up the boycott. We did. We knew this hurt and puzzled many of our colleagues, especially those South African teachers of English who had been active against apartheid in their own country. We were also aware of the powerful argument about academic freedom.

Looking back on our decision and subsequent events, in spite of the hurt to friends, I still believe we did what we had to, and that time has vindicated us. The South African government has had to bow to international pressure and make changes. The extraordinary violence and outrageous racism of the militant white groups in South Africa currently protesting that decision of their government, demonstrates the seriousness of the situation still. It shows that half-hearted measures would not have been enough to bring to bear on that country. I am glad we were clear on the matter.

Right from the beginning, from the powhiri (the welcome to strangers), all of us as conference participants sensed that more than token acknowledgement was being given to different voices, to different styles of learning and behaving. I was constantly being reminded of the challenges handed out to us in Mike Rose's book, *Lives on the Boundary*, published just the year before the conference, that if we are to meet the needs of those called the underachievers and outsiders in our world of "higher learning," it is we who will have to make changes. At least, we will have to make as many moves towards change as they do when they enter our schools and institutions.

Learning is more likely to take place in a dynamic environment than in one of one-way compulsion. Dynamic teaching does not impel learners mechanistically. It focuses on learning as much as on teaching. Both learner and teacher are equally necessary and valuable in the process of becoming literate. One is not more important than the other. If teachers emphasise the learning processes with their students and try them out, too, they will remain aware of the different ways progress and competence in language can be achieved. They may also value the different strengths and weaknesses of other learners in their classrooms if they are constantly being reminded of their own.

I have been making my way towards this understanding for many years, and I know my practice has increasingly demonstrated it. It has been one of my strongest messages to my students who are learning to teach English. I try to show them my processes at work, how I go about planning and making classroom decisions, for example. I constantly choose texts which are new to me so that they can see me dealing with the new material.

The IFTE Conference increased my commitment to this way of teaching; this way of making the processes open and clear; this emphasis on remembering the learner's point of view to new encounters. It did this because I saw how my colleagues, very experienced and esteemed teachers, struggled with the new formats and approaches to learning with which the conference challenged us. Unfamiliar settings, different languages, use of different learning styles, holistic language practices, acknowledgement of the spiritual side, expression of personal, often emotional responses were some of the new experiences encountered by many delegates more used to the traditional international conference format.

I struggled with some of them myself, particularly the place of a spiritual element in schooling. I'm still not comfortable with it. In fact, I am still resisting it strongly. But what that is making me do is articulate clearly what it is I disagree with, what it is that makes me feel anxious and uncomfortable. I may never resolve it, but I am having to experience being an outsider, being inexperienced, not knowing "the language" and the accustomed way of doing things. For a confident, assured, language-efficient person like myself, it is not easy. I experience self-doubt, which flows over into other areas of my thinking as well. I am being a learner.

Some may have felt that the conference did not address the politics of language directly enough. It is true that we did not arrive at new statements of policy, nor did we articulate a new direction for

IFTE and its members to move towards. But what we did have to do was implement the policies and directions we have been talking about over the last twenty years. Many realised that talk and written statement are easier than practice. Our policy statements are not enough. We may readily recite them in business meetings, seminar rooms, prestigious publications, and conference platforms, but until our classrooms, our own behaviour and language exemplify them, we need meetings such as "Different Voices, Aotearoa 1990," to give us the opportunity for some revision.

27 From Auckland to New York: A Look Ahead to 1995

John S. Mayher

In the decades since the 1966 Dartmouth Seminar inaugurated a transatlantic conversation among teachers of the English language arts, that dialogue has now become worldwide. Although it is never clear to what extent this is only one conversation—the legend of Dartmouth certainly supports the view that the British and American participants of that era represent two very distinct academic cultures divided by a common language—it is clear that many of us continue to find it exciting and intellectually nourishing. In person and in print, I've developed a taste for multiple accents and multiple perspectives, which is why I volunteered to be the convener of the next IFTE Conference in New York in 1995. The Sixth International Conference will strive to continue and enrich these conversations by looking back at where we've been and, especially, looking ahead to the issues and problems that will confront English language arts teachers in the next century.

The 1995 conference will be different from the others in a lot of ways—being in New York will ensure it—but one of the most significant differences is that it will have a deliberate focus out from the profession to the social and political world we live in. The increasing standardization pressures on teachers and students, for example, come from outside the classroom, and no amount of reform within the classroom will relieve those pressures. National tests, national curricula, national standards, even national hysteria are either in place or on the horizon in all of the IFTE member countries. While IFTE has not been concerned much with such things in the past, it seems clear that it is precisely its *international* character which may make it a unique forum for discussion of such issues and provides it with a unique platform from which to at least attempt to influence policy in such areas. No one can be naive enough to think that politicians and policymakers will all share our perspective and endorse our positions, but if they don't even know what they are, we certainly have given up the possibility of impact before we have even begun. Among other efforts which will characterize the conference, therefore, will be as many attempts as possible to find ways to reach politicians and policymakers, as well as the rest of our profession, to enable them to share our talk and to understand our perspectives.

My sense of the history of the English language arts teaching and learning field since 1966 is that a broad consensus has emerged around a set of theoretical practices. These were summarized in the U. S. by the Joint Section Document of NCTE and parallel statements have been developed in other countries. The spread around the world of the whole language movement, the national writing project, the Early Literacy Inservice Course (ELIC), reader-response approaches to the teaching of literature, writing process approaches to composition instruction, and multiculturalism and diversifying the traditional literary canon are aspects of this emerging consensus. Only the last, however, has "made the papers" and rarely in a way which has made these shifts seem like progress.

As I write the list, of course, I am immediately aware of all of the controversy and discord that lurks beneath that consensus list. But while I am certainly all for critique and dissonance, I think the essential framework within which those disagreements are taking place can still be communicated to the public and to policymakers without stifling debate or distorting the issues. At least that is the challenge that the 1995 conference planners have set for ourselves: to articulate the underlying unit within which our current debates are taking place in such a way that we can have an impact on the world outside the school which is so intent on "reforming" us without our consent.

Theme

To these ends, the theme of the New York Conference will be: *Reconstructing Language and Learning for the 21st Century*. This theme hopes to embody both this forward-looking spirit of where we need to go next, and also to put special emphasis on our roles as *language* educators concerned with promoting student *learning* from a *constructivist* perspective. I'll expand on each of these ideas briefly here, but it should be emphasized that my views on these matters will provide only part of the input to the conversations of the conference, and I certainly don't expect them to be either uncontroversial or universally shared. In fact, it seems clear that for the conference to be both exciting and productive we need to explore our controversies and our differences (the theme of the Ottawa Conference in 1986) as well as our shared beliefs and assumptions.

Thinking of ourselves as language educators implies a definite shift from the more traditional notions of English teaching. While most of us are, to be sure, teaching English, many of the traditional conceptions of English teaching have proved to be barriers to be overcome rather than liberating ideas. For example, the Auckland Conference was attended by very few, if any, primary/elementary teachers, thereby limiting its diversity and range of concerns. Since most N–6 teachers don't think of themselves as English teachers, we need to expand our scope and our language to make them feel comfortably included. Similarly, English teaching in university departments has been almost exclusively focused on literature which has had a corresponding (negative?) effect in many secondary school programs, and, especially, in the self-definition of many secondary school teachers. The struggle of the compositionists to find a voice and a place in traditional American English departments is one effect of this focus, and the fact that virtually none of the other IFTE countries teach composition at all at the university level shows another effect. The point here is that one of the benefits of sharing across oceans and borders can be that the things Americans take for granted may not be similarly assumed by our colleagues around the world, and opening up those assumptions for questioning and scrutiny must be one of the foci of such international gatherings.

The stress of learning, which is the theme of the conference, is intended to provide a new way of framing some of our traditional debates. One such debate has sometimes been cast as an opposition between student-centered and teacher-centered pedagogies. A parallel version is the dispute between a process-focused and a product-focused pedagogy. The student-centered position seemed to be strengthened by the growth theorists at Dartmouth and their descendants while teacher-centered (or perhaps subject-centered?) views seem embodied, albeit differently, in the skills and cultural heritage models which Dixon critiqued in *Growth through English* (1967). A look at classrooms around the world, however, suggests that whatever labels are used for these debates, it seems clear that the Dartmouth tensions among theories and practices are still with us in many guises. The U. S. Coalition Conference at Wye Plantation in 1987 showed a shift in the American position toward something akin to the growth model, but the gap between the coalition's vision expressed in *Democ-*

racy through Language and the actual practices of most classrooms provide another issue for us to explore in New York.

In some respects the profession's leadership may be more united now than it was at Dartmouth, but certainly the public and the political leadership of all of the IFTE countries still holds pretty traditional views. This is certainly being reflected in many of the calls for national standards and national testing in the U. S. And in the case of England and Wales, the conservative notions of what English teaching is for has strongly influenced both the creation of and much of the implementation of the national curriculum. While it is still a bit early to tell how similar debates will play out in the other member countries, it seems clear that one of the issues we must grapple with is whether or not we can influence public opinion in positive ways.

Shifting our focus to learning from teaching might be a positive step in this direction. At least some of our disputes with the more conservative and nostalgic members of the press and public and the politicians who respond to them are not about ends, at least not about broad goals and outcomes. By focusing on learning and making it clear that we are committed to all students becoming powerful language users who can read, write, speak, and listen, we can emphasize that we do care about products, that we have high standards, and so on. In remarks at an IFTE Plenary held at the 1987 AATE Conference in Melbourne, I emphasized that the English language education community had virtually abandoned the language of excellence to the traditionalists. This has enabled such people as E. D. Hirsch, Allan Bloom, and Diane Ravitch in the U. S. and their counterparts around the world to label us as soft, fuzzy, and tender-minded. I like soft and fuzzy as well as the next person, but in a hard, clear-cut, and tough-minded world, we must find a way to reclaim, renew, and recast the language of excellence in our own terms.

We claim to be language experts, but where is our rhetorical brilliance in the educational policy arena? How much influence have we had and are we having on the processes of standard setting? Of assessment development? Of national and local testing programs? Our success in resisting the conservative and internationally competitive rhetoric of the politicians of our respective countries has not been outstanding. Even worse, we have sometimes been critical of those of our colleagues who have tried to join the debate, to get involved in the policy arena, fearful apparently that we would lose our purity, compromise our integrity, and be coopted by the enemy. While these may be risks, the alternative seems to be becoming even more and more marginalized with no other recourse than to weep together in a forgotten corner. How does that help the next generation of students or of teachers?

We must be involved in these debates and processes not only because our own interests are at stake, but because no one else will speak for the children. Parents can and should be our natural allies in these struggles because they, too, care about their kids, but until we become better at articulating why what we know will help, not hurt, their children, they will continue to be as susceptible to our critics as the rest of the public. Part of the conference, therefore, will be focused on developing such outreach and involvement strategies partly by sharing successes where we can find them from around the world and partly by building new approaches to these problems.

Learning-centered schools could become a unifying vision for teachers and parents and even the public at large if we can find a way to connect learning with the pressure for accountability on the one hand and our recognition that schools as currently conceived are simply not helping all students achieve to their maximum potential. This can be just another slogan, of course—although it might be nice to have it be *our* slogan for a change—unless we work to actually find ways to embody these ideas in real school contexts with real end-of-century children and their teachers. Concreteness, therefore, will be one of the aims of the conference, and we hope to encourage conferees to share their good practices with each other and the world. This will not be done as lore to be exchanged among teachers, but as windows on classrooms which can serve as exemplars of how learning happens, and why this kind of learning is essential if we are going to develop students who can meet the language ability levels needed to be successful in the workplaces, universities, and families of the twenty-first century.

While it is hard to predict what the world will be like in 1995 and beyond, it seems unlikely that people around the world will have decided that the schools are OK and that no further attention to them is necessary. The notion of reconstructing remains central, therefore, both because it suggests the extent of the overhaul of schooling that will be required, and because it embodies the key notion of knowledge construction which is at the core of contemporary thinking about effective language education. Even here, of course, there are disputes, but from my perspective these are more internal than external disputes because they focus more on means than on ends. It seems highly healthy that such disputes and debates exist, because that is the nature of our process for coming to better understand how we do what we do. Opportunities for arguments and debate on these issues will be structured into the conference formally and informally and should provide for many lively occasions.

One central feature of the knowledge construction debates must focus on assessment. Most of us have long recognized that whether we like it or not, the assessment tail wags the instructional dog. Of more recent vintage is our recognition that we have to be involved directly in the assessment debates, in the development of assessment procedures, and so on. Americans now know that we can no longer abdicate our responsibilities to the psychometricians and the Educational Testing Service. People in other countries are finding the testers cropping up behind most of the calls for higher standards and world-class competition and coming to recognize that even long traditions of other kinds of assessment—some good, some bad—won't necessarily save them from the short-answer testers. It didn't save New South Wales, and the threat grows daily all over the IFTE world.

Lurking behind the assessment debates is another version of the "What is English?" question which has been one of the subtexts of all the international conversations. One can't decide about assessment until one decides what we are looking for as benchmarks of growth, as necessary knowledge to possess, and as vital abilities to demonstrate. These questions, in turn, rest on the epistemological bedrock of our conceptions of the nature of knowledge and of learning. We need therefore to be both open to continued exploration of these questions and able to recognize that most of our debates assume a broadly constructivist view on these matters of the sort expressed in the coalition reports, in the joint section report of the Elementary, Secondary, and College Sections of NCTE. My own view of it in *Uncommon Sense* suggests that one of our real problems is finding a way to help each other—and parents, students, administrators, and the public—come to challenge our assumptions and reconstruct our teaching, learning, and assessment practices.

The key, once again, may be proactivity: to seize the high ground for our own collective vision of what and how language learning and achievement can and should be assessed. Our traditional ostrich postures and our fears that we were somehow too pure to dirty our hands with such nitty-gritty problems are disappearing to some extent, but we still haven't gotten to the point where we are taking the lead in these matters in a way that compels attention from policymakers and their testing allies. Since this issue, too, seems clearly to be a worldwide problem, we can benefit from sharing strategies, exemplars, and outreach approaches aimed at helping us win the respect we deserve.

Structure

This theme and the many sub-themes implied within it will play a key role in structuring the 1995 IFTE Conference. Many of the detailed decisions as to particular issues and themes are still being developed at this time in consultation with teachers around the world. Some fundamental structural decisions have been made, however, and understanding these may be helpful to anyone who hopes to join us in 1995.

The most important structural decision that has been made is that there will be two parts to the 1995 Conference: an open weekend conference on the last weekend in May, which we hope will attract a large number of teachers at all levels from around the world (referred to here as Part I), and a follow-up week-long conference which will be limited to approximately three hundred participants (called here Part II). The two parts will be thematically integrated and interrelated in terms of people, but the focus of the first part will be sharing where we are in an international context, while the second will be designed to look ahead to the next century by pushing those within the professional conversation along, as well as by developing position statements which can be contributions to the larger public conversations in the policy worlds that affect us.

Both parts will have opportunities for participants to talk with each other about issues and problems in our theoretical practices, but only the weekend conference will have formal speeches and presentations. The goal is to use those formal presentations as plenary conversation starters for the various working parties who will be talking and writing together during the week-long second part. While the logistical details of how to do this are still being developed, the conceptual framework here is that participants in both parts will choose an issue/topic/sub-theme to concentrate on and their participation will be limited by that choice. For each individual, therefore, there will be some sacrifice of breadth to depth, but we hope to develop ways through such things as desk-top publishing, on-line inkshedding, and other across-group bulletins to at least keep people informed as to how things are going in the other groups.

Approximately half of the group involved in Part II will be delegations selected by each of the national associations to make up

IFTE. While the criteria for selection are still being developed, our goal is to have a diverse group in terms of teaching level, areas of concern, and experience chosen by each nation. We hope that diversity of background and commonality of purpose will make for richly interactive groups. The rest of the Part II participants will be assembled from people with particular concerns for and expertise in the areas covered by the themes and sub-themes. We anticipate that most of these will be drawn from the English education community in all its variety around the world, but we also hope to include relevant thinkers from other disciplines who may be able to shed light on policy and theory issues from other perspectives. Also included in the second group will be representatives of countries where English is a major educational language but not, strictly speaking, a native one. Again, processes for selecting and inviting such people are still under development.

One thing seems clear, however, that if the conference is to really be a working session, some of the work will have to have been done by participants before they arrive. We anticipate, therefore, trying to set up various pre-conference writing tasks which can then be shared more or less formally with other participants before they arrive in New York so that the discussion and drafting processes will be under way immediately. Many of the presentation/information-sharing aspects of the conference, therefore, will actually take place before the face-to-face transactions, and anyone anticipating being a participant in Part II of the conference will be signing on to write before, during, and after it.

Final Thoughts

The Sixth International Conference will attempt, therefore, to move beyond the classroom and teaching and learning transactions within it to the larger context in which such transactions take place. While I am convinced that such a move is long overdue, having this focus for an IFTE Conference will not, in itself, be enough to have the kind of impact we need. Each of the various national associations which make up IFTE has, to one degree or another, begun to move more actively in its own local and national political arenas by developing political action strategies, by becoming involved in the political processes of curriculum and assessment development, and so on. Some of these are survival strategies; the best of them are trying to lead rather than merely react to outside threats. My hope is that the nineties will continue to see such efforts expanded and that the sociopolitical themes of the 1995 Conference will be part of a growing effort to take control of our own destiny.

For this to happen *internationally* as well as nationally and locally, it will undoubtedly require continual rethinking of IFTE's purpose and structures. The current structure of IFTE grew out of the vision of Garth Boomer and Steven Tchudi, who were, respectively, presidents of the Australian and U.S. English teaching associations. They modeled it on the Australian national association, which exists as a federation of state organizations so that potential members join their state group and are automatically a member of the national group. The national group has virtually no independent bureaucracy and its annual meetings, for example, are not run centrally but rotated among the various state associations. While this seems to work well enough in Australia, it is less clear that it is a useful model for an international organization.

Some of the questions that seem pertinent if IFTE is to become a group with the potential to speak on broad policy questions across national boundaries might include: Should individuals be able to join IFTE directly in some way or should it continue to be, exclusively, a loose confederation of national associations? How could each national association make more efforts to make the existence and purposes of IFTE more visible to its membership? What sort of efforts could be made to make IFTE a more proactive organization and what would be the costs involved in doing so? Are there benefits which might accrue from such efforts? How could funds be generated to support them? For me the benefits of dialogue and interchange among the IFTE countries with our colleagues in other countries where English is a major language have been personally rewarding. More important, however, I am convinced that the networks that have been built and the contacts that have been made through these international conferences and conversations have provided enormous support to the force of progressive language education throughout the English-speaking world. The consensus I have tried to articulate here is, strikingly, an *international* consensus. The curricular initiatives identified earlier have moved around the globe as have such assessment practices as those of the primary language record, portfolio assessment, and the like.

And most important, of course, has been the internationalization of our bookshelves. I don't dare list all of those involved for fear of leaving someone out inadvertently, but if I had been restricted to reading U.S.-based authors alone on the issues that have concerned me during the last twenty-five years, all aspects of my professional life would be the poorer for it. While some of this happened before Dartmouth, it was remarkably little, and the cross-pollination engendered since has clearly enabled us to enrich our understanding of language education as well as to build the consensus explored here.

I am convinced that our collective international resources could enable us to seize the policy initiatives in our own countries more effectively than we ever could without them. To do that we need strong networks and a dynamic International Federation for the Teaching of English.

Come join us in New York as we take the next steps down that road!

Editors

Joe Milner is chair of the Department of Education at Wake Forest University, chair of the Conference on English Education, director of the North Carolina Writing Project, a member of the Board of Directors of the North Carolina Science and Math Alliance, and a member of the National Humanities faculty. He has served as an editor of an affiliate journal, has written books in English education, including *Bridging English;* has published critical essays on Stevens and Agee; pedagogical essays in *English Journal, English Education, Children's Literature,* and other journals; and research studies in *Kappan* and the *Journal of Genetic Psychology.*

Carol Pope is associate professor of English Language Arts Education at North Carolina State University in Raleigh, North Carolina, where she works in the undergraduate program with students who will become middle-grades language arts teachers and in the graduate program with English education students. Previously, she was an assistant professor of English education at the University of Houston, taught high school English for ten years in North Carolina, served as a system-level coordinator of English language arts in Albemarle County Schools, Charlottesville, Virginia, and as a consultant with the Department of Public Instruction in North Carolina.

Contributors

Bruce C. Appleby is professor of English and professor of curriculum and instruction at Southern Illinois University in Carbondale. He has taught at all grade levels and does teacher preparation for all grade levels. In addition to his many journal articles and book chapters, he was coeditor (with Nancy McCracken) of *Gender Issues in the Teaching of English* (Boynton/Cook, 1992). Appleby does workshops and inservice work in a wide variety of areas, including gender, sexual harassment, computers, and writing across the curriculum—both nationally and internationally. He makes presentations regularly at NCTE and CCCC and for numerous affiliates.

Bertadean Baker is currently employed as assistant principal of Mariam Boyd and Hawkins elementary schools and also as a teaching specialist for Teach for America. She has devoted twenty-nine years to assisting children in North Carolina public schools. Baker has conducted workshops in creative writing, sex bias, classroom management, cooperative learning, and developmentally appropriate practices for classroom teachers, administrators, and parents.

Dennise M. Bartelo is associate professor of education and coordinator of elementary education at Plymouth State College of the University System of New Hampshire. She has been a classroom teacher, reading specialist, special education teacher, and English as a second language teacher in grades K–12. Her dissertation, *The Linkages Across the Language Processes*, investigated young children's response to reading and writing, and was co-chaired by Donald Graves of the University of New Hampshire and Barbara Hutson of Virginia Polytechnic Institute and State University. She has presented workshops on language and literacy at local, state, national, and international conferences, and has been a consultant with the American International Schools overseas. Her recent research project involves evaluating writing across the curriculum at the college level.

Catherine Beavis is a lecturer in English education at Deakin University, where she coordinates Studies in Teaching English. She has worked in secondary education in various capacities: as a classroom teacher, a consultant, a researcher, through the subject association (AATE) and through VCAB, the body responsible for curriculum and assessment in the final years of schooling in Victoria, Australia. She has been active in the development and implementation of the new literature course at this level, and regularly offers workshops and presentations at ARA, VATE, and AATE conferences.

Carole B. Bencich is associate professor of English at Indiana University of Pennsylvania and founding co-director of the Southcentral PA Writing Project. She has taught high school English, worked as a language arts consultant in Florida, and served as president of the Florida Council of Teachers of English. In addition to teaching and supervising in IUP's English education program, she makes presentations regularly at NCTE conventions and writes for local and state publications.

Sheridan Blau teaches in the departments of English and education at the University of California, Santa Barbara, where he is director of the South Coast Writing Project and the Literature Institute for Teachers. He serves as senior advisor to California's language arts test development team for statewide testing in reading and writing. He is also a member of the National Writing Project Advisory Board, the Executive Committee of the Conference on English Education, and the task force for the National Standards Project for English Language Arts. He has published widely in the areas of seventeenth-century literature, composition theory, professional development for teachers, and the teaching of composition and literature.

William Boswell taught for over thirty years with the Protestant School Board of Greater Montreal and from 1965 was an English department head. Since retirement in 1985, he has been teaching at McGill's Centre for the Study and Teaching of Writing and working on a consultative committee for Quebec's Ministry of Education. He has been involved in the following projects: Ministry of Education language arts curriculum guides; Writers' Development Trust Guides for the teaching of Canadian literature; *Crossroads*, a two-volume collection of Canadian literature for high schools; and *The Writer's Voice*, a writing program for grades 10–12.

Rita Brause is a professor in the graduate school of education of Fordham University and director of teacher education. She has taught at all levels of schooling and served as consultant to teacher-researchers, English language arts departments, and faculties rethinking schooling. A recipient of an NCTE Promising Researcher Award, she has published journal articles and chapters in books as well as *Enduring School: Problems and Possibilities*, and coedited with John Mayher, *Search and Research: What the Inquiring Teacher Needs to Know*, both published by Falmer Press/Taylor & Francis. A regular attendee at NCTE conferences, and the rock and roll dances, she served as chair of the Conference on English Education's 1992 Conference.

Marian Cooper Bryan teaches in the H.O.T.S. (higher-order thinking skills) program in Wilmington, North Carolina, public schools and teaches educational psychology part time at the University of North Carolina, Wilmington. As a National Writing Project Fellow, she has studied writing process and whole language in England, Wales, and New Zealand and contributed chapters to and served on the editorial board for *Writing in Trust: A Tapestry of Teachers' Voices*. She serves on the NCTE Committee on Tracking and Grouping Practices and has contributed to the NCTE publication *Tracked for Failure/Tracked for Success*. She has also published and presented in the areas of writing process, printless books, and classroom management.

Jenny Buist is head of the English department at Wellington East Girls' College in New Zealand. She has been active in English teaching associations for many years and held the position of president of the New Zealand Association for the Teaching of English in 1991 and 1992. She was a member of the National Syllabus Committee which wrote the initial draft Forms Six and Seven English Syllabus for New Zealand. She has participated in the New Zealand Writing Project. In addition to her role in organising national conferences for teachers of English, she has made regular presentations at a regional and national level and has been a member of advisory groups for the International Association for the Evaluation of Educational Achievement literacy research and for the development of achievement-based assessment methods.

Winifred Crombie is the director of the University of Waikato Language Institute in New Zealand, where she is responsible for an operation which runs a range of research and postgraduate programmes in applied linguistics and language teaching, a language-testing and support programme for university students, inservice courses for practising teachers, and courses in English and other languages for students from New Zealand and overseas. In addition to journal articles and book chapters, she has written books on stylistics, discourse analysis, and syllabus design. She worked mainly in England and France before moving to New Zealand in 1991.

Patricia Gillard (formerly Palmer) is research fellow and associate professor in the Department of Communication Studies, Royal Melbourne Institute of Technology. She was previously head of research and development for ABC Television, Australia's national public broadcaster. She has been an English teacher, lecturer in English curriculum, and associate director of the *TV: The Child's View* project at the University of Sydney. For three years she was a member of the Children's Program Committee which advised the Australian Broadcasting Tribunal on the regulation of children's television. Research publications include *Girls and Television* (1986) and *The Lively Audience* (1986), which explore the place of television in children's lives and their use of its content.

Janet Giltrow is senior lecturer in English in the Department of English at Simon Fraser University, Burnaby, British Columbia. She has published articles on composition instruction, linguistic and pragmatic description of style, and cultural contexts of language learning, as well as a textbook on academic writing.

Patsy Ginns teaches English at Chestnut Grove Junior High in Stokes County, North Carolina. In 1991 she was named statewide Academically Gifted Teacher of the Year. Other teaching assignments have been in Alaska and South Carolina. Among her publications are two volumes of oral history: *Rough Weather Makes Good Timber* and *Snowbird Gravy and Dishpan Pie*, published by the University Press in Chapel Hill. She serves on the editorial board of the *North Carolina English Teacher* and is a Level III Pioneer with the North Carolina Writing Project.

Gerald Grace is head of the School of Education, University of Durham, United Kingdom. He has taught previously at Kings College, University of London, the University of Cambridge (where he was Fellow of Wolfson College) and Victoria University of Wellington, New Zealand, where he was professor of education and head of department, 1987–89. He is the author of *Teachers, Ideology and Control* (1978); the editor of *Education and the City* (1984), and the coeditor of *Teachers: The Culture and Politics of Work* (1987) and of *Teacher Supply and Teacher Quality: Issues for the 1990s* (1991). During his sabbatical year (1993–94) he will be making presentations at conferences in the United States, Australia, and New Zealand.

Mary K. Healy is director of the English Credential Program in the graduate school of education at the University of California, Berkeley, and coeditor of the NCTE journal *English Education*. She is the former research and training director of the Puente Project in the office of the president, University of California, and was co-director of the Bay Area Writing Project. For the past ten years, she has taught summer courses on writing and learning and classroom-based research for teachers in Sweden, Norway, and Finland.

Stella D. Holmes is a reading strategist consultant at William J. Johnston Middle School in Colchester, Connecticut, and teacher/consultant for the University of Connecticut Writing Project. She has taught K–12 grades as well as summer college-level courses. Her expertise was crucial in the restructuring of a junior high school to a middle school. She has an electric approach to teaching language arts and reading through content courses which has made her a highly valued and commendable teacher in the Connecticut public school system.

Deborah James is professor of literature and language at the University of North Carolina at Asheville. She also directs the University Writing

Contributors

Center and teaches in the Basic Writing Program there. She has co-directed the North Carolina Mountain Area Writing Project. She has been most recently involved in teaching and helping to develop a first-year program for African American students on a predominantly white campus under the direction of Dwight Mullen. She has given several presentations at CCCC conventions. Her current writing project grows out of her ethnographic research in basic writing.

Claire Lacattiva, associate professor at St. John's University in New York, is a senior faculty member who teaches courses in educational methodology. During the past ten years, her research has focused on cross-cultural issues. She has presented research and lectured in Europe, Asia, Australia, and New Zealand, as well as in the United States. She is listed in eight directories, including *World's Who's Who of Women*.

Nancy Lester is adjunct associate professor of teacher education at New York University in New York City, New York, and co-director of The Write Company, an inservice education partnership also based in New York City. In both arenas, her interests are in promoting and supporting critical reflections on teaching and learning and connecting these to reconstruing relationships among members of educational communities as the basis for changing schooling. In addition to articles published in professional journals like *English Education* and *Language Arts*, she has coedited (with Garth Boomer, Cindy Onore, and Jon Cook) *Negotiating the Curriculum: Educating for the 21st Century* (Falmer, 1992), and coauthored (with Cindy Onore) *Learning Change: One School District Meets Language Across the Curriculum* (Boynton/Cook-Heinemann, 1990) and (with John S. Mayher and Gordon Pradl) *Learning to Write/Writing to Learn* (Boynton/Cook-Heinemann, 1983).

Helga Lewis is currently a first-grade teacher in the New Hanover County Schools in North Carolina. For the past seven years, she was an assistant lecturer in the English department of the University of North Carolina at Wilmington as well as a full-time Chapter 1 remedial reading teacher in the New Hanover County Schools. She has been affiliated with the North Carolina Writing Project since 1983.

John S. Mayher is professor of English education at New York University. He will be the convener of the 1995 Conference of the International Federation for the Teaching of English to be held in New York in May 1995. He has taught junior and senior high school English and worked as a consultant on writing and learning across the curriculum in many schools. His *Uncommon Sense: Theoretical Practice in Language Education* won the 1991 David H. Russell Award for Distinguished Research in the Teaching of English from NCTE. He is also the author of numerous articles and the coauthor of *Learning to Write/Writing to Learn* (with

Nancy Lester and Gordon Pradl) and *Search and Research: What the Inquiring Teacher Needs to Know* (with Rita Brause). From 1990 to 1992 he was chair of the Conference on English Education of NCTE.

Edward Milner is a computer teacher at East Mecklenburg High School in Charlotte, North Carolina. He is teaching in Scotland at Blantyre High School as a Fulbright Exchange Teacher. He has made presentations at the Society for the Scientific Study of Religion, the American Philosophical Association, the American Studies Association, the American Vocational Association, and the Council for Exceptional Children. He has written articles for *Periscope, the Journal for Curriculum Theorizing*, and the *NCVA Journal;* editorial critiques for *The Clearing House;* a chapter in *Qualitative Evaluation;* as well as poems and songs for various magazines. He has observed teaching in schools in New Zealand, and in England, Wales, Northern Ireland, and Scotland in the United Kingdom. He is now working on an article comparing computer teaching in the United Kingdom with that in the United States.

Andrew Overstreet is superintendent of schools for the Orange County School System in the Research Triangle area of North Carolina. He has also worked as a teacher, principal, and superintendent in Virginia.

P. B. Parris is assistant professor at the University of North Carolina at Asheville, where she established computer-assisted instruction in freshman composition in 1988, and continues to teach regularly in the program, as well as encouraging others in the use of CAI. In addition, she teaches a full range of creative writing courses. Her publications include journal articles, poems, short stories, and a novel, *Waltzing in the Attic,* which has also appeared in Canada, Germany, Austria, Switzerland, and the United Kingdom.

Katharine Perera is professor of educational linguistics in the Department of Linguistics at the University of Manchester, United Kingdom. She taught English in Malaysia for Voluntary Service Overseas and then taught for a number of years in schools in the United Kingdom and lectured in a college of teacher education before moving to Manchester University. From 1988 to 1989 she was a member of the Government Committee (the "Cox Committee") which drew up the United Kingdom National Curriculum in English. She is editor of the *Journal of Child Language* (Cambridge University Press). Her publications include *Children's Writing and Reading* (Blackwell) and *Understanding Language* (NATE).

David Philips is a senior policy analyst in the learning and assessment policy section of the New Zealand Ministry of Education. A former high school English teacher, he has conducted research on the teaching of writing in schools and has been a development consultant with the

Education Review Office. In addition to articles, research reports (e.g., with A. O'Rourke, *Responding Effectively to Pupils' Writing*, NZCER, Wellington, 1989), and book chapters, he collaborated with A. Carruthers, P. Scanlan, and E. Rathgen on *The Word Process*, Longman Paul, Auckland, 1991, and edited *Best of Set: Writing*, NZCER, Wellington, 1992. He is currently writing a handbook on assessment across the curriculum and studying part time for a Ph.D. in educational policy. He has also made presentations at local and overseas conferences on language issues.

Ruie Jane Pritchard is associate professor of English education at North Carolina State University and co-director of the Capital Area Writing Project. She was a high school English teacher before getting her Ph.D. at the University of Missouri–Columbia. In addition to journal articles and book chapters, she collaborated on *Ideas and Insights: Language Arts in the Elementary Grades* (NCTE). She worked with the New Zealand Writing Project and the Ministry of Education as a Fulbright Senior Researcher/Lecturer, and has returned many times for follow-up work in New Zealand. She is a frequent presenter at professional conferences in the United States and abroad.

Elody Rathgen is principal lecturer in English education at the Christchurch College of Education. She has been a head of department in English in high school, an adviser to teachers, and a curriculum developer in high school English. She is coauthor with Pauline Scanlan of *Say It with Words*, a text for senior English, and of *The Word Process*. Currently, she is a Commonwealth Relations Trust Fellow, working on a Ph.D. in feminist critique of teaching and learning theory.

Ann Buhman Renninger is curriculum director (K–12) for Colonial School District, Plymouth Meeting, Pennsylvania, where she was formerly language/reading arts coordinator as well as a secondary English teacher. Recently, she coedited and contributed sections to *Tracked for Failure/Tracked for Success: Derailing the Negative Effects of Ability Grouping*, NCTE, 1993. She also co-wrote, with Morton Botel and Bonnie Botel-Sheppard, "Integrating Language Arts: Facilitating Change in Schools," a chapter which appears in *Controversy to Consensus* (Allyn and Bacon, 1993). She will complete her Ph.D. in English education at New York University in spring 1993. She regularly presents at NCTE, ASCD, IFTE, and other conferences, and serves as an independent consultant in English/language arts.

Robert E. Shafer is professor emeritus of English at Arizona State University. He has taught English in high schools in Wisconsin and Virginia and is the founder of NCTE's International Assembly. In addition to his journal articles, book chapters, and textbooks, he recently collaborated with James Britton and Ken Watson on *Teaching and Learning English Worldwide*. His most recent research is on assessment in the English language arts and on attitudes toward the content of English as a school subject.

R. Baird Shuman is professor of English emeritus at the University of Illinois at Urbana-Champaign, and research professor of curriculum and instruction at the University of Nevada at Las Vegas. He has taught in Philadelphia's inner city, at Drexel University, San Jose State University, and Duke University. He holds the Ph.D. in English from the University of Pennsylvania. He is the author of over 750 articles and reviews and has written or edited twenty-seven books, including *Teaching English through the Arts* (with Denny Wolfe), *Resources for Writers; Classroom Encounters; William Inge; American Drama, 1918–1960;* and *Georgia O'Keeffe*. He frequently lectures in the United States and abroad on the teaching of English.

Joan Naomi (Mittelstaedt) Steiner has recently earned her doctorate in English education at New York University. She has taught English at Menasha High School in Menasha, Wisconsin, for twenty years. She is a consultant for the University of Wisconsin Educational Research Center, where she is developing on-demand performance assessment instruments for Wisconsin students. She chairs NCTE's Committee on Tracking and Grouping Practices, K–12 and is coeditor of *Tracked for Failure/Tracked for Success: An Action Packet for Derailing the Negative Effects of Ability Grouping*. In addition to book chapters and articles, she is author of *A Comparative Study of the Educational Stances of Madeline Hunter and James Britton*, published by NCTE. She frequently presents at NCTE conventions, affiliate conferences, and ASCD.

Wendy Strachan teaches in the language education department at the University of British Columbia. She has taught English, language arts, and social studies at most grade levels in both Canadian and international schools. She initiated and developed the National Writing Project-affiliated *East Asia* and the *Athens Writing* projects and has worked as a consultant on the teaching of writing in international schools all over Asia, the Middle East, and Europe. She is currently director of *Writing Project Europe*. She has published articles and book chapters on writing, classroom research, and literacy development. One of her present teaching and research interests is in approaches to developing aboriginal language literacy among Indian and Inuit adults of Canada's Northwest Territories.

Nancy Thompson is associate professor of English at the University of South Carolina, where she has helped to create the composition and rhetoric graduate degree programs. Her teaching interests include helping students at all levels from freshmen through graduate students become better writers, especially those who come to the university as "basic writers." Her research and publications focus on "mainstreaming" basic writers; using media in education; studying and practicing "imaging" as a mental process students can wield to their advantage; and on writing about New Zealand's famous teacher, Sylvia Ashton-Warner, upon whose life and work she has done extensive research. She is active in NCTE, especially its International Assembly.

Natalie White is assistant professor of education at Rowan College of New Jersey. A specialist on international and multicultural perspectives on the teaching of English, she has conducted research on ethnopoetics, myth, and story.

Merle Yvonne Williams-Price is employed as a K–12 instructional specialist for the schools of Weldon, North Carolina. Before moving to Weldon, she worked as a Teacher-on-Loan for the North Carolina State Department of Public Instruction, making language arts and whole language presentations. During the summers of 1983 to 1987, she organized and implemented week-long communication skills workshops for 6–12 teachers. In addition to twenty-one years of public school teaching, she has worked for the North Carolina Community College system as an instructor of freshman composition and the adult GED program.

Denny Wolfe holds B.A. and M.A. degrees in English, as well as the Ph.D. in English education from Duke University. Currently, he is professor of English education, director of the Tidewater Virginia Writing Project, and associate dean in the Darden College of Education at Old Dominion University, Norfolk, Virginia. He has published more than sixty articles on various aspects of teaching English, as well as three books, *Writing for Learning in the Content Areas*, *Making the Grade: Evaluating and Judging Student Writing*, and *Teaching English through the Arts*. In 1984, he won the Sarah and Rufus Tonelson Award for Excellence in Teaching, Service, and Research in the Darden College of Education at Old Dominion University.

Noeline Wright is currently working as an adviser to secondary schools through the Education Advisory Service of the University of Waikato's School of Education in Hamilton, New Zealand. She has taught high school English in a number of schools both in New Zealand and overseas. On a national level, she is vice president of NZATE (the New Zealand Association for the Teaching of English) and has contributed workshops at national conferences and articles for the journal *English in Aotearoa*.